Bloom's Modern Critical Interpretations

The Adventures of
  Huckleberry Finn
The Age of Innocence
Alice's Adventures in
  Wonderland
All Quiet on the
  Western Front
As You Like It
The Ballad of the Sad
  Café
Beloved
Beowulf
Black Boy
The Bluest Eye
The Canterbury Tales
Cat on a Hot Tin Roof
The Catcher in the Rye
Catch-22
The Chronicles of
  Narnia
The Color Purple
Crime and
  Punishment
The Crucible
Darkness at Noon
Death of a Salesman
The Death of Artemio
  Cruz
Don Quixote
Emerson's Essays
Emma
Fahrenheit 451
A Farewell to Arms
Frankenstein
The Glass Menagerie

The Grapes of Wrath
Great Expectations
The Great Gatsby
Gulliver's Travels
Hamlet
The Handmaid's Tale
Heart of Darkness
I Know Why the
  Caged Bird Sings
The Iliad
Jane Eyre
The Joy Luck Club
The Jungle
Long Day's Journey
  Into Night
Lord of the Flies
The Lord of the Rings
Love in the Time of
  Cholera
The Man Without
  Qualities
The Metamorphosis
Miss Lonelyhearts
Moby-Dick
My Ántonia
Native Son
Night
1984
The Odyssey
Oedipus Rex
The Old Man and the
  Sea
On the Road
One Flew Over the
  Cuckoo's Nest

One Hundred Years of
  Solitude
Persuasion
Portnoy's Complaint
Pride and Prejudice
Ragtime
The Red Badge of
  Courage
Romeo and Juliet
The Rubáiyát of Omar
  Khayyám
The Scarlet Letter
A Separate Peace
Silas Marner
Song of Solomon
The Sound and the
  Fury
The Stranger
A Streetcar Named
  Desire
Sula
The Tale of Genji
A Tale of Two Cities
"The Tell-Tale Heart"
  and Other Stories
Their Eyes Were
  Watching God
Things Fall Apart
To Kill a Mockingbird
Ulysses
Waiting for Godot
The Waste Land
Wuthering Heights
Young Goodman
  Brown

Bloom's Modern Critical Interpretations

Amy Tan's
The Joy Luck Club
New Edition

Edited and with an introduction by
Harold Bloom
Sterling Professor of the Humanities
Yale University

BLOOM'S
LITERARY CRITICISM
An imprint of Infobase Publishing

Bloom's Modern Critical Interpretations: The Joy Luck Club—New Edition
Copyright © 2009 by Infobase Publishing
Introduction © 2009 by Harold Bloom

Bloom's Literary Criticism
An imprint of Infobase Publishing
132 West 31st Street
New York NY 10001

Library of Congress Cataloging-in-Publication Data
Amy Tan's Joy Luck Club / edited and with an introduction by Harold Bloom. — New
ed.
       p. cm. — (Bloom's modern critical interpretations)
    Includes bibliographical references and index.
    ISBN 978-1-60413-399-8
  1. Tan, Amy. Joy Luck Club.   2. Mothers and daughters in literature.   3. Chinese
Americans in literature.   I. Bloom, Harold.   II. Title.   III. Series.
    PS3570.A48J632 2009
    813'.54—dc22   2008052355

You can find Chelsea House on the World Wide Web at
http://www.chelseahouse.com

Contributing editor: Pamela Loos
Cover designed by Takeshi Takahashi

Printed in the United States of America
IBT IBT 10 9 8 7 6 5 4 3 2 1

This book is printed on acid-free paper.

Contents

Editor's Note   vii

Introduction   1
     Harold Bloom

Born of a Stranger: Mother–Daughter Relationships
     and Storytelling in Amy Tan's *The Joy Luck Club*   3
     Gloria Shen

Voice, Mind, Self: Mother–Daughter Relationships in Amy Tan's
     The Joy Luck Club and *The Kitchen God's Wife*   17
     M. Marie Booth Foster

Hanyu at the Joy Luck Club   35
     Steven P. Sondrup

Discovering the Ethnic Name and the Genealogical Tie in
     Amy Tan's *The Joy Luck Club*   45
     Zenobia Mistri

The Role of Mah Jong in Amy Tan's *The Joy Luck Club*   53
     Ronald Emerick

Feng Shui, Astrology, and the Five Elements: Traditional
     Chinese Belief in Amy Tan's *The Joy Luck Club*   63
     Patricia L. Hamilton

Moving Forward to Reach the Past: The Dialogics of
    Time in Amy Tan's *The Joy Luck Club*   83
    Marc Singer

Mothers' "China Narrative": Recollection and Translation in Amy
    Tan's *The Joy Luck Club* and *The Kitchen God's Wife*   109
    Yuan Yuan

Identity-in-Difference: Re-Generating Debate about Intergenerational
    Relationships in Amy Tan's *The Joy Luck Club*   123
    Bella Adams

Choosing Hope and Remaking Kinship: Amy Tan's
    The Joy Luck Club   139
    Magali Cornier Michael

Chronology   173

Contributors   175

Bibliography   177

Acknowledgments   181

Index   183

Editor's Note

My introduction briefly questions the permanent place in an American canon of Amy Tan's indubitably charming *The Joy Luck Club*.

All ten essayists would disagree with my doubts. Canonical disputes can be resolved only by time.

Mother-daughter relationships are the inevitable topic for all the essayists, including those who extend their view to *The Kitchen God's Wife*. It would be absurd of me to express a preference between one of Amy Tan's admirers and another, as they are compelled to center on her one dominant theme. That there should be a certain sameness in their comments may or may not indicate a limitation in Tan's vision.

HAROLD BLOOM

Introduction

In an accomplished essay, Myra Jehlen sees Amy Tan, against all odds, returning to Whitman's stance and singing a latter-day *Song of Myself.* That implicitly is high praise and, if justified, might give *The Joy Luck Club* an aesthetic dignity beyond the popular success it continues to enjoy. Will it be a permanent part of the revised canon of an American literature "opened up" by consideration of gender and ethnicity, or will it prove only another period piece, in which we currently abound?

Amy Tan is a skilled storyteller and a remarkable personality. Jehlen charmingly says: "Amy Tan has read her Emerson, and she doesn't believe him. This is not surprising, as he probably would have doubted her." I would murmur that it all depends upon *which* Emerson Tan has read, as there are so many. Having met and admired Tan, I would recommend *The Conduct of Life,* which is consonant with her rugged but amiable stance toward reality.

Jehlen eloquently concludes by stating both Tan's relation to Whitman and the significant differences:

> Jing-Mei becomes herself finally when, like Whitman, she can be the writer of the Body and the writer of the Soul, can sing both others and herself. If she is Whitman's critic as well as his descendant, it is because America has lost its innocence in the matter of individualism. Moreover, the duplicities of the notion of the universal self have been revealed in our time especially by the protestations of people of Amy Tan's kind: women and non-whites. It is not surprising that Jing-Mei's claim be not as universal as

1

Whitman's, nor that its costs be apparent. It is surprising to find her claiming the old transcendent, appropriating self at all, and, in the name of culture, singing a latter-day "Song of Myself."

Jehlen is aware, as I am, that Whitman attempted to speak for women as for men and for all ethnic strains. What she doubts is the Whitmanian possibility of universal representation, since we are in a time of group identities: gendered, diversely oriented sexual preferences, ethnicities. And yet Whitman, at his best, permanently has reached and held a universal audience. *Song of Myself* is not a period piece.

GLORIA SHEN

Born of a Stranger: Mother–Daughter Relationships and Storytelling in Amy Tan's The Joy Luck Club

Amy Tan's first work, *The Joy Luck Club* (1989),[1] is a challenge to the novel as a "narrative paradigm" (Jameson, 151) in several ways: form, narrative structure, and narrative techniques. It is not a novel in the sense that only one story, "his story" is presented; it is a work of sixteen "her stories." The stories are "presented" not by one single third-person narrator either from her particular perspective or from the various "points of view" of the characters. These are narrative techniques conventionally associated with the novel of the nineteenth and twentieth centuries. The book is divided into four main sections; the stories are told from the viewpoints of four Chinese mothers and their Chinese American daughters. The only exception is Suyuan Woo, who, having recently died, speaks not for herself but through her daughter, Jing-mei. The daughter tells her mother's stories as she takes her mother's place at the mahjong table and on the fateful trip to China. The stories, "told" by the three mothers and four daughters at different times and in different settings, resemble fragments of stories collected by a sociologist and randomly put together, rather than carefully constructed narratives set in a deliberate order by an author. In other words, *The Joy Luck Club* employs an unusual narrative strategy. In this chapter, I explore the connection between the narrative strategy employed in *The Joy Luck Club* and the relationships between the Chinese mothers and their American-born daughters.

From *International Women's Writing: New Landscapes of Identity*, edited by Anne E. Brown and Marjanne E. Goozé, pp. 233–244. © 1995 by Anne E. Brown and Marjanne E. Goozé.

3

In *The Joy Luck Club*, important themes are repeated in the stories like musical leitmotifs and presented from slightly different angles in order to give the reader a continuous sense of life as well as a full understanding of the significance of each event. The unique structure of *The Joy Luck Club* allows the unconnected fragments of life, revealed from different but somewhat overlapping perspectives by all the "reliable" narrators, to unfold into a meaningful, continuous whole so that the persistent tensions and powerful bonds between mother and daughter, between generations, may be illuminated through a montage effect on the reader.

The traditional novel as a "narrative paradigm" (Jameson, 151) entails a set of rules that bestow legitimacy upon certain narrative forms and preclude certain other forms. Jameson expounds the notion of "narrative paradigm" by claiming that the "forms" of the novel as the "inherited narrative paradigms" are: "the raw material on which the novel works, transforming their 'telling' into its 'showing,' estranging commonplaces against the freshness of some unexpected 'real,' foregrounding convention itself as that through which readers have hitherto received their notions of events, psychology, experience, space, and time" (151). The "inherited narrative paradigms" determine rules of the game and illustrate how they are to be applied. The rules define what has the right to be said and done in the culture in question. Oral narrative forms, such as popular stories, myths, legends, and tales, are thus viewed as belonging to a "savage, primitive, underdeveloped, backward, alienated" mentality, composed of opinions, prejudice, ignorance and ideology (Lyotard, 19). As Lyotard notes, oral narrative forms have been deemed fit for women and children only and have not been rightly considered as appropriate or competent forms to be subsumed under the category of the novel. As a Western-conceived notion, the "narrative paradigm" of the novel thus excludes various minority subnarrative traditions, including women's. Structurally, *The Joy Luck Club* is an interesting example because it rejects artificial unity and espouses the fragmentary, one of the main features of postmodernism.[2]

The dissolution of unity in the traditional novel, best manifested in the "fragmentation" of the work, serves to highlight different themes that evolve around the mother–daughter relationship. *The Joy Luck Club* is divided into four sections, each of which consists of four stories. Each of the four sections of the book begins with a prologue, a brief narrative illustrative of the theme of that section. The Joy Luck Club is a monthly mahjong gathering to which the generation of the Chinese mothers has belonged for decades and with which the generation of the American daughters has grown up. Like four Chinese boxes, the complexity of the narrative structure is revealed through stories told within stories by the mothers to the daughters. In this manner, Tan directly puts forward the views, feelings, emotions, and thoughts of her characters, stressing the mixture of action, consciousness, and subconsciousness. In the chapter "Without Wood," a daughter tells about a dream she once had as a child that reveals subconsciously the daughter's strong desire to resist the clutching influence of the mother on her. In this dream, the daughter finds herself in a playground filled with rows of sandboxes. In each sandbox there is a doll. Haunted by the feeling that her mother knows exactly which doll she will pick, the daughter deliberately chooses a different one. When the mother orders the guardian of the gate to the dreamworld to stop her, the little girl becomes so frightened that she remains frozen in place (186).

Tan's storytelling technique reveals the complexity of the dark, invisible mind of cultural consciousness and subconsciousness best portrayed by the stories within stories. In *The Joy Luck Club*, Tan moves with swiftness and ease from one story to another, from one symbol or image to another. In a sense, *The Joy Luck Club* can be properly called a collection of intricate and haunting memories couched in carefully wrought stories. Tan has purposely externalized the eight characters' mental world by allowing each of them to tell her own story in a deceptively simple manner, thus allowing the reader to plunge into the mind of the characters. The motives, desires, pains, pleasures, and concerns of the characters are thereby effectively dramatized. This particular writing strategy allows Tan to transcend the conventional novelistic dichotomy of preferred "showing" and undesirable "telling." The stories thus tell us a great deal about individual characters, their reaction to each other, and their activities together. Because the stories are all told in the mothers' and the daughters' own voices, we are spared the pressing question with which the reader of a conventional novel is constantly bombarded: Am I dealing with a "reliable" or "unreliable" narrator? While immersed in particular and individual perspectives, the reader of *The Joy Luck Club* also confronts the more general and lasting concerns of many generations. Unlike Maxine Hong Kingston's *The Woman Warrior*, which relates the life experience of one woman and concentrates on one single family, the stories in *The Joy Luck Club*, with its characters and circumstances skilfully interwoven, presents a continuous whole more meaningful than the sum of its parts.

In *The Joy Luck Club*, Tan probes the problematic mother–daughter relationship in sixteen separate stories spanning two generations of eight women. Though the eight characters are divided into four families, the book itself is concerned more with an unmistakable bifurcation along generational lines: mothers, whose stories all took place in China, and daughters, whose stories deal with their lives in America. Though the mothers all have different names and individual stories, they seem interchangeable in that they all have similar personalities—strong, determined, and endowed with mysterious power— and that they all show similar concerns about their daughters' welfare. As a result, the mothers are possessively trying to hold onto their daughters, and the daughters are battling to get away from their mothers. The four mothers and four daughters are different, but their differences remain insignificant as the action of the novel is focused on the persistent tensions and powerful bonds between them.

Tan's characters are seen in both detail and outline. The first-person testimonies allow the reader to examine each of the characters closely and to develop a sense of empathy with each of them; but, at the same time, the testimonies reveal a pattern, particularly in the way the mothers and daughters relate to one another. The purpose of this treatment is obvious: to portray the mother and daughter relationship as both typical and universal.

In Tan's novel, The Joy Luck Club is a bridge uniting both space and time. The Joy Luck Club connects the sixteen intricately interlocking stories and helps to reveal and explain the infinite range and complexity of mother–daughter relationships. Within the narrative, it joins two continents and unites the experiences of the mothers and the daughters. The American daughters are alien to Chinese culture as much as they are to their mothers' uncanny, Chinese ways of thinking. To the daughters, cultural and ethnic identity is possible only when they can fully identify themselves with their mothers through their maturation into womanhood. The sharing of cultural experiences between mothers and daughters through the device of storytelling transforms structurally isolated monologues into meaningful dialogues between mother and mother, daughter and daughter, and, more important, mother and daughter and coalesces the sixteen monologues into a coherent whole. While the mother and daughter relationships are unique in the ethnic context of Tan's novel, they also have a universal aspect. Indeed, all women share this experience, regardless of time and space. An-mei Hsu is puzzled by both the specific and universal qualities of the mother–daughter relationship. Raised traditionally, she was taught to swallow her desires, her bitterness, and the misery of others. Rejecting her upbringing, she tries to instill in her daughter a strong sense of self. Unfortunately, her daughter is a passive individual. An-mei Hsu is thus convinced that regardless of their respective upbringing, mothers and daughters are somehow condemned to being similar: "And even though I taught my daughter the opposite, still she came out the same way! Maybe it is because she was born to me and she was born a girl. And I was born to my mother and I was born a girl. All of us are like stairs, one step after another, going up and down, but all going the same way" (215).

Through her structural experiments with the elements of fiction and her storytelling device, and with the testimonial mode of characterization, Tan has pushed her novel beyond the merely conventional practice of the novel (to mimic the convention of the appearance of life, as done by many traditional novelists). Instead, she tries to do away with "his story" and present "her life" from the perspectives of the individual women characters in the form of loosely connected monologues. These monologues serve to translate as faithfully as possible the intricate relationship that can exist between a mother and her daughter.

Tan's extensive use of symbols and images creates a mood of expression that reveals and explains the infinite range and complexity of these mother–daughter relationships. Each of the four sections of *The Joy Luck Club* begins with a prologue, defining the theme of that section while disclosing certain aspects of the problem in the mother–daughter relationship. The first prologue contains a cluster of images that highlight the nature of this relationship in the book and summarize the whole novel. This prologue centers around an old woman who remembers that, while still in Shanghai, she bought a swan for a small sum. The swan, according to the vendor, was once a duck who had managed to stretch his neck in the hope of becoming a goose. On the boat sailing to America, the old woman swore to the swan that she would one day have a daughter whom no one would look down upon, for she would speak only perfect English. In order for this daughter to know her mother's meaning, she would give her the swan (17).

However, upon arriving in America, the swan is confiscated, and the old woman is left with only one of the swan's feathers. This feather is far too insignificant for her to convince anyone, least of all her daughter, how beautiful the swan was. Furthermore, the daughter she had hoped for has become an unsympathetic "stranger" who does not even speak her language. The prologue thus ends on a poignant note. Indeed, year after year, the mother waits for the moment when she would be able to tell her daughter in perfect American English that the feather is far from worthless, for it symbolizes all of her "good intentions" (17).

The prologue sets the tone and the reasons for the tensions and conflicts in the mother–daughter relationship. The "swan" and the "old woman" who sailed across the ocean together, "stretching their necks toward America" (17), are an emblem of the four mothers who came to the United States, hoping to give their daughters a better life than the one they had in China. The "good intentions" are clearly stated. But the mother, left with an almost worthless feather, is condemned to wait patiently many years until the daughter is finally mature enough to come back to her, to appreciate her, and to reconstruct the beautiful swan from the feather. The swan is therefore emblematic of both the mother's new life in America and, more important, her past one in China, an experience the mother wants to communicate to her daughter. However, only a mature daughter, who has overcome the psychological and cultural gap separating her from her mother is capable of coming to terms with this experience.

The mother–daughter relationship is the central issue and focal point in the dialogues between the mothers and daughters in Tan's book. The novel traces the psychological development of the American daughter and her final acceptance of the Chinese mother and what the Chinese mother stands for. Jing-mei Woo, who replaces her recently deceased mother at the mahjong table, is the first to tell a story on behalf of her mother; she is also the very last daughter to recount her own story. It is interesting to note that when she is asked by her three "aunts" to go to China in order to fulfill her mother's long-cherished wish to meet her lost twin babies, Jing-mei shocks and upsets them with her confused yet honest remark that she would not know what to tell her sisters because she did not really know her mother: "What will I say? What can I tell them about my mother?" (40).

The mothers are all frightened by this response. Indeed, they sense in it the confusion of their own daughters. In Jing-mei, they recognize their own daughters, all as ignorant and as unmindful of the truths and hopes their mothers brought over with them from China (40). Ironically, the accomplishment of the mother's dream for her daughter, a dream that entailed her physical removal from the motherland, results in multifarious problems in the relationship with her daughter.

In Tan's novel, the Chinese mothers are all strong-willed, persistent, hard to please, and overly critical. They often make their presence and their goodwill look like outrageous impositions rather than tacit influences. When, for example, Jing-mei Woo describes her mother's New Year crab dinner, we learn that, although she does not like this dish, she is obliged to eat it since her refusal to do so would constitute a rejection of her mother's love (202). The food and the advice offered by the mothers are hard to refuse not only because they are a symbol of love but also because they tend to carry the full weight of maternal authority. That is why Waverly Jong is convinced that telling one's mother to be quiet would be tantamount to committing suicide (173). In another example, Waverly tries to make her mother accept her American boyfriend by showing her a fur coat that he has given her as a token of his love. Totally dejected by her mother's antagonism toward her boyfriend, whom the mother does not consider good enough for her daughter, Waverly Jong feels distressed at not being able to shake off her mother's clutching influence. When she looks once again at the coat her mother has just finished criticizing, she becomes convinced that it is, indeed, shabby (169).

The mother's wish for the daughter to live a better life than the one she had back in China is revealed in the conversation between the Chinese woman and her swan on her journey to America in the novel's first prologue.

Ironically, this wish becomes the very source of the conflicts and tensions in their relationship. This is made perfectly clear by Jing-mei Woo when she half jokingly, half-remorsefully recalls her ever-agonizing childhood, a period during which her mother unsuccessfully attempts to transform her into a child prodigy. In order to prepare Jing-mei for a future that she hopes will be brilliant, Suyuan Woo nightly submits Jing-mei to a series of tests while forcing her to listen to countless stories about amazing children (133–34). Mother and daughter finally settle on Jing-mei's becoming a concert pianist, and Jing-mei begins to take piano lessons from Mr. Old Chong, a retired piano teacher who happens to be deaf. As a result, the daughter manages to get away with playing more or less competently while her teacher conducts an imaginary piece of music in his head (148).

Another daughter, Rose Hsu Jordan, is married to a "foreigner" who wishes to divorce her. Her mother, An-mei Hsu, urges her to speak up in the hope of saving her marriage. She does this by juxtaposing the Chinese way with the American way. The Chinese way consists of not expressing one's desires, not speaking up, and not making choices. The American way consists of exercising choices and speaking up for oneself. An-mei Hsu raised Rose in the American way. She hoped that this would allow her daughter to lead a better life than the one she had in China. Indeed, in China people had no choice. Since they could not speak up, they were forced to accept whatever fate befell them (241). An-mei Hsu reminds Rose that by not speaking up, she "can lose her chance forever" (215).

The frustration that Waverly's mother, Lindo Jong, feels is shared by all the mothers. This frustration is best summarized in her painful and poignant confession during the course of which she accuses herself of being responsible for the way Waverly has turned out. Her sense of responsibility stems from the fact that she is the one who wanted Waverly to have the best of both worlds, and it leads her to openly berate herself for not being able to foresee that her daughter's American circumstances would not necessarily mix well with her Chinese reality (254).

The alienation between mother and daughter often stems either from a lack of understanding or from various forms of miscommunication. While the daughters, all born in America, entirely adapt to the customs and language of the new land, the immigrant mothers still hold onto those of China. All the mothers feel their daughters' impatience when they speak Chinese and are convinced that their daughters think they are stupid when they attempt to communicate with them in broken English (40–41). If Jing-mei is initially reluctant to carry out her mother's long-cherished wish to be reunited with her two lost sisters, it is mainly because she believes that she and her mother have never understood one another. The language barrier that existed between them was such that both mother and daughter imperfectly translated each other's words and meanings (37).

In a tragicomic incident that exemplifies the futile attempt to bridge the mother–daughter gap, Lindo Jong is proudly speaking to her daughter about Taiyuan, her birthplace. Waverly mistakes Taiyuan for Taiwan and is subsequently visibly irritated when her mother loudly corrects her. The daughter's unintentional mistake, combined with the mother's anger, destroys their attempt to communicate. Consequently, they are both plunged, once again, into a steely silence (183). In another example of Tan's lightness of touch straining with ambivalence, Lena St. Clair defines her mother as a "displaced person" who has difficulties expressing herself in English. Born in Wushi, near Shanghai, she speaks Mandarin and only a little English. Lena's father, who spoke only a few canned Chinese expressions, always insisted that his wife learn English. Unable to express herself clearly in English, she communicates through gestures and looks and sometimes in a broken English punctuated by hesitations and frustration. Her husband thus feels justified in putting words in her mouth (106).

The mothers' inability to speak perfect American English has multiple ramifications. For one thing, as they themselves have not lived in a foreign country, the daughters are left with the false impression that their mothers are not intelligent. As a result, the daughters often feel justified in believing that their mothers have nothing worthwhile to say. Furthermore, when mother and daughter share neither the same realm of experience and knowledge nor the same concerns, their differences are not marked by a slip of the tongue or the lack of linguistic adroitness or even by a generational gap, but rather by a deep geographical and cultural cleft. When the mother talks about American ways, the daughter is willing to listen; when the mother shows her Chinese ways, the daughter ignores her. The mother is thus unable to teach her daughter the Chinese ways of obeying parents, of listening to the mother's mind, of hiding her thoughts, of knowing her own worth without becoming vain, and, most important of understanding why "Chinese thinking is best" (254).

The gulf between the Old World and the New, between Chinese mother and American daughter, is exacerbated by the ethnic and racial biases against the Chinese that the young daughter has to deal with on a regular basis. A conversation between Waverly and her mother, Lindo Jong, shows that even as a young child, the daughter is fully aware of the hurtful effect these prejudices have had on the Chinese mother, who has not adjusted well to the life and customs of the new land. One night, while Lindo Jong is brushing her daughter's hair, Waverly, who has overheard a boy in her class discuss Chinese torture, wickedly asks her the following question: "Ma, what is Chinese torture?" Visibly disturbed by this question, Lindo Jong sharply nicks her daughter's skull with a hairpin. She then softly but proudly answers that Chinese people are proficient in many areas. They "do business, do medicine, do painting . . . do torture. Best torture" (91).

While the Chinese mother seems able readily to shrug off the detrimental influence of ethnic and racial biases, she cannot help but feel the effect of them upon her daughter. Lindo Jong is unable to overcome the painful reality that sets her apart from her daughter. She is ashamed because she knows that the daughter she is so proud of is ashamed of her and of her Chinese ways (255). The constantly growing cleavage of ethnic and national identity drives the daughter to make persistent efforts to Americanize herself in order to lessen her mother's commanding influence.

The daughters' battles for autonomy and independence from powerful imposing mothers are relentless, and the confrontations between mothers and daughters are fierce. In the chapter "Without Wood," daughter Rose Hsu Jordan describes the decision she made as a child in her dream to pick a different doll from the one her mother expected her to choose (186). Another daughter, Jing-mei, adopts a self-defensive strategy against her mother's expectation that she be a child prodigy by disappointing her whenever she can. She does this by getting average grades, by not becoming class president, by not being accepted into Stanford University, and finally by dropping out of college (142). By consistently failing her mother, Jing-mei manages to assert her own will.

The struggle between mother and daughter is equally ferocious. It often takes the form of psychological warfare between the two. Waverly Jong, a child prodigy chess player, envisages this struggle as a chess game in which her mother is transformed into a fierce opponent whose eyes are reduced to "two angry black slits" (100). The struggle is also expressed in physical and verbal fights. When, for example, the daughter Lena St. Clair overhears a mother and daughter who live next door shouting and fighting, she is not overly surprised when she learns from the daughter that both of them "do this kind of stuff all the time" (142).

This type of painful and dramatic confrontation also characterizes the relationship between Jing-mei Woo and her mother, Suyuan. Following a rather violent physical fight, Jing-mei Woo accuses her mother of wanting her to be someone she is not. Suyuan responds to this accusation by telling her that only two types of daughters exist: obedient daughters and disobedient daughters. Following this pronouncement, the daughter screams that she wishes that she was not her mother's daughter. When Suyuan reminds her that this is something that cannot be changed, Jing-mei utters the worst possible thing that a Chinese daughter could ever say to her mother: "Then I wish I'd never been born! I wish I were dead! Like them" (142). This "them" refers to the twin babies whom her mother was forced to abandon in China while attempting to escape the invading Japanese troops. Before Jing-mei realizes what a mindless thing she has just said, Suyuan, badly hurt, falls silent, backs out of the room, and like a small leaf in the wind, appears "thin, brittle, lifeless" (142).

In spite of the daughters' successful resistance and rejection of their influence, the mothers valiantly refuse to give up. After having tried many different strategies throughout their lives, the mothers finally discover that storytelling is the best way to reach the hearts and minds of their daughters. Realizing that sharing her past with her daughter might be the last and only trump card she has in order to "save" her daughter, Ying-ying St. Clair decides to give it a try. Her decision, nevertheless, reflects her awareness of the nature of the clash—the daughter's lack of ethnic and cultural identity, which Ying-ying is convinced will lead to her daughter's unhappiness. By telling her past to a daughter who has spent all of her life trying to slip away from her, Ying-ying St. Clair hopes to reclaim her, "to penetrate her skin and pull her to where she can be saved" (242). Jing-mei Woo's dying mother also realizes that her daughter's problem similarly stems from her refusal to embrace her Chinese roots. Indeed, before her trip to China, Jing-mei relentlessly denies her Chinese heritage. On the train to China from Hong Kong, Jing-mei finally comes to terms with her true identity. Reflecting on her past, she admits to feeling different. Furthermore, she is now prepared to concede: "[M]y mother was right. I am becoming Chinese" (267).

The device of storytelling by women to women is employed extensively throughout the novel as a means to achieve various ends. For instance, it is the means by which Lindo Jong is physically set free. As a young girl, Lindo managed to get out of an arranged marriage. She accomplished this feat by inventing stories about her husband's ancestor's wish for him to marry a servant girl. The mothers also resort to storytelling when trying to impart daily truths and knowledge to the daughters. Through storytelling, they hope to help their daughters rise above negative circumstances or simply avoid unknown dangers. Waverly Jong remembers her mother's telling her a story about a girl who carelessly ran into a street and was subsequently killed by a taxi (90). Lena St. Clair remembers the story her mother made up about a young woman who fell in love with an irresponsible man and had a baby out of wedlock (106). After her mother's maid tells the child An-mei Hsu about the rape that led to her mother's shameful position as the third concubine of a wealthy man, An-mei Hsu realizes that she is now better able to grasp the meaning of many of the things that previously escaped her (237). For the mother, Ying-ying St. Clair, telling her daughter about her past is a tangible proof of her love. In sharing her past with her daughter, she hopes to counter the fact that her daughter has no *chi*, no spirit. Lena's lack of *chi* is Ying-ying's greatest shame, and her stories become a means by which she hopes to help her submissive daughter regain her "tiger spirit" (252).

Telling Lena about her past is absolutely necessary because both mother and daughter are "tigers" and both are "lost . . . unseen and not seeing, unheard and not hearing" (67). By learning about her mother's past, Lena becomes better equipped to fight back and restore her happiness (marital happiness, in her case) in much the same way her mother did in the course of her own life. For Ying-ying St. Clair, who has already waited far too long to tell Lena her story, storytelling is also a positive experience since it allows her to find herself, to remember that long ago she "wished to be found" (83).

Through the sharing of personal experiences, a reconciliation between mothers and daughters is reached. The daughters realize that their mothers have always had their best interests at heart. Echoing the old woman and the swan in the first prologue at the beginning of the novel, mother Lindo Jong explains her feelings most poignantly: "I wanted everything for you to be better. I wanted you to have the best circumstances, the best character. I didn't want you to regret anything" (265). Because their own lives in China had been circumscribed by social and parental constraints that invariably led to pain, humiliation, and tragedy, the mothers all came to America to give their daughters a better life. However, daughters must first understand the real circumstances surrounding their mothers: how they arrived in their new country, how they married, how hard they tried to hold onto their Chinese roots. Once they have understood this, the daughters are better able to understand why they themselves are the way they are. Ultimately, this understanding will also lead them to finally appreciate their mothers. The mothers try very hard to leave an imprint of themselves on their daughters through various means. For the mother Lindo Jong, names carry a symbolic significance. She tells her daughter that the reason she named her Waverly is that, when she gave birth to her, they lived on a street with the same name. In naming her thus, she was convinced that her daughter would feel that she belonged on that street and that when it would come time for her to leave home, she would take with her a "piece" of her mother (265). While Waverly is left with a "piece" of her mother in her name, An-mei Hsu inherits from her mother a ring of watery blue sapphire, and Jing-mei receives a necklace with a jade pendant from hers. These pieces of jewelry are also symbolic of their mothers' continued presence in their lives. However, the daughters' acceptance of, and identification with, their mothers does not take place until all of them come into contact with their mothers' past through stories. Thus, after her mother's death, when she sets foot on Chinese land for the first time in her life, Jing-mei learns about her mother's long-cherished wish. Also during this trip, she discovers the meaning of her mother's name as well as the meaning of her own name: her mother's, Suyuan, means "Long-cherished Wish," and hers, Jing-mei, means "Younger Sister of Pure Essence." After learning the hidden meanings of these names, Jing-mei is full of remorse: "I think about this. My mother's long-cherished wish. Me, the younger sister who was supposed to be the essence of the others. I feed myself with the old grief, wondering how disappointed my mother must have been" (281).

The sharing of cultural experience between mother and daughter through the device of storytelling transforms the naive, self-protective daughters, who try hard to move away from, or surpass, their ethnic roots, into the mature daughters who are appreciative of their mothers' Chinese ways. Through storytelling, the daughters come to accept their mothers' and their own race and are willing to seek their ethnic and cultural roots. Jing-mei goes to China and reunites with her twin sisters. Waverly and her American husband go to China together with her mother and spend their honeymoon there (184).

With a new consciousness, the mature daughter sees her mother in a new light. As Waverly Jong puts it: "[I]n the brief instant that I had peered over the barriers I could finally see what was really there: an old woman, a wok for her armor, a knitting needle for her sword, getting a little crabby as she waited patiently for her daughter to invite her in" (183–84). The daughter's defiance turns out to be baseless, and the "scheming ways" of the mother who seemed relentless in her pursuit of her daughter's weakest spots prove to be unfounded (180). After her mother's death, Jing-mei Woo also realizes, for the first time, that Schumann's music, which as a child she had played at a fateful recital, is in fact, composed of two parts: "Pleading Child" and "Perfectly Contented." Interestingly, it is the former piece that she played so poorly. While in mourning for her mother, Jing-mei also comes to the realization that she has always been biased by a one-sided view of life and by a poor opinion of her mother. When she plays the two pieces of music together, she suddenly understands that they are "two halves of the same song" (144). Schumann's music thus serves as a metaphor used by Tan to highlight the relationship between mother and daughter. This relationship encompasses, like Schumann's music, two phases of the human experience. At times, these phases may appear to be contradictory, but, in fact, they are really two natural and complementary stages of life. Tan thus seems to imply that a complete and holistic experience of life requires an understanding and an acceptance of both phases.

The novel ends with the arrival of Jing-mei Woo in China, the "motherland," where the three sisters are reunited and where Jing-mei finally accepts her Chinese identity. Jing-mei had to leave the West and travel all the way to China before she was able to realize that both her mother and China are in her blood. Only when she has reached maturity is she able to close the geographical gap and come to terms with her ethnic, cultural, and racial background. In doing so, she transcends the psychological gap that had alienated her from her mother and from herself. When the struggles and battles are over, when the daughter is mature enough to be able to accept the mother and identify with what she stood for, what was formerly considered a hateful bondage is revealed to be a cherished bond.

Notes

I wish to thank Anne Brown and Marjanne Goozé for their thoughtful reading, critique, and assistance with this chapter.

1. Amy Tan was born in Oakland, California, in 1952. Her parents left China and came to the United States in 1949, leaving behind three young daughters. The communist revolution of 1949 prevented them from sending for their daughters after they had settled down in the United States. Tan was twelve years old before she learned of her sisters' existence. Recently, Tan and her mother were reunited with them in China. Tan wrote her first short story in 1985 after having joined Squaw Valley, a writers' workshop. In 1989, she published her first novel, *The Joy Luck Club*. See Amy Ling's *Between Worlds* for a brief description of Amy Tan's life.

2. The rejection of organic unity and concentration on the fragmentation of language games, of time, of the human subject, of society itself, are an attitude widely shared among postmodernists. For detailed discussions on various attempts made against totality by postmodernists, see Jean-François Lyotard's *The Postmodern Condition* and Fredric Jameson's *The Political Unconscious*.

References

Hong Kingston, Maxine. *The Woman Warrior: Memoirs of a Girlhood Among Ghosts*. New York: Random House, 1977.

Jameson, Fredric. *The Political Unconscious: Narrative as a Socially Symbolic Act*. Ithaca, NY: Cornell University Press, 1981.

Ling, Amy. *Between Worlds: Women Writers of Chinese Ancestry*. New York: Pergamon Press, 1990, 137–38.

Lyotard, Jean-François. *The Postmodern Condition: A Report on Knowledge*. Manchester: Manchester University Press, 1984.

Ong, Walter J. *Orality and Literacy. The Technologizing of the Word*. New York: Methuen, 1982.

Tan, Amy. *The Joy Luck Club*. New York: Putnam, 1989.

M. MARIE BOOTH FOSTER

Voice, Mind, Self: Mother-Daughter Relationships in Amy Tan's The Joy Luck Club and The Kitchen God's Wife

In *The Joy Luck Club* and *The Kitchen God's Wife*, Amy Tan uses stories from her own history and myth to explore the voices of mothers and daughters of Chinese ancestry. Each woman tells a story indicative of the uniqueness of her voice. Mary Field Belensky, in *Women's Ways of Knowing*, argues that voice is "more than an academic shorthand for a person's point of view ... it is a metaphor that can apply to many aspects of women's experience and development.... Women repeatedly used the metaphor of voice to depict their intellectual and ethical development; ... the development of a sense of voice, mind, and self were intricately intertwined" (18). In Tan's fiction, the daughters' sense of self is intricately linked to an ability to speak and be heard by their mothers. Similarly, the mothers experience growth as they broaden communication lines with their daughters. Tan's women are very much like the women Belensky portrays in *Women's Ways of Knowing*: "In describing their lives, women commonly talked about voice and silence: 'speaking up,' 'speaking out,' 'being silenced,' 'not being heard,' 'really listening,' 'really talking,' 'words as weapons,' 'feeling deaf and dumb,' 'having no words,' 'saying what you mean,' 'listening to be heard'" (18). Until Tan's women connect as mothers and daughters, they experience strong feelings of isolation, a sense of disenfranchisement and fragmentation. These feelings often are a result of male domination, as Margery Wolf and Roxanne Witke describe in *Women in Chinese Society* (1–11).

From *Women of Color: Mother–Daughter Relationships in 20th-Century Literature*, edited by Elizabeth Brown-Guillory, pp. 208–227. © 1996 by the University of Texas Press.

17

A photo that is in part a pictorial history of Tan's foremothers is the inspiration for many of her portrayals of women. Tan writes in "Lost Lives of Women" of a picture of her mother, grandmother, aunts, cousins:

> When I first saw this photo as a child, I thought it was exotic and remote, of a far-away time and place, with people who had no connection to my American life. Look at their bound feet! Look at that funny lady with the plucked forehead. The solemn little girl was in fact, my mother. And leaning against the rock is my grandmother, Jing mei. . . . This is also a picture of secrets and tragedies. . . . This is the picture I see when I write. These are the secrets I was supposed to keep. These are the women who never let me forget why stories need to be told. (90)

In her remembrances, Tan presents Chinese American women who are forging identities beyond the pictures of concubinage and bound feet, women encountering new dragons, many of which are derived from being "hyphenated" American females. She views mother–daughter relationships in the same vein as Kathie Carlson, who argues, "This relationship is the birthplace of a woman's ego identity, her sense of security in the world, her feelings about herself, her body and other women. From her mother, a woman receives her first impression of how to be a woman" (xi).

The Joy Luck Club and *The Kitchen God's Wife* are studies in balance—balancing hyphenation and the roles of daughter, wife, mother, sister, career woman. In achieving balance, voice is important: in order to achieve voice, hyphenated women must engage in self-exploration, recognition and appreciation of their culture(s), and they must know their histories. The quest for voice becomes an archetypal journey for all of the women. The mothers come to the United States and have to adapt to a new culture, to redefine voice and self. The daughters' journeys become rites of passage; before they can find voice or define self they must acknowledge the history and myth of their mothers—"her-stories" of life in China, passage to the United States, and assimilation. And each must come to grips with being her mother's daughter.

The Joy Luck Club is a series of stories by and about narrators whose lives are interconnected as a result of friendship and membership in the Joy Luck Club: Suyuan and Jing-mei Woo, An-mei Hsu and Rose Hsu Jordan, Lindo and Waverly Jong, and Ying-ying and Lena St. Clair. The stories illuminate the multiplicity of experiences of Chinese women who are struggling to fashion a voice for themselves in a culture where women are conditioned to be silent. The stories are narrated by seven of the eight women in the group—four daughters and three mothers; one mother has recently died of a cerebral aneurysm. Jing-mei, nicknamed June, must be her mother's voice. The book is divided into four sections: Feathers from a Thousand *Li* Away, The Twenty-six Malignant Gates, American Translation, and Queen Mother of the Western Skies. Each chapter is prefaced with an introductory thematic tale or myth, all of which tend to stress the advice given by mothers.

Tan tells her mother's stories, the secret ones she began to tell after the death of Tan's father and brother in *The Kitchen God's Wife*. Patti Doten notes that Tan's mother told stories of her marriage to another man in China and of three daughters left behind when she came to the United States in 1949 (14), a story that is in part remembered in *The Joy Luck Club* with An-mei's saga. In *The Kitchen God's Wife*, a mother and daughter, Winnie Louie and Pearl Louie Brandt, share their stories, revealing the secrets that hide mind and self—and history—and veil and mask their voices. Winnie Louie's tale is of the loss of her mother as a young girl, marriage to a sadistic man who sexually abused her, children stillborn or dying young, a patriarchal society that allowed little room for escape from domestic violence (especially against the backdrop of war), and her flight to America and the love of a "good man." Daughter Pearl Louie Brandt's secrets include her pain upon the loss of her father and the unpredictable disease, multiple sclerosis, that inhibits her body and her life.

Tan's characters are of necessity storytellers and even historians, empowered by relating what they know about their beginnings and the insufficiencies of their present lives. Storytelling—relating memories—allows for review, analysis, and sometimes understanding of ancestry and thus themselves. The storytelling, however, is inundated with ambivalences and contradictions which, as Suzanna Danuta Walters argues, often take the form of blame in mother–daughter relationships (1).

Voice balances—or imbalances—voice as Chinese American mothers and daughters narrate their sagas. Because both mothers and daughters share the telling, the biases of a singular point of view are alleviated. Marianne Hirsch writes, "The story of female development, both in fiction and theory, needs to be written in the voice of mothers as well as in that of daughters. . . . Only in combining both voices, in finding a double voice that would yield a multiple female consciousness, can we begin to envision ways to live 'life afresh'" (161). Tan's fiction presents ambivalences and contradictions in the complicated interactions of mothers' and daughters' voices.

Regardless of how much the daughters try to deny it, it is through their mothers that they find their voice, their mind, their selfhood. Voice finds its form in the process of interaction, even if that interaction is conflict. "Recognition by the daughter that her voice is not entirely her own" comes in time and with experiences (one of the five interconnecting themes referred to by Nan Bauer Maglin in *The Literature of Matrilineage* as a recurring theme in such literature [258]). The experiences in review perhaps allow the daughters to know just how much they are dependent upon their mothers in their journey to voice. The mothers do not let them forget their own importance as the daughters attempt to achieve self-importance.

As Jing-mei "June" Woo tells her story and that of her deceased mother, the importance of the mother and daughter voices resonating, growing out of and being strengthened by each other, is apparent in her state of confusion and lack of direction and success. Perhaps her name is symbolic of her confusion: she is the only daughter with both a Chinese and an American name. As she recalls life with her mother, Jing-mei/June relates that she is constantly told by her mother, Suyuan Woo, that she does not try and therefore cannot achieve success. June's journey to voice and balance requires self-discovery—which must begin with knowing her mother. June has to use memories as a guide instead of her mother, whose tale she tells and whose saga she must complete. She must meet the ending to the tale of life in China and daughters left behind that her mother has told her over and over again, a story that she thought was a dark fairy tale.

The dark tale is of a previous life that includes a husband and daughters. Suyuan's first husband, an officer with the Kuomintang, takes her to Kweilin, a place she has dreamed of visiting. It has become a war refuge, no longer idyllic. Suyuan Woo and three other officers' wives start the Joy Luck Club to take their minds off the terrible smells of too many people in the city and the screams of humans and animals in pain. They attempt to raise their spirits with mah jong, jokes, and food.

Warned of impending danger, June's mother leaves the city with her two babies and her most valuable possessions. On the road to Chungking, she abandons first the wheelbarrow in which she has been carrying her babies and her goods, then more goods. Finally, her body weakened by fatigue and dysentery, she leaves the babies with jewelry to provide for them until they can be brought to her family. America does not make Suyuan forget the daughters she left as she fled. June Woo secretly views her mother's story as a fairy tale because the ending always changed. Perhaps herein lies the cause of their conflict: neither mother nor daughter listens to be heard, so each complains of not being heard. June Woo's disinterest and lack of knowledge of her mother's history exacerbate her own voicelessness, her lack of wholeness.

At a mah jong table where, appropriately, June takes her mother's place, she is requested by her mother's friends to go to China and meet the daughters of her mother. Thus her journey to voice continues and begins: it is a journey started at birth, but it is only now that she starts to recognize that she needs to know about her mother in order to achieve self-knowledge. She is to tell her sisters about their mother. The mothers' worst fears are realized when

June asks what she can possibly tell her mother's daughters. The mothers see their daughters in June's response, daughters who get irritated when their mothers speak in Chinese or explain things in broken English.

Although it startles her mother's friends, June's question is a valid one for a daughter whose relationship with her mother was defined by distance that developed slowly and grew. According to June, she and her mother never understood each other. She says they translated each other's meanings: she seemed to hear less than what was said, and her mother heard more. It is a complaint leveled by mothers and daughters throughout *The Joy Luck Club* and later in *The Kitchen God's Wife*. Both women want to be heard, but do not listen to be heard. They must come to understand that a voice is not a voice unless there is someone there to hear it.

Jing-mei is no longer sitting at the mah jong table but is en route to China when she summons up memories of her mother that will empower her to tell the daughters her mother's story. In the title story and in the short story "A Pair of Tickets," she occupies her mother's place in the storytelling, much as she occupies it at the mah jong table, and she is concerned with the responsibilities left by her mother. In her own stories, "Two Kinds" and "Best Quality," she is concerned with her selves: Jing-mei and June—the Chinese and the American, her mother's expectations and her belief in herself. Her stories are quest stories, described by Susan Koppelman in *Between Mothers and Daughters* as "a daughter's search for understanding" of her mother and herself (xxii). As June makes soup for her father, she sees the stray cat that she thought her mother had killed, since she had not seen it for some time. She makes motions to scare the cat and then recognizes the motions as her mother's; the cat reacts to her just as he had to her mother. She is reminded that she is her mother's daughter.

According to Judith Arcana in *Our Mothers' Daughters*, "we hold the belief that mothers love their daughters by definition and we fear any signal from our own mother that this love, which includes acceptance, affection, admiration and approval does not exist or is incomplete" (5). It does not matter to Jing-mei that she is not her mother's only disappointment (she says her mother always seemed displeased with everyone). Jing-mei recalls that something was not in balance and that something always needed improving for her mother. The friends do not seem to care; with all of her faults, she is their friend. Perhaps it is a "daughter's" expectations that June uses to judge her mother. Suyuan tells the rebellious June that she can be the best at anything as she attempts to mold her child into a piano-playing prodigy. She tells June she's not the best because she's not trying. After the request by the Joy Luck Club mothers June, in really listening to the voice of her mother as reserved in her memory, discovers that she might have been able to demonstrate ability had she tried: "for unlike my mother I did not believe I could be anything I wanted to be. I could only be me" (154). But she does not recognize that the "me" is the one who has made every attempt to escape development. The pendant her late mother gave her is symbolic. It was given to her as her life's importance. The latter part of the message is in Chinese, the voice of wisdom versus the provider of American circumstances.

In archetypal journeys, there is always a god or goddess who supports the "traveler" along his or her way. In *The Kitchen God's Wife*, Lady Sorrowfree is created by Winnie Louie, mother of Pearl, when the Kitchen God is determined by her to be an unfit god for her daughter's altar, inherited from an adopted aunt. The Kitchen God is unfit primarily because he became a god despite his mistreatment of his good wife. A porcelain figurine is taken from a storeroom where she has been placed as a "mistake" and is made into a goddess for Pearl, Lady Sorrowfree. Note Winnie's celebration of Lady Sorrowfree:

> I heard she once had many hardships in her life. . . . But her smile is genuine, wise, and innocent at the same time. And her hand, see how she just raised it. That means she is about to speak, or maybe she is telling you to speak. She is ready to listen. She understands English. You should tell her everything. . . . But sometimes, when you are afraid, you can talk to her. She will listen. She will wash away everything sad with her tears. She will use her stick to chase away everything bad. See her name: Lady Sorrowfree, happiness winning over bitterness, no regrets in this world. (414–415)

Perhaps Tan's mothers want to be like Lady Sorrowfree; they are in a sense goddesses whose altars their daughters are invited to come to for nurturance, compassion, empathy, inspiration, and direction. They are driven by the feeling of need to support those daughters, to give to them "the swan" brought from China—symbolic of their her-stories and wisdom, and the advantages of America, like the mother in the preface to the first round of stories. In the tale, all that is left of the mother's swan that she has brought from China after it is taken by customs officials is one feather; the mother wants to tell her daughter that the feather may look worthless, but it comes from her homeland and carries with it all good intentions. But she waits to tell her in perfect English, in essence keeping secrets. The mothers think that everything is possible for the daughters if the mothers will it. The daughters may come willingly to the altar or may rebelliously deny the sagacity of their mothers.

The mothers struggle to tell their daughters the consequences of not listening to them. The mother in the tale prefacing the section "Twenty-six Malignant Gates" tells her daughter not to ride her bike around the corner where she cannot see her because she will fall down and cry. The daughter questions how her mother knows, and she tells her that it is written in the book *Twenty-six Malignant Gates* that evil things can happen when a child goes outside the protection of the house. The daughter wants evidence, but her mother tells her that it is written in Chinese. When her mother does not tell her all twenty-six of the Malignant Gates, the girl runs out of the house and around the corner and falls, the consequence of not listening to her mother. Rebellion causes conflict—a conflict Lady Sorrowfree would not have to endure. June Woo and Waverly Jong seem to be daughters who thrive on the conflict that results from rebellion and sometimes even the need to win their mothers' approval. June trudges off every day to piano lessons taught by an old man who is hard of hearing. Defying her mother, she learns very little, as she reveals at a piano recital to which her mother has invited all of her friends. June notes the blank look on her mother's face that says she has lost everything. Waverly wins at chess, which pleases her mother, but out of defiance she stops playing until she discovers that she really enjoyed her mother's approval. As an adult she wants her mother to approve of the man who will be her second husband; mother and daughter assume the positions of chess players.

Tan's mothers frequently preach that children are to make their mothers proud so that they can brag about them to other mothers. The mothers engage in fierce competition with each other. Suyuan Woo brags about her daughter even after June's poorly performed piano recital. All of the mothers find fault with their daughters, but this is something revealed to the daughters, not to the community.

Much as Lindo Jong credits herself with daughter Waverly's ability to play chess, she blames herself for Waverly's faults as a person and assumes failures in raising her daughter: "It is my fault she is this way—selfish. I wanted my children to have the best combination: American circumstances and Chinese character. How could I know these things do not mix?" (289). Waverly knows how American circumstances work, but Lindo can't teach her about Chinese character: "How to obey parents and listen to your mother's mind. How not to show your own thoughts, to put your feelings behind your face so you can take advantage of hidden opportunities. . . . Why Chinese thinking is best" (289). What she gets is a daughter who wants to be Chinese because it is fashionable, a daughter who likes to speak back and question what she says, and a daughter to whom promises mean nothing. Nonetheless, she is a daughter of whom Lindo is proud.

Lindo Jong is cunning, shrewd, resourceful; Waverly Jong is her mother's daughter. Waverly manages to irritate her mother when she resists parental guidance. Judith Arcana posits that "some daughters spend all or most of their energy trying futilely to be as different from their mothers as possible in behavior, appearance, relations with friends, lovers, children, husbands" (9). Waverly is a strategist in getting her brother to teach her to play chess, in winning at chess, in gaining her mother's forgiveness when she is rude and getting her mother's acceptance of the man she plans to marry. Lindo proudly reminds Waverly that she has inherited her ability to win from her.

In literature that focuses on mother/daughter relationships, feminists see "context—historical time and social and cultural group" as important (Rosinsky, 285). Lindo relates in "The Red Candle" that she once sacrificed her life to keep her parents' promise; she married as arranged. Chinese tradition permits Lindo's parents to give her to Huang Tai for her son—to determine her fate—but Lindo takes control of her destiny. On the day of her wedding, as she prepares for the ceremony, she schemes her way out of the planned marriage and into America, where "nobody says you have to keep the circumstances somebody else gives to you" (289).

It takes determination to achieve voice and selfhood, to take control of one's mind and one's life from another, making one's self heard, overcoming silence. Lindo does not resign herself to her circumstances in China. Waverly reveals that she learns some of her strategies from her mother: "I was six when my mother taught me the art of invisible strength. It was a strategy for winning arguments, respect from others, and eventually, though neither of us knew it at the time, chess games" (89). Therein lies Lindo's contribution to her daughter's voice.

Lindo uses the same brand of ingenuity to play a life chess game with and to teach her daughter. Adrienne Rich writes in *Of Woman Born*: "Probably there is nothing in human nature more resonant with charges than the flow of energy between two biologically alike bodies, one which has lain in amniotic bliss inside the other, one which has labored to give birth to the other. The materials are there for the deepest mutuality and the most painful estrangement" (226). Lindo has to contend with a headstrong daughter: "'Finish your coffee,' I told her yesterday. 'Don't throw your blessings away.' 'Don't be old-fashioned, Ma,' she told me, finishing her coffee down the sink. 'I'm my own person.' And I think, how can she be her own person? When did I give her up?" (290).

Waverly is champion of the chess game, but she is no match for her mother in a life chess game. She knows her chances of winning in a contest against her mother, who taught her to be strong like the wind. Waverly learns during the "chess years" that her mother was a champion strategist. Though she is a tax attorney able to bully even the Internal Revenue Service, she fears the wrath of her mother if she is told to mind her business: "Well, I don't know if it's explicitly stated in the law, but you can't ever tell a Chinese mother to shut up. You could be charged as an accessory to your own murder" (191). What Waverly perceives as an impending battle for her mother's approval of her fiancé is nothing more than the opportunity for her mother and her to communicate with each other. She strategically plans to win her mother's approval of her fiancé, Rick, just as if she is playing a game of chess. She is afraid to tell her mother that they are going to be married because she is afraid that her mother will not approve. The conversation ends with her recognition that her mother also needs to be heard and with her mother's unstated approval of her fiancé. Waverly Jong recognizes her mother's strategies in their verbal jousts, but she also recognizes that, just like her, her mother is in search of something. What she sees is an old woman waiting to be invited into her daughter's life. Like the other mothers, Lindo views herself as standing outside her daughter's life—a most undesirable place.

Sometimes Tan's mothers find it necessary to intrude in order to teach the daughters to save themselves; they criticize, manage, and manipulate with an iron fist. An-mei Hsu and Ying-ying St. Clair play this role. "My mother once told me why I was so confused all the time," says Rose Hsu during her first story, "Without Wood" (212). "She said that I was without wood. Born without wood so that I listened to too many people. She knew this because she had almost become this way" (212). Suyuan Woo tells June Woo that such weaknesses are present in the mother, An-mei Hsu: "Each person is made of five elements. . . . Too little wood and you bend too quickly to listen to other people's ideas, unable to stand on your own. This was like my Auntie An-mei" (19). Rose's mother tells her that she must stand tall and listen to her mother standing next to her. If she bends to listen to strangers, she'll grow weak and be destroyed. Rose Hsu is in the process of divorce from a husband who has labeled her indecisive and useless as a marriage partner. She is guilty of allowing her husband to mold her. He does not want her to be a partner in family decisions until he makes a mistake in his practice as a plastic surgeon. Then he complains that she is unable to make decisions: he is dissatisfied with his creation. Finding it difficult to accept divorce, she confusedly runs to her friends and a psychiatrist seeking guidance.

Over and over again her mother tells her to count on a mother because a mother is best and knows what is inside of her daughter. "A psyche-atricks will only make you hulihudu, make you heimongmong" (210). The psychiatrist leaves her confused, as her mother predicts. She becomes even more confused as she tells each of her friends and her psychiatrist a different story. Her mother advises her to stand up to her husband, to speak up. She assumes the role of Lady Sorrowfree. When Rose does as her mother advises, she notices that her husband seems scared and confused. She stands up to him and forces him to retreat. She is her mother's daughter. She listens to her mother and finds her voice—her self.

Like the other mothers, An-mei demonstrates some of the qualities of "Lady Sorrowfree." An-mei is concerned that her daughter sees herself as having no options. A psychologist's explanation is "to the extent that women perceive themselves as having no choice, they correspondingly excuse themselves from the responsibility that decision entails" (Gilligan, 67). An-mei was "raised the Chinese way": "I was taught to desire nothing, to swallow other people's misery, to eat my own bitterness" (241). She uses the tale of the magpies to indicate that one can either make the choice to be in charge of one's life or continue to let others be in control. For thousands of years magpies came to the fields of a group of peasants just after they had sown their seeds and watered them with their tears. The magpies ate the seeds and drank the tears. Then one day the peasants decided to end their suffering and silence. They clapped their hands and banged sticks together, making noise that startled and confused the magpies. This continued for days until the magpies died of hunger and exhaustion from waiting for the noise to stop so that they could land and eat. The sounds from the hands and sticks were their voices. Her daughter should face her tormentor.

An-mei tells stories of her pain, a pain she does not wish her daughter to endure. Memory is, in part, voices calling out to her, reminding her of what she has endured and of a relationship wished for: "it was her voice that confused me," "a familiar sound from a forgotten dream," "she cried with a wailing voice," "voices praising," "voices murmuring," "my mother's voice went away" (41–45). The voices of her mothers confused her. She was a young girl in need of a mother's clear voice that would strengthen her circumstances and her context. The voices remind her, in "Scar," of wounds that heal but leave their imprint and of the importance of taking control out of the hands of those who have the ability to devour their victims, as in the story "Magpies." A scar resulting from a severe burn from a pot of boiling soup reminds her of when her mother was considered a ghost: her mother was dead to her family because she became a rich merchant's concubine. With time the scar "became pale and shiny and I had no memory of my mother. That is the way it is with a wound. The wound begins to close in on itself, to protect what is hurting so much. And once it is closed, you no longer see what is underneath, what started the pain" (40). It is also the way of persons attempting to assimilate—the wounds of getting to America, the wounds of hyphenation, close in on themselves and then it is difficult to see where it all began.

An-mei remembers the scar and the pain when her mother returns to her grandmother Poppo's deathbed. Upon the death of Poppo, she leaves with her mother, who shortly afterward commits suicide. Poppo tells An-mei that when a person loses face, it's like dropping a necklace down a well: the only way you can get it back is to jump in after it. From her mother An-mei learns that tears cannot wash away sorrows; they only feed someone else's joy. Her mother tells her to swallow her own tears.

An-mei knows strength and she knows forgetting. Perhaps that is why her daughter tells the story of her loss. It is Rose Hsu who tells the story of her brother's drowning and her mother's faith that he would be found. She refuses to believe that he is dead; without any driving lessons, she steers the car to the ocean side to search once more for him. After her son Bing's death, An-mei places the Bible that she has always carried to the First Chinese Baptist Church under a short table leg as a way of correcting the imbalances of life. She gives her daughter advice on how to correct imbalances in her life. The tale prefacing the section "Queen of the Western Skies" is also a fitting message for Rose Hsu. A woman playing with her granddaughter wonders at the baby's happiness and laughter, remembering that she was once carefree before she shed her innocence and began to look critically and suspiciously at everything. She asks the babbling child if it is Syi Wang, Queen Mother of the Western Skies, come back to provide her with some answers: "Then you must teach my daughter this same lesson. How to lose your innocence but not your hope. How to laugh forever" (159).

Like all the other daughters, Lena must recognize and respect the characteristics of Lady Sorrowfree that are inherent in her mother, Ying-ying. Ying-ying describes her daughter as being devoid of wisdom. Lena laughs at her mother when she says "arty-tecky" (architecture) to her sister-in-law. Ying-ying admits that she should have slapped Lena more as a child for disrespect. Though Ying-ying serves as Lena's goddess, Lena initially does not view her mother as capable of advice on balance. Ying-ying's telling of her story is very important to seeing her in a true mothering role; her daughter's first story makes one think that the mother is mentally unbalanced.

Evelyn Reed in *Woman's Evolution* writes: "A mother's victimization does not merely humiliate her, it mutilates her daughter who watches her for clues as to what it means to be a woman. Like the traditional foot-bound Chinese woman, she passes on her affliction. The mother's self-hatred and low expectations are binding rags for the psyche of the daughter" (293). Ying-ying, whose name means "Clear Reflection," becomes a ghost. As a young girl she liked to unbraid her hair and wear it loose. She recalls a scolding from her mother, who once told her that she was like the lady ghosts at the bottom of the lake. Her daughter is unaware of her mother's previous marriage to a man in China twenty years before Lena's birth. Ying-ying falls in love with him because he strokes her cheek and tells her that she has tiger eyes, that they gather fire in the day and shine golden at night. Her husband opts to run off with another woman during her pregnancy, and she aborts the baby because she has come to hate her husband with a passion. Ying-ying tells Lena that she was born a tiger in a year when babies were dying and because she was strong she survived. After ten years of reclusive living with cousins in the country, she goes to the city to live and work. There she meets Lena's father, an American she marries after being courted for four years, and continues to be a ghost. Ying-ying says that she willingly gave up her spirit.

In Ying-ying's first story, "The Moon Lady," when she sees her daughter lounging by the pool she realizes that they are lost, invisible creatures. Neither, at this point, recognizes the importance of "listening harder to the silence beneath their voices" (Maglin, 260). Their being lost reminds her of the family outing to Tai Lake as a child, when she falls into the lake, is rescued, and is put on shore only to discover that the moon lady she has been anxiously awaiting to tell her secret wish is male. The experience is so traumatic that she forgets her wish. Now that she is old and is watching her daughter, she remembers that she had wished to be found. And now she wishes for her daughter to be found—to find herself.

Lena, as a young girl, sees her mother being devoured by her fears until she becomes a ghost. Ying-ying believes that she is already a ghost. She does not want her daughter to become a ghost like her, "an unseen spirit" (285). Ying-ying begins life carefree. She is loved almost to a fault by her mother and her nursemaid, Amah. She is spoiled by her family's riches and wasteful. When she unties her hair and floats through the house, her mother tells her that she resembles the "lady ghosts . . . ladies who drowned in shame and floated in living people's houses with their hair undone to show everlasting despair" (276). She knows despair when the north wind that she thinks has blown her luck chills her heart by blowing her first husband past her to other women.

Lena, Ying-ying's daughter, is a partner in a marriage where she has a voice in the rules; but when the game is played, she loses her turn many times. Carolyn See argues that "in the name of feminism and right thinking, this husband is taking Lena for every cent she's got, but she's so demoralized, so 'out of balance' in the Chinese sense, that she can't do a thing about it" (11). In the introductory anecdote to the section "American Translation," a mother warns her daughter that she cannot put mirrors at the foot of the bed because all of her marriage happiness will bounce back and tumble the opposite way. Her mother takes from her bag a mirror that she plans to give the daughter as a wedding gift so that it faces the other mirror. The mirrors then reflect the happiness of the daughter. Lena's mother, as does Rose's mother, provides her with the mirror to balance her happiness; the mirror is a mother's advice or wisdom. It is Lena's mother's credo that a woman is out of balance if something goes against her nature. She does not want to be like her mother, but her mother foresees that she too will become a ghost; her husband will transform her according to his desires. Ying-ying recalls that she became "Betty" and was given a new date of birth by a husband who never learned to speak her language. Her review of her own story makes her know that she must influence her daughter's "story" that is in the making. Lena sees herself with her husband in the midst of problems so deep that she can't see where the bottom is. In the guise of a functional relationship is a dysfunctional one. Her mother predicts that the house will break into pieces. When a too-large vase on a too-weak table crashes to the floor, Lena admits that she knew it would happen. Her mother asks her why she did not take steps to keep the house from falling, meaning her marriage as well as the vase.

The goddess role becomes all important to Ying-ying as she becomes more determined to prevent her daughter from becoming a ghost. She fights the daughter that she has raised, "watching from another shore" and "accept[ing] her American ways" (286). After she uses the sharp pain of what she knows to "penetrate [her] daughter's tough skin and cut the tiger spirit loose," she waits for her to come into the room, like a tiger waiting between the trees, and pounces. Ying-ying wins the fight and gives her daughter her spirit, "because this is the way a mother loves her daughter" (286). Lady Sorrowfree helps her "charge" achieve voice.

From the daughter with too much water, to the mother and daughter with too much wood, to the tiger ghosts and just plain ghosts, to the chess queens, Tan's women in *The Joy Luck Club* find themselves capable of forging their own identities, moving beyond passivity to assertiveness—speaking up. They are a piece of the portrait that represents Amy Tan's family history—her own story included; they are, in composite, her family's secrets and tragedies. Tan is unlike some Asian American writers who have had to try to piece together and sort out the meaning of the past from shreds of stories overheard or faded photographs. As in her stories, her mother tells her the stories and explains the photographs. Bell Gale Chevigny writes that "women writing about other women will symbolically reflect their internalized relations with their mothers and in some measure re-create them" (80). From Tan's own accounts, her interaction with her mother is reflected in her fiction.

Tan's women with their American husbands attempt often without knowing it to balance East and West, the past and the future of their lives. A level of transcendence is apparent in the storytelling, as it is in *The Kitchen God's Wife*. Mothers and daughters must gain from the storytelling in order to have healthy relationships with each other.

In *The Kitchen God's Wife*, Winnie Louie and her daughter Pearl Louie Brandt are both keepers of secrets that accent the distance that characterizes their relationship. Pearl thinks after a trip to her mother's home: "Mile after mile, all of it familiar, yet not this distance that separates us, me from my mother" (57). She is unsure of how this distance was created. Winnie says of their relationship: "That is how she is. That is how I am. Always careful to be polite, always trying not to bump into each other, just like strangers" (82). When their secrets begin to weigh down their friends who have known them for years, who threaten to tell each of the other's secrets, Winnie Louie decides that it is time for revelation. The process of the revelation is ritual: "recitation of the relationship between mother and daughter," "assessment of the relationship," and "the projection of the future into the relationship" (Koppelman, xxvii). At the same time revelation is a journey to voice, the voice that they must have with each other. Again, voice is a metaphor for speaking up, being heard, listening to be heard. No longer will stories begin as Pearl's does: "Whenever my mother talks to me, she begins the conversation as if we were already in the middle of an argument" (11). That they argue or are in conflict is not problematic; it is the "talks to" that should be replaced with "talks with." As much as Pearl needs to know her mother's secrets, Winnie Louie needs to tell them in order to build a relationship that is nurturing for both mother and daughter.

Pearl's secret is multiple sclerosis. At first she does not tell her mother because she fears her mother's theories on her illness. What becomes her secret is the anger she feels toward her father, the inner turmoil that began with his dying and death. Sometimes the mother's voice drowns the voice of the daughter as she attempts to control or explain every aspect of the daughter's existence. "If I had not lost my mother so young, I would not have listened to Old Aunt," says Winnie Louie (65) as she begins her story. These might also be the words of her daughter, though Pearl's loss of mother was not a physical loss. The opportunity for the resonating of mother and daughter voices seems to be the difference between balance and imbalance. American circumstances are to be blamed for the distance; the need to keep secrets grows out of the perceived necessity of assimilation and clean slates. Because her mother was not there, Winnie "listened to Old Aunt" (65). Winnie Louie's dark secret begins with her mother, who disappeared without telling her why; she still awaits some appearance by her mother to explain. Her mother's story is also hers: an arranged marriage—in her mother's case, to curb her rebelliousness; realization that she has a lesser place in marriage than purported; and a daughter as the single lasting joy derived from the marriage. The difference is that Winnie's mother escaped, to be heard from no more.

Winnie's family abides by all of the customs in giving her hand in marriage to Wen Fu: "Getting married in those days was like buying real estate. Here you see a house you want to live in, you find a real estate agent. Back in China, you saw a rich family with a daughter, you found a go-between who knew how to make a good business deal" (134). Winnie tells her daughter, "If asked how I felt when they told me I would marry Wen Fu, I can only say this: It was like being told I had won a big prize. And it was also like being told my head was going to be chopped off. Something between those two feelings" (136). Winnie experiences very little mercy in her marriage to the monstrous Wen Fu.

Wen Fu serves as an officer in the Chinese army, so during World War II they move about China with other air force officers and their wives. Throughout the marriage, Winnie knows abuse and witnesses the death of her babies. She tries to free herself from the tyranny of the marriage, but her husband enjoys abusing her too much to let her go. Her story is a long one, a lifetime of sorrow, death, marriage, imprisonment, lost children, lost friends and family. Jimmie Louie saves her life by helping her to escape Wen Fu and to come to the United States. She loves Jimmie Louie and marries him. The darkest part of her secret she reveals to Pearl almost nonchalantly: Pearl is the daughter of the tyrant Wen Fu.

The daughter asks her mother: "Tell me again . . . why you had to keep it a secret." The mother answers: "Because then you would know. . . . You would know how weak I was. You would think I was a bad mother" (398). Winnie's actions and response are not unexpected. She is every mother who wants her daughter to think of her as having lived a blemish-free existence. She is every mother who forgets that her daughter is living life and knows blemishes. Secrets revealed, the women begin to talk. No longer does Winnie have to think that the year her second husband, Jimmie Louie, died was "when everyone stopped listening to me" (81). Pearl knows her mother's story and can respect her more, not less, for her endurance. She is then able to see a woman molded by her experiences and her secrets—a woman who has lived with two lives. With the tiptoeing around ended, the distance dissipates. By sharing their secrets, they help each other to achieve voice. The gift of Lady Sorrowfree is symbolic of their bonding; this goddess has all of the characteristics of the nurturing, caring, listening mother. Her imperfections lie in her creation; experiences make her. She has none of the characteristics of the Kitchen God.

The story of the Kitchen God and his wife angers Winnie Louie; she looks at the god as a bad man who was rewarded for admitting that he was a bad man. As the story goes, a wealthy farmer, Zhang, who had a good wife who saw to it that his farm flourished, brought home a pretty woman and made his wife cook for her. The pretty woman ran his wife off without any objection from the farmer. She helped him use up all of his riches foolishly and left him a beggar. He was discovered hungry and suffering by a servant who took him home to care for him. When he saw his wife, whose home it was, he attempted to hide in the kitchen fireplace; his wife could not save him. The Jade Emperor, because Zhang admitted he was wrong, made him Kitchen God with the duty to watch over people's behavior. Winnie tells Pearl that people give generously to the Kitchen God to keep him happy in the hopes that he will give a good report to the Jade Emperor. Winnie thinks that he is not the god for her daughter. How can one trust a god who would cheat on his wife? How can he be a good judge of behavior? The wife is the good one. She finds another god for her daughter's altar, Lady Sorrowfree. After all, she has already given her a father.

Even as Winnie tells her story, one senses that the women are unaware of the strength of the bond between them that partly originates in the biological connection and partly in their womanness. Storytelling/revealing secrets gives both of them the opportunity for review; Winnie Louie tells Pearl that she has taught her lessons with love, that she has combined all of the love that she had for the three she lost during the war and all of those that she did not allow to be born and has given it to Pearl. She speaks of her desire "to believe in something good" (152), her lost hope and innocence: "So I let those other babies die. In my heart I was being kind. . . . I was a young woman then. I had no more hope left, no trust, no innocence" (312). In telling her story, she does not ask for sympathy or forgiveness; she simply wants to be free of the pain that "comes from keeping everything inside, waiting until it is too late" (88).

Perhaps this goddess, Lady Sorrowfree, to whom they burn incense will cause them never to forget the importance of voice and listening. On the heels of listening there is balance as both Winnie and Pearl tell their secrets and are brought closer by them. East and West, mother and daughter, are bonded for the better. Arcana notes that "mother/daughter sisterhood is the consciousness we must seek to make this basic woman bond loving and fruitful, powerful and deep . . ." (34). It ensures that women do not smother each other and squelch the voice of the other or cause each other to retreat into silence.

In exploring the problems of mother–daughter voices in relationships, Tan unveils some of the problems of biculturalism—of Chinese ancestry and American circumstances. She presents daughters who do not know their mothers' "importance" and thus cannot know their own; most seem never to have been told or even cared to hear their mothers' history. Until they do, they can never achieve voice. They assimilate; they marry American men and put on American faces. They adapt. In the meantime, their mothers sit like Lady Sorrowfree on her altar, waiting to listen. The daughters' journeys to voice are completed only after they come to the altars of their Chinese mothers.

Works Cited and Consulted

Arcana, Judith. *Our Mothers' Daughters*. Berkeley: Shameless Hussy Press, 1979.

Belensky, Mary Field, et al. *Women's Ways of Knowing*. New York: Basic Books, 1986.

Blicksilver, Edith. *The Ethnic American Woman: Problems, Protests, Lifestyle*. Dubuque, Ia.: Kendall/Hunt Publishing, 1978.

Carlson, Kathie. *In Her Image: The Unhealed Daughter's Search for Her Mother*. Boston: Shambhala, 1990.

Chevigny, Bell Gale. "Daughters Writing: Toward a Theory of Women's Biography." *Feminist Studies* 9 (1983): 79–102.

Chodorow, Nancy. *Feminism and Psychoanalytic Theory*. New Haven: Yale University Press, 1989.

Doten, Patti. "Sharing Her Mother's Secrets." *Boston Globe*, June 21, 1991, E9–14.

Friday, Nancy. *My Mother/My Self*. New York: Delacorte Press, 1977.

Gardiner, Judith Kegan. "Mind Mother: Psychoanalysis and Feminism." In *Making a Difference: Feminist Literary Criticism*, ed. Gayle Greene and Coppélia Kahn, 113–145. New York: Methuen, 1985.

Gilligan, Carol. *In a Different Voice*. Cambridge, Mass.: Harvard University Press, 1982.

Hirsch, Marianne. *The Mother–Daughter Plot: Narrative, Psychoanalysis, Feminism*. Bloomington: Indiana University Press, 1989.

Hirsch, Marianne, and Evelyn Fox Feller. *Conflicts in Feminism*. New York: Routledge, 1990.

Kim, Elaine H. *Asian American Literature: An Introduction to the Writings and Their Social Context*. Philadelphia: Temple University Press, 1982.

Koppelman, Susan. *Between Mothers and Daughters, Stories across a Generation*. New York: Feminist Press at the City University of New York, 1985.

Maglin, Nan Bauer. "The Literature of Matrilineage." In *The Lost Tradition: Mothers and Daughters in Literature*, ed. Cathy N. Davidson and E. M. Broner, 257–267. New York: Frederick Ungar, 1980.

Marbella, Jean. "Amy Tan: Luck But Not Joy." *Baltimore Sun*, June 30, 1991, E–11.

"Mother with a Past." *Maclean's* (July 15, 1991): 47.

Reed, Evelyn. *Woman's Evolution*. New York: Pathfinder Press, 1975.

Rich, Adrienne. *Of Woman Born: Motherhood as Experience and Institution*. New York: Norton, 1976, 1986.

Rosinsky, Natalie M. "Mothers and Daughters: Another Minority Group." In *The Lost Tradition: Mothers and Daughters in Literature*, ed. Cathy N. Davidson and E. M. Broner, 281–303. New York: Frederick Ungar, 1980.

See, Carolyn. "Drowning in America, Starving in China." *Los Angeles Times Book Review*, March 12, 1989, 1, 11.

Spence, Jonathan D. *The Search for Modern China*. New York: W. W. Norton, 1990.

Tan, Amy. *The Joy Luck Club*. New York: Ivy Books, 1989.

———. *The Kitchen God's Wife*. New York: G. P. Putnam's Sons, 1991.

———. "Lost Lives of Women." *Life* (April 1991), 90–91.

Walters, Suzanna Danuta. *Lives Together/Worlds Apart: Mothers and Daughters in Popular Culture*. Berkeley: University of California Press, 1992.

Wolf, Margery, and Roxanne Witke. *Women in Chinese Society*. Stanford: Stanford University Press, 1975.

Yamada, Mitsuye. "Invisibility Is an Unnatural Disaster: Reflections of an Asian American Woman." In *This Bridge Called My Back: Writings of Radical Women of Color*, ed. Cherríe Moraga and Gloria Anzaldúa, 35–40. Latham, N.Y.: Kitchen Table/Women of Color Press, 1982.

STEVEN P. SONDRUP

Hanyu at the Joy Luck Club

Immigration as a social phenomenon presents a complex array of divided loyalties, hierarchies, and systems of reference. In the case of immigrants themselves, marginalization of many different kinds is a complicated and often deeply disorienting experience. On the one hand, the immigrant feels varying degrees of alienation in the new culture: unfamiliar customs, habits, laws, and language exert a powerful centrifugal force toward the outer edges of society. On the other hand, the immigrant also experiences an alienation from the home culture as well. The forces that combined to occasion emigration—a departure from the familiar, the including, and the defining—often come more clearly and painfully into focus. Not only do the motives and forces that prompted the original emigration loom large, but the distance between the old and the new culture grows ever greater. While the emigrant is living away from the natal culture, that culture continues to change, transform itself, and develop in ways that the emigrant may not have been able to anticipate or even understand. Local and regional dialects often give way to a nationally standardized language in which the emigrant may feel deracinated after an absence. The bind is, thus, double: the emigrant will typically experience at least a degree of marginalization in the new culture but will constantly become ever more alienated from the changing native culture. For the children of immigrants born in the new culture, the tension between assimilation

From *Cultural Dialogue and Misreading*, edited by Mabel Lee and Meng Hua, pp. 400–408. © 1997 by Wild Peony Pty. Ltd. and contributors.

35

on the one hand and retention of some kind of link to the values, traditions, and language of their parents on the other can be considerable. Many factors play a role in heightening or narrowing, in complicating or resolving, or in exacerbating or relieving the tension. The archetypal generation gap in such families is complicated by one additional and often very complex factor.

The expansion of the canon of American literature begun in the 1960s and continuing into the present has brought the literature and criticism of many minority groups within the United States of America to the attention of much larger audiences. Asian American literature is a strategically constructed term stressing a unitary if not monolithic identity but coined to counter marginalization or complete exclusion.[1] In the late 1970s Elaine H. Kim attempted to define Asian American literature as 'work published in English by writers of Chinese, Japanese, Korean, and Filipino ancestry about the experiences of Asians in America' (1982:xi). By any standard, Asian American literature has thrived in a most remarkable way over the last twenty-five years and achieved extraordinary prominence during the early 1990s. The popular, commercial and critical success of Maxine Hong Kingston's *The Woman Warrior*, Henry Hwang's *M. Butterfly*, and Amy Tan's *The Joy Luck Club* and *The Kitchen God's Wife* are indicative of this new pre-eminence. Notably, the new prominence of Asian American novels, poetry, and drama is well balanced by the numerous articles and books by scholars specializing in Asian American literature.

In presuming to discuss Asian American literature and more specifically one aspect of *The Joy Luck Club*, I am acutely aware of the precariousness of my critical stance. As a Danish American male, I have no access to distinctly insider Chinese cultural knowledge, no facility with a methodology that might be group-specific, and no first-hand experience with mother–daughter relationships that are certainly an extremely important matrix of the novel.[2] Although sensitive, I hope, to the uniqueness and particularity of each of these foci of understanding, I am persuaded, along with those adhering to the approach frequently known as the ethnicity school, that more is to be gained than lost by allowing broad critical entree to minority literatures.[3]

The issue I wish to raise, albeit as an outsider, is that of the status of the Chinese language in a narratological sense in *The Joy Luck Club*.[4] By definition the Chinese American novel—a specific species of the Asian American novel—is written in English, but Chinese, usually either Yue (or Cantonese as it is more typically known in the United States) or Mandarin, is part of the texture of the novel, a texture that conspicuously plays a role in the narrative strategy in some cases or in others is so smooth it almost vanishes. *The Joy Luck Club* is decidedly of the former type. The question of language is problematized in the opening lines of the novel:

In America I will have a daughter just like me. But over there nobody will say her worth is measured by the loudness of her husband's belch. Over there nobody will look down on her, because I will make her speak only perfect American English.... Now the woman was old. And she had a daughter who grew up speaking only English and swallowing more Coca-Cola than sorrow. (3)

The speaking of perfect American English is initially a token of full assimilation into American society, a society that is naively thought to be free of social injustices and prejudices. But disappointingly, the mastery of American English at the expense of Mandarin is no warrant of happiness, but rather a source of misunderstanding and at least transitory alienation. To learn perfect American English is to rebel against traditional Chinese cultural expectations and to resist, forget, or suppress the official language in which they are embedded.

The Joy Luck Club narrates the maturation of four second-generation Chinese women and their eventual bonding with their mothers, all of whom had left China in the hope of finding a better life. Each of these four mothers who played mah-jong together for decades tries in the course of many years to tell her daughter about her past and especially her relationship with her mother in a way in which the values of traditional China, the Chinese diaspora, and male Eurocentrism are engaged. The nature and dynamics of storytelling which create an alternative space and a different history distinct from the official accounts of war and political strife in China during the 1930s and 1940s are foregrounded and become one of the principle axes of the novel.

The linguistic competence of the major characters in the novel is clearly presented. The mothers are all native speakers of Mandarin and are thus a distinct minority in the Chinese American community which is made up of about eighty-six per cent speakers of Cantonese (Ramsey 1987:98). This marginalization within a marginalized community, however, is an issue that is touched upon only in passing. The daughters grow up hearing varying amounts of Mandarin spoken at home and understand their mothers when they speak Mandarin but do not achieve any significant degree of oral fluency themselves. Notably, none can read Chinese, a fact which is a difficulty in that spoken Chinese is much more strongly linked to writing than Western languages are to their respective written forms. The attempt to clarify which meaning of a particular homophone is intended by reference to the appropriate character is incomprehensible and alien to the second generation. The daughters' inability to read Chinese characters, however, stresses the importance of the spoken language and immediate interpersonal relationships as opposed to depersonalized abstractions. The value of the intimacy of an oral tradition that strongly contrasts with the official and public tradition and in many ways subverts it is forcefully adduced.

Oliver Stone's film adaptation of the novel heightens the linguistic contrast in competence between the first and second generation. Early in the film, Jing-mei cautions her aunties not to speak Chinese at the mah-jong table lest she, not being able to understand them, think they are cheating. Yet, when at the end she finally meets her two sisters in China, she is able to speak remarkably fluent Mandarin. The stressing of the difference between the Chinese culture of the mothers and the basically American culture of the daughters takes place very forcefully in linguistic terms in other ways as well. In the film, none of the daughters is ever portrayed speaking Mandarin or giving any evidence of understanding it at all, whereas the novel clearly indicates that they have at least rudimentary control of the language. Moreover, in the film all of the episodes that take place in China are performed in Mandarin accompanied by English subtitles. The novel, of course, contains no extended passages in Mandarin, and the descriptions of life in China prior to emigration are entirely in English. This cinematic innovation changes one of the fundamental structural aspects of the novel. Whereas the mothers in the novel illustrate the proposition that subalterns can never speak for themselves, that they can only find a voice through others—in this case their daughters who have been brought up to speak perfect American English—in the film they are given their own very distinctive voice which is not only not mediated by their daughters but completely alien to their daughters.[5] The powerful sense of cultural otherness created by Mandarin dialogue is only enhanced by the mothers' gaining of the power of narrative in their own right that is not dependent on the perfect American English of their daughters. Because the cinematic gap between self and other is so much more pronounced in that the other has its own contrasting voice that is not subsumed within the voice of the self, the ultimate resolution of the painful separation of self and (m)other at the end is even more poignant.

Some of the most obvious misunderstandings between the immigrant mothers and those around them have to do with their less than complete mastery of English. Language difficulties have long been part of the caricature of Chinese Americans in American popular culture and take place on many levels. Direct quotations of the mothers' speech are often unidiomatic in English but fully reveal the Chinese syntax lying just below the surface. After a heated description on the difference between Taiyuan and Taiwan, Lindo Jong triumphantly proclaims, 'Now you understand my meaning' (203). Although the intent is perfectly clear, the statement seems peculiar in English but can easily be recognized as a word for word translation of *xianzai ni mingbai wode yisi*. The phonological struggles with English in *The*

Joy Luck Club, however, are often witty and provide a telling commentary on contemporary American culture. When Ying-ying St. Clair refers to her social security (the government mandated system of retirement payments) as 'so-so security' (275), the contemporary American will easily understand how such a misunderstanding on the phonetic level could take place but also that 'so-so' in the sense of mediocre and barely adequate is not an altogether inappropriate description of the current state of the system. On another occasion, Suyuan Woo misunderstands a vulgar insult directed toward her in a neighbourhood disagreement in a wonderfully ironic manner. Reporting on the verbal exchange, she says:

> 'And that man, he raise his hand like this, show me his ugly fist and call me worst Fukien landlady. I not from Fukien. Huuh! He know nothing!' she said satisfied she had put him in his place. (224)

Her inability or refusal to understand the single most vulgar and socially unacceptable word in American English is a misprision that rejects the common and base (albeit in the new culture), insists literally on social legitimacy, and reaffirms her insistence on things of only the best quality, the explicit theme of the chapter in which the exchange takes place but more generally the novel as a whole.

The misunderstanding, though, is doing something more. The reader who is also familiar with Chinese will recognize in the word *Fukien* not a standard place name but rather a variation of *Fujian*, that is, Fujian province. To interpret and make sense of her angry neighbour's vulgar appellation which she does not understand or refuses to understand in English requires recourse to Chinese and specifically a dialectical form. Although Suyuan Woo is not in fact from Fujian province, the interpretive process legitimizes Chinese, dialectical Chinese, and English in a complex referential system. This incident is but one example of the rich polyvalence resulting from the interplay of Chinese and English.

Many pages of the novel have several romanized Chinese words or phrases printed in italics so they will stand out from the body text. Often the literal English translation follows immediately, but the syntax of the sentences is so carefully crafted that the non-Chinese-speaking reader may not realize that the translation is a translation. The Chinese thus functions on one level to create the feeling of a situation where cultures overlap and languages are freely mixed; that is, the effect of the real. But in creating the effect of the real, the novel is also less than fully candid with the non-Chinese-speaking reader. Words like *taitai* and *popo* are treated as proper names rather than titles or relationships and the translations that are given are, to say the least, somewhat idiosyncratic. More striking, however, is the romanization of the Chinese. The romanization does not adhere to any one of the major systems but appears to be principally a combination of the Pinyin and Yale systems, with occasional forms that belong to neither.[6] The unsystematic and non-standard romanization probably has no impact on the reader unfamiliar with the various systems of romanization, but for the reader able to take part at least to a degree on both the Chinese as well as the American side of the cultural dialogue, the effect is arresting. In its effort to recreate in presumably the American ear the sound of what was said, it stresses the underlying orality of the experiences being related. These experiences are not typically chronicled in official histories, but rather histories of a different kind, histories that are told by mothers to their daughters. But perhaps even more significantly, when these fundamentally oral experiences are written, their writing subverts and disrupts the established norms of official written discourse to create a special mode of discourse—an alternative narrative space—adequate to the narration of the histories of four women. Just as the official accounts of the civil wars, the Japanese invasion, and the great upheavals of the period are recorded in officially sanctioned and correct forms of the language, the suffering, disappointments, hopes, and joy—the history that is uniquely the women's and not a part of public record—requires a commensurate mode of expression that diverges from publicly accredited norms.[7]

This intersection of generations, cultures, and languages—both official and unsanctioned—constitutes a particularly rich signifying system and complex narrative architecture. One of the most arresting examples is the use of the Chinese word *bing*. It first occurs in the account of the childhood of Rose Hsu Jordan as the name of one of her four brothers: Matthew, Mark, Luke, and Bing. Particularly in the context of a chapter that begins with a description of An-Mei Hsu's Christian faith, the appearance of the name Bing at the end of a list of the New Testament evangelists is particularly disarming. Neither Christian tradition nor mainstream American culture seems to offer any obvious explanation for this curious series of names. Seeking an explanation in terms of what could be a Chinese name is, moreover, problematic because no Chinese tone is marked so the precise reading and meaning is indeterminable. The range of possible meanings is broad. If one assumes the first tone, among the possibilities are: a soldier or a pawn; or ice, icicles, or frost. Assuming the third tone: bright, luminous; to grasp or to hold; or cakes, biscuits, or pastry. Assuming the fourth tone: sickness, disease, a fault or defect, or to be distressed about; together with, incorporate, merge, combine, united; even or equal; or to drive off, to expel, or to arrange. Although this array would not present itself in a Chinese text because each sense would be represented by a different character, this specially forged narrative language—part English, part Chinese, part standardized, part free invention, and part a hybrid combination—offers wide-ranging interpretive possibilities. The immediate narrative situation helps isolate some meanings that may be heuristically helpful. Bing is the youngest of four brothers. On a family excursion to the beach, he wanders off and is drowned in the ocean never to be seen again. In this context, the cluster of meanings associated with sickness, disease, defect and distress certainly suggest themselves. Bing's tragic death would certainly justify an epithet suggesting defect and distress. Although the information that one of the possible readings of Bing provides adds to the character and power of the situation, it does not go very far in accounting for his presence among Matthew, Mark, and Luke.

The word, however, appears in another context. When Waverly Jong becomes very angry with her mother's manipulation and condescending insults, she angrily goes to her parents' home. In a discussion that begins with Waverly's confusing Taiyuan, her mother's home, with Taiwan, her mother in exasperation explains that another name for Taiyuan is Bing and writes the character, though to no avail. The character, however, is very important. The ancient form has been interpreted as two people walking down the same road together, and indeed that chapter of the novel ends with an image of Waverly and Lindo Jong perhaps being able to set aside differences and walk the same path. Although in modern usage, *bing* means side by side, united, together, simultaneously, or merged (as with a small state and a large state), in classical Chinese, particularly during the Zhou dynasty, the more abstract sense of united, or two people or things closely associated, was more pronounced.[8] To the extent that the ancient conflation in one character of a city name and the sense of being side by side or united resonates in the chaotic cultural space of the narrated immigrant community, it enriches, strengthens, and broadens the force of the narrative.

What connection, though, is there between Bing as the alternative name of Taiyuan and the child named Bing who drowned? What interpretive strategy suggests that the two are anything but unrelated homophones? The only response is that the novel seems to invite the juxtaposition. In its portrayal of immigrant life on the fragmented margins of both Chinese and American culture, *The Joy Luck Club* is so conspicuously structured to disrupt any sense of the linear flow of time, conventional narrative practice, or normative language usage in order to make connections that otherwise would not be made that the tentative conjunction of the two seems almost required.

If the little boy's name is interpreted in terms of the idea of being side by side or united, his name is a deeply ironic and tragic contrast to his fate. Being held by the Coiled Dragon (138) beneath the sea, he is completely separated from his family and particularly his mother. The poignancy of the loss is staggering. What, though, of Bing's relationship to his brothers, Matthew, Mark, and Luke in the biblical framework these names suggest? The Apostle John, whose place Bing has taken in the catalogue of the evangelists, has a very rich tradition associated with him: the beloved Apostle, the Apostle who elected to remain on earth until the second coming of Jesus, and the Apostle who beheld the apocalyptic end of the earth and recorded his vision. The element of the Johanine tradition most relevant here, though, is the emphasis throughout his gospel and to a lesser degree in the epistles on unity, on the community of believers, and on the mystical union of the trinity.[9] What links Bing to the evangelist John is, thus, the theme of unity deriving on the one hand from a major theme in the Gospel of John and on the other from one of the earliest senses of the Chinese word *bing*. In the episode dealing with the boy named Bing, he represents the tragically ironic reversal of what his name suggests and, unlike the Apostle John, he is precisely the one who is not permitted to linger.

Chinese at the Joy Luck Club obviously fulfills all of the immediate expectations. It provides the effect of the real by creating the ambience and linguistic color expected in a Chinese immigrant community. It also serves as a reliable index of assimilation: the poorer the mastery of Chinese, the greater the assimilation into American society. But beyond these rather obvious and predictable roles, Chinese significantly enhances the narrative power of the novel. The disruption of its norms by the first generation of immigrants parallels their distortions of English as non-native speakers and creates an alternative narrative space and a special mode of discourse that challenges official conventions but is exactly what is required for the telling of their stories. A medium of communication arises in which the seemingly most disparate of elements can find common ground and walk together just as the novel as a whole can be seen to hinge on the arduous, alienating and almost life-threatening challenge of finding common ground on which different generations, different cultures, different hopes, as well as the self and the other, can meet and walk together.

NOTES

1. See Lemuel Ignacio's *Asian Americans and Pacific Islanders: Is There Such an Ethnic Group?* for historical background on the term. See also Kim, pp. xi–xii. Lynn Pan's *Sons of the Yellow Emperor: A History of the Chinese Diaspora* provides a useful survey of Chinese emigration to the United States.

2. See Xiaomei Chen's 'Reading Mother's Tale—Reconstructing Women's Space in Amy Tan and Zhang Jie'. See also the 'Introduction' and 'Occidentalism as Counterdiscourse' in *Occidentalism*. See also Susan Cahill's *Mother's Memories, Dreams, and Reflections by Literary Daughters*.

3. Sau-ling Cynthia Wong's *Reading Asian American Literature: From Necessity to Extravagance* deals specifically with reading strategies appropriate for Asian American Literature. See especially pp. 3–5 for a cogent formulation of the issue. See also Werner Sollors, *Beyond Ethnicity: Consent and Descent in American Culture*, especially pp. 3–19.

4. For a general introduction to the issues centring on language and ethnicity, see Harald Haarmann, *Language in Ethnicity: A View of Basic Ecological Relations*.

5. Although subaltern studies originated with Indian scholars their theoretical implications are finding fruitful application in other areas. See Gail Hershatter 'The Subaltern Talks Back: Reflections on Subaltern Theory and Chinese History'. The richest sources of information on subaltern studies is Oxford University Press's *Subaltern Studies*. See also Spivak's two essays in *In Other Worlds*, 'Subaltern Studies: Deconstructing Historiography' (pp. 197–221) and 'A Literary Representation of the Subaltern: A Woman's Text from the Third World' (pp. 241–68).

6. Notably, the Wade-Giles system does not seem to have played any role at all in any of the romanization except in personal names, for example, An-mei Hsu. Although it may have some advantages in terms of phonetic precision, the complex combination of consonants would probably not be helpful to most readers.

7. The broader question of the extent to which *The Joy Luck Club* fractures normative, patriarchal narrative conventions in creating a distinctly feminist mode of discourse invites further investigation.

8. For example, *Zheng zhong xing yin yi zhong he da zi dian* (Comprehensive Large Dictionary of Forms, Pronunciations, and Definitions, 2nd revised edition) under the entry for *bing* quotes Lin Yi-guang in pointing out that in Zhou Dynasty bronze script the word signified two people standing side by side united as one. And Couvreur's *Dictionnaire classique de la langue chinoise* (1963) offers the straightforward definition: 'deux personnes ou deux choses associées ensemble, associer ensemble deux personnes ou deux choses.'

9. The point is nowhere clearer than in John 17: 21–3: 'Jesus prays, that they all may be one; as thou, Father, art in me, and I in thee, that they also may be one in us: that the world may believe that thou hast sent me. And the glory which thou gavest me I have give them; that they may be one, even as we are one: I in them, and thou in me, that they may be made perfect in one; and that the world may know that thou hast sent me, and hast loved them, as thou hast loved me.' The view represented in the *Anchor Bible Dictionary* (Doubleday 1992) is typical: 'Oneness is the key to proper interpretation of the gospel of John. The key to unity in John is christological unity, specifically the unity of the Son with the Father. Jesus is the one shepherd, the one who is the exclusive shepherd of God's people (10:16). In 10:30 the christological oneness is stated most clearly: I and the Father are one (4:752).'

WORKS CITED

Cahill, Susan (ed.) 1988 *Mothers: Memories, Dreams, and Reflections by Literary Daughters*. Menton, New York:

Chen, Xiaomei 1994 'Reading Mother's Tale—Reconstructing Women's Space' in Amy Tan and Zhang Jie *Chinese Literature, Essay, Articles, Reviews* 16: pp. 111–32.

———. 1995 *Occidentalism: A Theory of Counterdiscourse in Post-Mao China*. Oxford University Press.

Haarmann, Harald 1986 *Language and Ethnicity: A View of Basic Ecological Relations*. Mouton de Gruyter, Berlin.

Hershatter, Gail 1993 'The Subaltern Talks Back: Reflections on Subaltern Theory and Chinese History' in *Positions* 1, 1: pp. 103–30.

Ignacio, Lemuel 1976 *Asian Americans and Pacific Islanders (Is There Such an Ethnic Group?)*. Philipino Development Association, San Jose, CA.

Kim, Elaine H. 1982 *Asian American Literature: An Introduction to the Writings and their Social Context*. Temple University Press, Philadelphia.

———. 1992 'Foreword' in Shirley Geok-lin Lim and Amy Ling (eds) *Reading Literatures of Asian Americans*. Temple University Press, Philadelphia.

Pan, Lynn 1990 *Sons of the Yellow Emperor: The History of the Chinese Diaspora*. Kodansha, New York.

Ramsey, S. Robert 1987 *The Languages of China*. Princeton University Press.

Sollors, Werner 1986 *Beyond Ethnicity: Consent and Descent in American Culture*. Oxford University Press.

Spivak, Gayatri Chakravorty 1988 *In Other Worlds: Essay in Cultural Politics*. Routledge, London.

Tan, Amy 1989 *The Joy Luck Club*. Ivy Books, New York.

Wong, Sau-ling Cynthia 1993 *Reading Asian American Literature: From Necessity to Extravagance*. Princeton University Press.

ZENOBIA MISTRI

Discovering the Ethnic Name and the Genealogical Tie in Amy Tan's The Joy Luck Club

In researching recent ideas in American Studies and ethnic literature, I have been struck by the work of William Boelhower and Werner Sollors, among others. In this essay, I would like to apply some of these ideas to thematic and structural elements in the ethnic American short story sequence as it relates to Amy Tan's *The Joy Luck Club*. Using Boelhower and Sollors's work, I propose to examine the tale of *The Joy Luck Club*'s June/Jing mei Woo, who becomes the axis for this short story cycle. June Woo's story acts a leitmotif in these tales of Chinese mothers and their American daughters who are unable to understand their mothers and their twin heritage. Boelhower's *Through a Glass Darkly: An Ethnic Semiosis in American Literature* provides a semiotic analysis of ethnicity that can be useful in understanding ethnic literature and is appropriate for this story sequence. Examining *The Joy Luck Club* using these approaches augments our understanding of this Chinese American story cycle and, in turn, permits the reader to see how ethnic semiosis can augment discussions of writers from different cultures.

Amy Tan's short story sequence, *The Joy Luck Club*, focuses on four Chinese mothers and their American daughters who are at odds with their mothers, their inheritance, and the power of their mothers' wisdom and strength. Interestingly, none of these mothers longs for her daughter to be Chinese following nothing but Chinese ways, for each woman has come to America with

From *Studies in Short Fiction* 35, no. 3 (Summer 1998): 251–257. © 1998 by Newberry College.

45

the intent of making a better life in which her family would know the fabled American successes. Each mother has her own powerful story of overcoming odds, of having learned the lesson of becoming strong through seeing her own mother suffer or by suffering herself. Each mother feels the anguish of the cultural separation between herself and her daughter. Each mother wants her daughter to know the power and advantage of joining the strengths of two cultures instead of embracing only one—the American; and importantly, each mother rescues her daughter from the specific danger that threatens her.

The structure of this short story sequence becomes a central metaphor for the thematic elements that link these stories to each other, involving an implicit conversation among the four mothers and their daughters as they tell their stories. The sequence is divided into four sections, each having four stories. Although the stories are about four mothers and their four daughters, only three mothers and four daughters tell their stories in these sections, for June Woo takes her dead mother's place in the first and last sections of the book. She alone has a story in each of the four sections, thus forming the central axis of the book; the first and last sections contain the mothers' stories. The second and third sections are given to the four daughters. Although we read the work sequentially, we continually look back. In theorizing on the short story *sequence* as opposed to the short story *cycle* and the implications of the former, Robert Luscher explains:

> ... we continually cast a backward glance to formulate the relationships of the past to the evolving whole. Such narrative organization is primarily spatial rather then temporal, since it subverts strict chronological progression. (Luscher 166)

The Joy Luck Club works spatially rather than chronologically. We discover pieces of the mothers' childhoods in China as we read their individual stories; we see the breach in the daughters' relationships with their mothers as we read their stories. We understand the repeated symbols, which expand with each use as the stories hold hands at crucial junctures. The theme rounds out with each mother's pain as it expands with each daughter's fear of disappointing her mother. We understand that the cultural divide causes these walls. Each story fits a space on the map that develops for us as we begin to observe the developing and continually shifting picture.

The thematic design for the book evolves through the central story of June Woo and her finding of her ethnic self through her mother. The supporting stories of the other three daughters stand as leitmotifs of the fractured relationships between the mothers and their daughters. None of these American-born daughters listens, understands, or respects the power, strength, and wisdom of her Chinese mother. Each of them sees her mother's behavior as if from another continent and is ashamed of her "strange" ways; each daughter fails to understand her mother's need to see American successes coupled with Chinese wisdom and secrets. As the daughters' stories coalesce, showing the lack of understanding, so the mothers' stories fuse showing their pain and feelings of loss—not at their daughters' inability but at their unwillingness to see the power of combining both American and Chinese heritage.

The first and last stories stand as structural and thematic bookends in this collection, and June Woo holds the answer to the puzzle of the 16 stories. Undoubtedly, these stories speak to issues dealing with a bicultural heritage. William Boelhower constructs an approach that cuts across several disciplines such as cultural geography, anthropology, semiotics, cartography, and cultural history. This critical approach makes spaces for those elements that we cannot place using traditional literary methods. In accessing the intricacies and nuances in ethnic literature, Boelhower asks Jean de Crèvecoeur's question, "Who is the American, this new Man?" Since de Crèvecoeur's time, the makeup of the American is very different. In answering the question, Boelhower suggests that to understand the American, one must understand *ethnicity* and *ethnic project* or undertaking, in which memory is the crucial factor. Boelhower explains, "Through the processing system of Memory and Project, the subject puts himself in touch with the foundational world of his ancestors, reproduces himself as a member of an ethnic community, and is able to produce ethnic discourse" (Boelhower 87). His analysis suggests germane possibilities for reading and understanding in a more intricate fashion than traditional analysis would permit.

The variety of textual strategies that Boelhower suggests revolve around issues dealing with *discovering the self implicit in the surname, the ethnic sign,* and *memory versus the written word*:

> The very ability of the protagonist to stand between the dominant and the ethnic cultures and between the American present and the foundational past of the immigrant generation without losing his «ancient soul» suggests how time and space are redefined.... (Boelhower 92)

This ability is apparent in each of the mothers in *Joy Luck Club*.

The opening story places June Woo in the uneasy situation of having to take her mother's place at the Joy Luck Club meeting; later, she is put in the precarious position of having to go to China to fulfill her dead mother's lifelong quest—of being reunited with her long-lost twin daughters. This journey becomes the spiritual, thematic, and structural design of the collection as

June Woo discovers her own bonds with her mother and with her ethnic self. Boelhower explains ethnic semiotics: "... in the beginning was the name.... By discovering the self implicit in the surname, one reproduces an ethnic seeing and understands himself as a social, an ethnic subject.... To speak of ethnicity is to speak of ancestry..." (82). June Woo discovers her mother and her ethnic self as she embarks on her journey to China to meet her recently discovered half-sisters. June's reluctance to go to China reflects on the tenuous relationship with her mother. "My mother and I had never really understood one another. We translated each other's meanings and I seemed to hear less than what was said, while my mother heard more" (Tan 37).

The trip to China becomes the way in which June Woo claims her name, and the other part of herself, Jing-mei Woo, that she has never understood or accepted. June Woo sets about rediscovering or reconstructing her American ethnic self. Significantly, she is the only daughter with both a Chinese and an American name. She sets the genealogical pattern of understanding her mother and so the ethnic self as she makes this journey to China to be reunited with her twin half-sisters whom she had long assumed to be dead. Boelhower explains how the reconstruction is achieved: "... the subject produces ethnic semiosis (signs) through a strategic use of memory which is nothing other than the topological and genealogical interrogation of the originating culture of his immigrant ancestors" (82). Memory floods June as she recalls the stories her mother told, in Chinese, of the inception of the *Joy Luck Club* in Kweilin. She recalls the retelling over the years: "Over the years she told me the same story, except for the ending, which grew darker, casting long shadows over her life, and eventually in mine" (Tan 42). Here we see the use of memory to reconstruct the moment in time when the twins were lost. At one level, June's project is the trip to tell the twins that Suyuan Woo is dead; at a deeper level, the trip becomes the journey into the being of her immigrant mother. Like so many immigrant parents, Suyuan Woo has wanted her daughter to be a fantastic American Chinese success. Instead, she has dropped out of college a number of times, changed majors, and is far from the traditionally accomplished immigrant. June Woo feels her own failure and misreads her mother's encouragement as disappointment.

In a sense this lack of communication is reflected in the lives of the other three mothers and daughters. Auntie An-mei expresses the imperative for the trip. "But most important, you must tell them about her life. The mother they did not know they must now know." June's reply is the reply of the other daughters. "What will I say? What can I tell them about my mother? I don't know anything. She was my mother" (Tan 40).

Auntie An-mei speaks to the genealogical tie in powerful ways: "Not know your own mother? ... How can you say? Your mother is in your bones!"

(Tan 40). As all the aunts chime in, coaching her on what she should tell about their mother, the nightmare shared by these Chinese mothers becomes clear to June:

> They are frightened. In me they see their own daughters, just as ignorant, just as unmindful of all the truths and hopes they have brought to America. They see daughters who grow impatient when their mothers talk in Chinese, who think they are stupid when they explain things in fractured English. They see that joy and luck do not mean the same thing to their daughters, that to these closed American born minds 'joy-luck' is not a word, it does not exist. They see daughters who will bear grandchildren born without any connecting hope passed from generation to generation. (Tan 40–41)

This passage illustrates the pain of being put aside as being inferior; it articulates the anguish of the forgotten and obliterated, of not having progeny who would look back at ancestral ties with the past. All the mothers, Suyuan Woo, An-mei Hsu, Lindo Jong, Ying-ying St. Clair, fear this genealogical obliteration. June recalls her mother's gift of the jade pendant in "American Translation." She remembers the conversation as a lesson in the blood knot of kinship: "'No, Ma,' I protested. 'I can't take this,' 'Nala, Nala'—'Take it, take it'—she said, as if she were scolding me." And then she continued in Chinese. "For a long time I wanted to give you this necklace. See, I wore this on my skin, so when you put it on your skin, then you know my meaning. This is your life's importance" (Tan 208).

An-mei Hsu's first story, "Scar," speaks to this blood bond with the mothers before her: "This is how a daughter honors her mother. It is *shou* so deep it is in your bones. . . . You must peel off your skin, and that of your mother, and her mother before her. Until there is nothing. No scar, no skin, no flesh." Lindo Jong fears her granddaughter will forget her heritage in "The Red Candle":

> It's too late to change you, but I'm telling you because I worry about your baby. I worry that someday she will say, 'Thank you, grandmother, for the gold bracelet. I'll never forget you.' But later she will forget she had a grandmother. (Tan 48)

Ying-ying St. Clair also feels the loss of closeness and the separation:

> I think this to myself even though I love my daughter. She and I have shared the same body. There is a part of her mind, which is

my mind. But when she was born, she sprang away from me like a slippery fish and has been swimming away ever since. All her life, I have watched her from another shore" (Tan 242).

These fears on the part of the mothers are the fears that the genealogical chain that links up with the foundational world of the ancestors will be broken. All the mothers have their memories of the past. Boelhower explains: ". . . it is not a question here of the ethnic subject living in the past but as Sowell says (1981:273), of the past living in him" (90).

These matrilineal fears compound in the book until the last section, where each mother reaches out and forcibly links up with her daughter, showing her the strength she needs to take from her mother and her mother's mother before her. Like women warriors, each mother takes up the challenge and meets it head on. Even timid Ying-ying St. Clair comes forth like the tiger between the trees to rescue her lost daughter. This metaphor of being part of the life substance of their daughters appears in each of the mother's stories.

Werner Sollors sees ethnicity as constructed from the conflict of what he calls issues of "consent and descent." Sollors does not make distinctions among the ethnic groups. Unlike him, I see *consent and descent* as applicable only to those ethnic groups, like most Asian Americans, who have *chosen* to immigrate to the United States. For Sollors, consent is the conscious choice an individual makes in deciding to become an American while descent is the tie to the place of one's origin. Sollors suggests the dynamics of ethnicity set in motion when descent and consent are in conflict and when the group fears for its survival (Sollors 6).

This theme of not understanding the mothers echoes through the daughters' stories. But it is June Woo who goes to the marrow of the issue in the last story of this cycle. She feels her bones ache with a familiar pain when the train leaves the Hong Kong border and enters China. She recalls her mother's words: "Once you are born Chinese, you cannot help but feel and think Chinese. . . . It is in your blood waiting to be let go" (Tan 267). Now on the train she dreams and imagines. Boelhower explains that without imagination there can be no project. He theorizes significant ethnic experiences in ethnic fiction as being generated from a *cultural encyclopedia*: "When the parents die, their cultural inheritance is passed on to the children; only now they must practice a politics of memory in order to piece together the original patrimony" (100).

June imagines her sisters' letter to their mother and slowly recovers her Chinese past through pieces of her father's stories coupled with remembering stories her mother had told her; these enable her to weave her generational story all the way back to China. Boelhower calls this a *memnotechnical strategy* of recovery. Here, June chooses to splice memory with the project at hand, which requires her to go forward.

The journey Jing-mei/June undertakes is organized geographically in the text; she goes from San Francisco to Hong Kong, to Shenshen, China, to Guangzhou to Shanghai. Yet, while it is organized geographically, there is a parallel journey being reconstructed for Jing-mei through her mother's and father's stories and recollections. This geographical journey undertaken by her parents in 1949 is recalled and brought back to her as she goes to China for the first time. Both stories—her parents' in the past, and hers in the present—serve to underscore and trace her mother's flight from Kweilin to Chungking, to Shanghai, to Canton, to Hong Kong, to Haiphong, and finally to San Francisco. As Boelhower might explain this: "here the goal is to interpret the past, not the past itself" (104).

The central "project" in *The Joy Luck Club* is Jing-mei's visit to her sisters. Implicit in her name lies the family story and her genealogical link. The pure essence (Jing) coupled with younger sister (mei) mingles. Symbolically, the three of them when united represent the essence of their mother, she who now lives in the faces and bones of her three daughters. They, in turn, signal the coming together of the other three mothers and their daughters. None of their "projects" could have been undertaken without the use of the ethnic encyclopedia—memory, stories, and the imagination. By the end of the journey, Jing-mei Woo understands the past as she understands what her mother means to her, as do the other daughters. The "Queen Mother of the Western Skies," the last story in the sequence, reflects on "The Joy Luck Club," the first story in which June Woo sits at her mother's place, facing East. The Western part of June Woo understands the Eastern inheritance of Jing-mei Woo as she asks her father to tell the missing part of her mother's Kweilin story. He starts in halting English, and she asks him to tell it in Chinese. Jing-mei Woo has arrived.

Works Cited

Boelhower, William. *Through A Glass Darkly: Ethnic Semiosis in American Literature*. New York: Oxford UP, 1987.

Luscher, Robert M. "The Short Story Sequence: An Open Book." Ed. Susan Lohafer and Jo Ellyn Clarey, *Short Story Theory at a Crossroads*. Baton Rouge: Louisiana State UP, 1986.

Sollors, Werner. *Beyond Ethnicity: Consent and Descent in American Culture*. New York: Oxford UP, 1986.

Tan, Amy. *The Joy Luck Club*. New York: Putnam, 1989.

RONALD EMERICK

The Role of Mah Jong in Amy Tan's The Joy Luck Club

At the beginning of Amy Tan's *The Joy Luck Club*, Jing-mei Woo, also known as June, takes the place of her recently deceased mother at the mah jong table with three of her mother's dearest friends. In accordance with the major theme of the novel—the relationship between mothers and daughters—it is appropriate and necessary that June recognize the bond between herself and her mother. Accepting her mother's role in the long-standing mah jong game is a symbolic first step in her journey toward understanding her mother and the mother–daughter relationship.

To date, much of the criticism of *The Joy Luck Club* focuses on the central theme of mother–daughter relationships. Ben Xu, for example, explains that all four mothers hold in common the experience of being a victim; as a result, they, like most traditional Chinese mothers, try to prepare their daughters for survival in harsh times. Although the daughters at first resist their mothers' attempts, they gradually move toward acquiescence by the end of the novel (13–15). Tracing a similar movement, Bonnie TuSmith points out that the mothers and daughters grow closer as the daughters mature. What begins as strife and "desperate confrontations" turns to mutual understanding, even a sense of community or oneness, by the end of the novel (67). Furthermore, Amy Ling explains that the distance between mothers and daughters is not just a generational gap but a "deep cultural and geographical chasm"

From *The CEA Critic* 61, nos. 2–3 (Winter and Spring/Summer 1999): 37–45. © 1999 by the College English Association.

(134). But as the daughters grow to understand their mothers' stories, "what was formerly considered a hated bondage is revealed to be a cherished bond" (141). Thus, Tan creates unity in the novel by her complex handling and resolution of the mother–daughter theme.[1]

Another area explored by the critics is the dialogic nature of the novel, its division into sixteen sections narrated by eight different characters. Gloria Shen, in her discussion of the significance of storytelling and narrative structure in the novel, points out that the sixteen sections "resemble fragments of stories collected by a sociologist and randomly put together, rather than carefully constructed narratives set in a deliberate order by an author" (233). Nevertheless, writes Shen, as the mothers and daughters share their viewpoints and experiences, "the device of storytelling transforms structurally isolated monologues into meaningful dialogues between mother and daughter . . . and coalesces the sixteen monologues into a coherent whole" (236).[2] In contrast, Stephen Souris, in his analysis of "inter-monologue dialogicity" in the novel, emphasizes the numerous gaps that occur as a result of the novel's dialogic approach. Since the mothers and daughters speak only to the reader, "no actual communication between mothers and daughters occurs" (107).[3]

Perhaps the novel's dialogic and somewhat fragmented structure has partially obscured another device Tan uses to create unity in the text: the mah jong game itself. In the first chapter of *The Joy Luck Club*, Tan provides information about the mah jong game and the specific positions occupied by each of the four mothers at the table: Suyuan Woo is in the East, where things begin; An-mei Hsu sits in the South; Lindo Jong represents the West; and Ying-ying St. Clair occupies the North. After the first chapter, the mah jong game seems to disappear as a central concern in the book. In fact, however, the role of mah jong is significant throughout the remainder of the novel; mah jong becomes a central metaphor and provides insights into the novel's structure, themes, imagery, and characterization.

A brief overview of mah jong should be sufficient to reveal how Tan employs the game in the novel. Originating centuries ago, mah jong is the national game of China (Kanai and Farrell 1). Although the game may seem unfamiliar and complicated to Westerners, it is similar to a game of gin rummy, using bamboo and bone or plastic tiles instead of cards, and requiring four players rather than two. As in rummy, the object of the game is to go out first by using tiles in various combinations to form three of a kind, three-tile straights, and a final pair. Unlike cards, in which there are four suits (spades, hearts, diamonds, and clubs), each containing thirteen cards, in mah jong there are only three "suits" (bamboo, balls or circles, and *wan* or Chinese characters), each suit containing nine tiles. In a deck of cards, there is only one of each card, whereas in a mah jong set there are four of each tile. Although there are no bonus cards in rummy, there are two types of bonus tiles in mah jong: four winds (east, south, west, and north) and three dragons (green, red, and white), making 136 tiles altogether. As in rummy, the game proceeds with each player, in succession, drawing tiles, using those tiles to make combinations, and discarding tiles until one player completes her hand and goes out. In rummy, any number of hands may be played until one player reaches the predetermined number of points—for example, five hundred—required to win. In mah jong, however, a minimum of sixteen hands must be played.

With just this brief overview of the game, it becomes obvious that Tan has incorporated elements of mah jong into *The Joy Luck Club*. First, the structure of the novel is the same as the structure of a mah jong game. A complete game of mah jong requires at least sixteen hands: four rounds, each consisting of four hands and each hand representing one of the four players—or one of the four winds. Thus, the East round is followed in succession by South, West and North rounds. Like a game of mah jong, the novel is structured into four major divisions, each division consisting of four parts and each part representing one of the four mothers or one of the four daughters. Therefore, the sixteen-chapter structure is the first indication that mah jong is a controlling metaphor for the novel.

In chapter 1, "The Joy Luck Club," Suyuan Woo explains to her daughter that the Chinese version of mah jong is different from the Jewish version because Chinese mah jong emphasizes strategy: "Jewish mah jong, they . . . play only with their eyes. . . . Chinese mah jong, you must play using your head, very tricky" (22–23). Each player devises a strategy designed not only to win but also to prevent other players from winning big. Throughout the novel, the four mothers advise their daughters to adopt strategies to improve their lives, particularly for solving problems with their husbands. Lindo Jong explains to her daughter, Waverly, that Waverly has inherited craftiness, the ability to use strategy to win chess games, from her mother's side of the family: "We are a smart people, very strong, tricky, and famous for winning wars. . . . We always know how to win" (202). Waverly calls this ability "the art of invisible strength. It was a strategy for winning arguments, respect from others, and eventually, . . . chess games" (89). An-mei Hsu urges her daughter, Rose, to develop courage and stand up to her husband, Ted; to stop listening to the opinions of others; and to heed her mother's advice: "'A girl is like a young tree,' she said. 'You must stand tall and listen to your mother standing next to you. That is the only way to grow strong and straight. But if you bend to listen to other people, you will grow crooked and weak. You will fall to the ground with the first strong wind'" (213).

And Ying-ying St. Clair tries to impart her *chi*, her fierce tiger nature, to her daughter, Lena, so that Lena will assert herself against her manipulative husband, Harold, and restore balance to her marriage: "I will use this sharp pain to penetrate my daughter's tough skin and cut her tiger spirit loose. She will fight me because this is the nature of two tigers. But I will win and give her my spirit, because this is the way a mother loves her daughter" (286). Therefore, just as each player must devise a strategy for winning at mah jong, each mother wants her daughter to devise a strategy for solving problems and being successful in life.

Bonus tiles—the winds and dragons—are particularly important in succeeding at mah jong. In addition, the start of each round of play requires the building of four walls of tiles in a square on the table. These mah jong elements—walls, winds, and dragons—are significant elements in *The Joy Luck Club*.

Walls—literal, metaphoric, and symbolic—recur throughout the novel. Walls operate as barriers between cultures, between mothers and daughters, between life and death. Concerning the central theme of the novel, mothers and daughters, the Chinese language and Chinese culture act as barriers between the four mothers and their daughters, preventing communication and understanding. When Suyuan attempts to explain mah jong to her daughter, June concludes, "These kinds of explanations made me feel my mother and I spoke two different languages. . . . I talked to her in English, she answered back in Chinese" (23).

In the preface to section 2, "The Twenty-six Malignant Gates," a mother attempts to warn her daughter about the misfortunes that can befall her outside her home. But the mother cannot translate the concepts from Chinese, and her impatient daughter shouts, "You can't tell me because you don't know! You don't know anything!" (87). Such failures to communicate occur throughout the novel and result in frustration for the mothers, who believe that their daughters do not properly honor and obey them, and exasperation for the daughters, who lose respect for their mothers and rebel against them. After a heated argument with Waverly, Lindo Jong regrets that she has been unable to communicate her essential Chinese nature to her daughter:

> I couldn't teach her about Chinese character. How to obey parents and listen to your mother's mind. How not to show your own thoughts, to put your feelings behind your face so you can take advantage of hidden opportunities. Why easy things are not worth pursuing. How to know your own worth and polish it. . . . Why Chinese thinking is best. (289)

The metaphor of the wall takes center stage in chapter 6, "The Voice from the Wall," in which Lena St. Clair tells a story that terrified her as a child. The ghost of a man whom her great-grandfather had sentenced to death returns from the dead and drags her great-grandfather through the wall that separates the dead from the living, to show him the horrors on the other side. The story haunts Lena throughout her childhood, and she associates the wall with the unknown dangers that await her in life (like the twenty-six malignant gates in the preface to this section of the novel). On the other side of Lena's bedroom wall lives another family, and late at night Lena hears screams. Imagining the worst scenario she can, Lena believes that the neighbor's daughter, perhaps a mirror image of herself, is suffering horrible abuse from her parents. Every night, the screaming and fighting resume beyond the wall:

> But the next night, the girl came back to life with more screams, more beating, her life once more in peril. And so it continued, night after night, a voice pressing against my wall telling me that this was the worst possible thing that could happen: the terror of not knowing when it would ever stop. (114)

Eventually, Lena meets Teresa, the daughter next door, and learns that her premonitions of disaster were incorrect, that the family is a boisterous but loving one, and that no harm has come from their constant screaming and fighting. Lena then hopes for a similar optimistic outcome for her own family, specifically for her mother, Ying-ying, who suffers bouts of severe depression and, in Lena's view, is turning into a ghost like the dead man who appeared to her great-grandfather. At the end of the chapter, Lena fantasizes about saving her mother from growing psychosis by establishing communication with her mother and thereby pulling her back from the barrier of despair that separates her from emotional health and from her family:

> And the daughter said, "Now you must come back, to the other side. Then you can see why you were wrong."
> And the girl grabbed her mother's hand and pulled her through the wall. (121)

Just as the walls must be broken to begin the mah jong game, walls must be torn down between mothers and daughters so that meaningful communication can occur and health can be restored.

Although walls in the novel are associated with danger and death, wind symbolizes power, and all four mothers are skillful at using the wind to their advantage. For example, Lindo Jong refers to the wind in recommending strategies for winning chess games to her daughter, Waverly. According to Lindo, wind is the source of invisible strength: "Wise guy, he not go against the wind.

In Chinese we say, Come from South, blow with wind—poom!—North will follow. Strongest wind cannot be seen" (89). "In other words," as Ling explains, "victory over hostile forces (the cold North wind) may be achieved not through direct confrontation but by apparent accommodation and giving in (warm South wind)" (132). Lindo sometimes attributes her daughter's success in chess to the power of the wind: "You don't have to be so smart to win chess. It is just tricks. You blow from the North, South, East, and West. The other person becomes confused. They don't know which way to run" (187).

Adopting her mother's metaphor of power, Waverly uses the wind to describe her mother's strategy for manipulating Waverly's thinking and behavior. She imagines her mother as a crafty opponent at the chess board: "Opposite me was my opponent, two angry black slits. She wore a triumphant smile. 'Strongest wind cannot be seen,' she said" (103). And, as usual, in chess as in life, Lindo overpowers Waverly and blows her away: "I felt myself growing light. I rose up into the air and flew out the window. Higher and higher, above the alley, over the tops of tiled roofs, where I was gathered up by the wind and pushed up toward the night sky" (103).

The wind is an equally powerful force in the life of Ying-ying St. Clair. In fact, Ying-ying blames the north wind for destroying her marriage and blowing her husband away. Describing her marriage and her husband's business trips and eventual affairs with other women, Ying-ying explains:

> I remembered that the north wind had blown luck and my husband my way, so at night when he was away, I opened wide my bedroom windows, even on cold nights, to blow his spirit and heart back my way.
>
> What I did not know is that the north wind is the coldest. It penetrates the heart and takes the warmth away. The wind gathered such a force that it blew my husband past my bedroom and out the back door. I found out from my youngest aunt that he had left me to live with an opera singer. (281)

The wind becomes a controlling metaphor in Ying-ying's vision of life, and she constantly reminds her daughter, Lena, that Lena's house and therefore her life are not in balance, because of the wind: "When something goes against your nature, you are not in balance. This house was built too steep, and a bad wind from the top blows all your strength back down the hill. So you can never get ahead. You are always rolling backward" (112).

Although Ying-ying uses the power of the wind to explain her failures, June Woo uses the wind to explain her mother's success, particularly her ability to win at mah jong. All the aunties agree that Suyuan Woo was the luckiest at mah jong, and June attributes her mother's winning to the fact that she had the strength of all four winds at her disposal. When June recounts her mother's ordeal in China before coming to San Francisco, she describes the misfortunes as character-building. Her mother's power increased as a result of her misfortunes; in a sense, she "came from many different directions" (223).

Like the four winds, the colored dragons are also powerful bonus tiles in mah jong. Although in European mythology dragons are destructive and evil forces, in Chinese mythology the dragon is a "well-meaning creature" and a guardian of seas, lakes, and rivers (Sanders 48). Ancient Chinese culture revered the dragon as a source of rain, fertility, awe-inspiring power, and luck, and ancient Chinese people celebrated the dragon in two popular festivals each year (Sanders 48–49; Smith 9). Thus, dragons are symbols of good fortune, just as red, green, and white dragons are good-luck tiles in the mah jong game. This desire for good fortune, or "joy luck," is a major theme in the novel and a major goal for all four mothers.

In chapter 1, Suyuan Woo tells June that she initiated the weekly mah jong game in China so that she and other wives could meet, have parties, tell stories, celebrate their happiness, and win at mah jong if they were lucky; thus, the name Joy Luck was born. When Suyuan came to San Francisco, she decided to continue the joy luck tradition with three new Chinese friends as a way of creating community and keeping alive their hopes for happiness and good fortune in America. However, as Xu points out, Suyuan had originally designed the mah jong game as a method of survival in troubled times, and it was necessary to reformulate the game so that it would become, "symbolically at least, a game with no losers" (9). In the same spirit as the reformulated game, all four mothers adopt the philosophy of joy luck as a way of maintaining hope in their lives. Although Lindo Jong teaches Waverly the power of the wind and the importance of strategy in winning at chess, she also attributes Waverly's success to luck, as if strategy alone is not enough. She tells Waverly about her own optimism as a young wife and mother and expresses her hopes for an even better life for her daughter: "I wanted everything for you to be better. I wanted you to have the best circumstances, the best character. I didn't want you to regret anything" (303).

Because of their belief in joy luck, the four mothers desire to teach their daughters the same philosophy, partly as a way of establishing a link between the two generations and the two cultures. Speculating about the fears and doubts of her mother's friends, June thinks:

> They see ... daughters ... unmindful of all the truths and hopes they have brought to America.... They see that joy and luck do not mean the same to their daughters, that to these closed

American-born minds "joy luck" is not a word, it does not exist. They see daughters who will bear grandchildren born without any connecting hope passed from generation to generation. (31)

In chapter 13, "Magpies," An-mei Hsu narrates the parable of the turtle and the magpies, which her own mother had imparted to her years before, a parable that teaches the joy luck philosophy. According to the parable, the turtle in the pond eats the tears, and thus swallows the misery, of unhappy children. Later, eggs pour out of the turtle's beak, and from the eggs burst forth magpies, birds of joy, which fly away laughing. Finally, the turtle explains the moral of the story: "Now you see . . . why it is useless to cry. Your tears do not wash away your sorrows. They feed someone else's joy. And that is why you must learn to swallow your own tears" (244). Just as her own mother had taught her to heed the turtle's warning, to hide her sorrow and to hope for joy and happiness, An-mei wants her daughter to adopt a similar philosophy.

In the final chapter of the novel, June Woo discovers the role that joy luck played in her deceased mother's life. June has previously learned that she has two sisters in China, and her mother's friends are paying June's fare to China, where she can fulfill her mother's lifelong hope of reunion. After June and her father arrive in China, her father tells June that the twin babies, whom her mother was forced to abandon when she was fleeing from Kwei-lin, were adopted by a good family who believed that twins were a sign of double luck. Her father also tells June that her mother's name, Suyuan, means "Long-Cherished Wish" and "Forever Never Forgotten." In a sense, Suyuan's name embodies the philosophy of her life and of the Joy Luck Club: Never give up hope of fulfilling your dreams. And as June finally meets and hugs her long-lost sisters in the novel's emotional ending, the book's two major themes, joy luck and the mother–daughter bond, come together. Laughing and crying tears of joy, June realizes, "I know we all see it: Together we look like our mother. Her same eyes, her same mouth, open in surprise to see, at last, her long-cherished wish" (332). By fulfilling her mother's "long-cherished wish," June has found her Chinese roots and become one with her mother. Thus, just as the colored dragons offer hope and good fortune to the players of mah jong, the joy luck philosophy offers hope for success and happiness to the mothers and daughters in the novel.

The game of mah jong is therefore more than just a convenient starting point for *The Joy Luck Club*. Mah jong influences structure, theme, imagery, and characterization in the novel. It informs the novel at every level. Most importantly, it symbolizes a link between mothers and daughters, a cultural bridge between the past and the present, a tradition that can be transferred from one generation to the next. The four daughters, like four players in a

mah jong game, must learn to combine strategy and luck if they hope to suc-
ceed in the game of life. Specifically, they must learn the joy luck philosophy
of the four experienced mah jong players of the novel, their mothers.

Notes

1. Gloria Shen points out that Tan creates unity in the novel by repeating
important themes "like musical leitmotifs . . . in order to give the reader a continuous
sense of life as well as a full understanding of the significance of each event" (233).
Despite the multiple themes, Shen agrees that the mother–daughter relationship is
the central issue in the dialogues between mothers and daughters: "The novel traces
the psychological development of the American daughter and her final acceptance of
the Chinese mother and what the Chinese mother stands for" (237).

2. Shen further relates the novel's structure to postmodernism because it
"rejects artificial unity and espouses the fragmentary" (234).

3. Ling also addresses the issue of dialogism in her discussion of the battles
between mothers and daughters. Although both mothers and daughters are strong
forces and spokespersons for their views, the mothers' stories are so poignant that the
author "more often takes a sympathetic stand toward the mother" (136).

Works Cited

Brown, Anne E., and Marjanne E. Goozé, eds. *International Women's Writing: New Landscapes of Identity.* Westport, CT: Greenwood, 1995.

Kanai, Shozo, and Margaret Farrell. *Mah Jong for Beginners.* Rutland, VT: Tuttle, 1955.

Ling, Amy. *Between Worlds: Women Writers of Chinese Ancestry.* New York: Pergamon, 1990.

Sanders, Tao Tao Liu. *Dragons, Gods & Spirits from Chinese Mythology.* New York: Schocken,
1980.

Shen, Gloria. "Born of a Stranger: Mother–Daughter Relationships and Storytelling in Amy
Tan's *The Joy Luck Club.*" Brown and Goozé. 233–44.

Smith, D. Howard. *Chinese Religions.* New York: Holt, 1968.

Souris, Stephen. "'Only Two Kinds of Daughters': Inter-Monologue Dialogicity in *The Joy
Luck Club.*" *MELUS* 19 (Summer 1994): 99–123.

Tan, Amy. *The Joy Luck Club.* New York: Ivy, 1989.

TuSmith, Bonnie. *All My Relatives: Community in Contemporary Ethnic American Literatures.*
Ann Arbor: U of Michigan P, 1993.

Xu, Ben. "Memory and the Ethnic Self: Reading Amy Tan's *The Joy Luck Club.*" *MELUS* 19
(Spring 1994): 3–18.

PATRICIA L. HAMILTON

Feng Shui, Astrology, and the Five Elements: Traditional Chinese Belief in Amy Tan's The Joy Luck Club

A persistent thematic concern in Amy Tan's *The Joy Luck Club* is the quest for identity. Tan represents the discovery process as arduous and fraught with peril. Each of the eight main characters faces the task of defining herself in the midst of great personal loss or interpersonal conflict. Lindo Jong recalls in "The Red Candle" that her early marriage into a family that did not want her shaped her character and caused her to vow never to forget who she was. Ying-ying St. Clair's story "Waiting Between the Trees" chronicles how betrayal, loss, and displacement caused her to become a "ghost." Rose Hsu Jordan recounts her effort to regain a sense of self and assert it against her philandering husband in "Without Wood." Framing all the other stories are a pair of linked narratives by Jing-mei Woo that describe her trip to China at the behest of her Joy Luck Club "aunties." The journey encompasses Jing-mei's attempts not only to understand her mother's tragic personal history but also to come to terms with her own familial and ethnic identity. In all the stories, whether narrated by the Chinese-born mothers or their American-born daughters, assertions of self are shaped by the cultural context surrounding them. However, there is a fundamental asymmetry in the mothers' and daughters' understanding of each other's native cultures. The mothers draw on a broad experiential base for their knowledge of American patterns of thought and behavior, but the daughters have only fragmentary,

---

From *MELUS* 24, no. 2 (Summer 1999): 125–145. © 1999 by MELUS.

second-hand knowledge of China derived from their mothers' oral histories and from proverbs, traditions, and folktales.[1] Incomplete cultural knowledge impedes understanding on both sides, but it particularly inhibits the daughters from appreciating the delicate negotiations their mothers have performed to sustain their identities across two cultures.

Language takes on a metonymic relation to culture in Tan's portrayal of the gap between the mothers and daughters in *The Joy Luck Club*. Jing-mei, recalling that she talked to her mother Suyuan in English and that her mother answered back in Chinese, concludes that they "never really understood one another": "We translated each other's meanings and I seemed to hear less than what was said, while my mother heard more" (37). What is needed for any accurate translation of meanings is not only receptiveness and language proficiency but also the ability to supply implied or missing context. The daughters' inability to understand the cultural referents behind their mothers' words is nowhere more apparent than when the mothers are trying to inculcate traditional Chinese values and beliefs in their children. The mothers inherited from their families a centuries-old spiritual framework, which, combined with rigid social constraints regarding class and gender, made the world into an ordered place for them. Personal misfortune and the effects of war have tested the women's allegiance to traditional ideas, at times challenging them to violate convention in order to survive. But the very fact of their survival is in large measure attributable to their belief that people can affect their own destinies. In the face of crisis the mothers adhere to ancient Chinese practices by which they try to manipulate fate to their advantage. Their beliefs and values are unexpectedly reinforced by the democratic social fabric and capitalist economy they encounter in their adopted country. Having immigrated from a land where women were allowed almost no personal freedom, all the Joy Luck mothers share the belief along with Suyuan Woo that "you could be anything you wanted to be in America" (132).

Ironically, the same spirit of individualism that seems so liberating to the older women makes their daughters resistant to maternal advice and criticism. Born into a culture in which a multiplicity of religious beliefs flourishes and the individual is permitted, even encouraged, to challenge tradition and authority, the younger women are reluctant to accept their mothers' values without question. Jing-mei confesses that she used to dismiss her mother's criticisms as "just more of her Chinese superstitions, beliefs that conveniently fit the circumstances" (31). Furthermore, the daughters experience themselves socially as a recognizable ethnic minority and want to eradicate the sense of "difference" they feel among their peers. They endeavor to dissociate themselves from their mothers' broken English and Chinese mannerisms,[2] and they reject as nonsense the fragments of traditional lore their mothers try to pass along to them. However, cut adrift from any spiritual moorings, the younger women are overwhelmed by the number of choices that their materialistic culture offers and are insecure about their ability to perform satisfactorily in multiple roles ranging from dutiful Chinese daughter to successful American career woman. When it dawns on Jing-mei that the aunties see that "joy and luck do not mean the same to their daughters, that to these closed American-born minds 'joy luck' is not a word, it does not exist," she realizes that there is a profound difference in how the two generations understand fate, hope, and personal responsibility. Devoid of a worldview that endows reality with unified meaning, the daughters "will bear grandchildren born without any connecting hope passed from generation to generation" (41).

Tan uses the contrast between the mothers' and daughters' beliefs and values to show the difficulties first-generation immigrants face in trans-mitting their native culture to their offspring. Ultimately, Tan endorses the mothers' traditional Chinese worldview because it offers the possibility of choice and action in a world where paralysis is frequently a threat. How-ever, readers who are not specialists in Chinese cosmology share the same problematic relation to the text as the daughters do to their mothers' native culture: they cannot always accurately translate meanings where the context is implied but not stated. Bits of traditional lore crop up in nearly every story, but divorced from a broader cultural context, they are likely to be seen as mere brushstrokes of local color or authentic detail. Readers may be tempted to accept at face value the daughters' pronouncements that their mothers' beliefs are no more than superstitious nonsense. To ensure that readers do not hear less than what Tan is actually saying about the mothers' belief sys-tems and their identities, references to Chinese cosmology in the text require explication and elaboration.

Astrology is probably the element of traditional Chinese belief that is most familiar to Westerners. According to the Chinese astrological system, a person's character is determined by the year of his or her birth. Personality traits are categorized according to a twelve-year calendrical cycle based on the Chinese zodiac. Each year of the cycle is associated with a different animal, as in "the year of the dog." According to one legend, in the sixth century B.C. Buddha invited all the animals in creation to come to him, but only twelve showed up: the Rat, Ox, Tiger, Rabbit, Dragon, Snake, Horse, Ram, Monkey, Cock, Dog, and Pig. Buddha rewarded each animal with a year bearing its personality traits (Scott). In addition to animals, years are associated with one of the Five Elements: Wood, Fire, Earth, Metal, and Water. Metal years end in zero or one on the lunar calendar; Water years end in two or three; Wood years end in four or five; Fire years end in six or seven; and Earth years end in eight or nine. Thus, depending on the year in which one is born, one might be a Fire Dragon, a Water Dragon, and so on. The entire animal-and-element cycle takes sixty years to complete.

Tan draws on astrology in *The Joy Luck Club* in order to shape character and conflict. Lindo Jong, born in 1918, is a Horse, "destined to be obstinate and frank to the point of tactlessness," according to her daughter Waverly (167). Other adjectives that describe the Horse include diligent, poised, quick, eloquent, ambitious, powerful, and ruthless (Rossbach 168). At one point or another in the four Jong narratives, Lindo manifests all of these qualities, confirming her identity as a Horse. In accordance with tradition, Lindo's first husband is selected by his birth year as being a compatible partner for her. The matchmaker in "The Red Candle" tells Lindo's mother and mother-in-law: "An earth horse for an earth sheep. This is the best marriage combination" (50). At Lindo's wedding ceremony the matchmaker reinforces her point by speaking about "birthdates and harmony and fertility" (59). In addition to determining compatibility, birth years can be used to predict personality clashes. Waverly notes of her mother Lindo, "She and I make a bad combination, because I'm a Rabbit, born in 1951, supposedly sensitive, with tendencies toward being thin-skinned and skittery at the first sign of criticism" (167). Lindo's friend Suyuan Woo, born in 1915, is also a Rabbit. No doubt the Joy Luck aunties have this in mind when they note that Suyuan "died just like a rabbit: quickly and with unfinished business left behind" (19). The friction between Horse and Rabbit mentioned by Waverly suggests why Lindo and Suyuan were not only best friends but also "arch enemies who spent a lifetime comparing their children" (37).[3]

Adherents of Chinese astrology contend that auspicious dates for important events can be calculated according to predictable fluctuations of *ch'i*, the positive life force, which is believed to vary according to the time of day, the season, and the lunar calendar. Thus, the matchmaker chooses "a lucky day, the fifteenth day of the eighth moon," for Lindo's wedding (57). Later, Lindo picks "an auspicious day, the third day of the third month," to stage her scheme to free herself from her marriage. Unlucky dates can be calculated as well. Rose Hsu Jordan recalls that her mother An-mei had a "superstition" that "children were predisposed to certain dangers on certain days, all depending on their Chinese birthdate. It was explained in a little Chinese book called *The Twenty-Six Malignant Gates*" (124). The problem for An-mei is how to translate the Chinese dates into American ones. Since the lunar calendar traditionally used in China is based on moon cycles, the number of days in a year varies. Lindo similarly faces the problem of translating dates when she wants to immigrate to San Francisco, but her Peking friend assures her that May 11, 1918 is the equivalent of her birthdate, "three months after the Chinese lunar new year" (258). Accuracy on this point would allow Lindo to calculate auspicious dates according to the Gregorian calendar used in the West. In a broader sense, Lindo's desire for exactness is a strategy for preserving her identity in a new culture.

Tan uses astrology to greatest effect in the life history of Ying-ying St. Clair, who does not fare at all well in the matter of translated dates or preserved identity. Ying-ying is a Tiger, born in 1914, "a very bad year to be born, a very good year to be a Tiger" (248). Tigers are typically passionate, courageous, charismatic, independent, and active, but they can also be undisciplined, vain, rash, and disrespectful (Jackson; Rossbach 167). Tiger traits are central to Ying-ying's character. As a teenager she is wild, stubborn, and vain. As a four-year-old in "The Moon Lady," she loves to run and shout, and she possesses a "restless nature" (72). According to Ruth Youngblood, "As youngsters [Tigers] are difficult to control, and if unchecked, can dominate their parents completely." Ying-ying's Amah tries to tame her into conformity to traditional Chinese gender roles: "Haven't I taught you—that it is wrong to think of your own needs? A girl can never ask, only listen" (70). Ying-ying's mother, too, admonishes her to curb her natural tendencies: "A boy can run and chase dragonflies, because that is his nature. But a girl should stand still" (72). By yielding to the social constraints placed on her gender and "standing perfectly still," Ying-ying discovers her shadow, the dark side of her nature that she learns to wield after her first husband leaves her.

Long before adulthood, however, Ying-ying experiences a trauma regarding her identity. Stripped of her bloodied Tiger outfit at the Moon Festival, she tumbles into Tai Lake and is separated from her family for several hours. Ying-ying's physical experience of being lost parallels her family's suppression of her active nature and curtailment of her freedom. Whenever she wears her hair loose, for example, her mother warns her that she will become like "the lady ghosts at the bottom of the lake" whose undone hair shows "their everlasting despair" (243). After Ying-ying falls into the lake, her braid becomes "unfurled," and as she drifts along in the fishing boat that picks her up, she fears that she is "lost forever" (79). When one of the fishermen surmises that she is a beggar girl, she thinks: "Maybe this was true. I had turned into a beggar girl, lost without my family" (80). Later she watches the Moon Lady telling her tragic story in a shadow play staged for the festival: "I understood her grief. In one small moment, we had both lost the world, and there was no way to get it back" (81). Even though Ying-ying is eventually rescued, she is afraid that her being found by her family is an illusion, "a wish granted that could not be trusted" (82). The temporary loss of her sense of security and belonging is so disturbing that her perception of her identity is forever altered. She is never able to believe her family has found "the same girl" (82).

Ying-ying's traumatic childhood experience prefigures the profound emotional loss and identity confusion she experiences as an adult. Looking back on her experience at the Moon Festival, she reflects that "it has happened many times in my life. The same innocence, trust, and restlessness, the wonder, fear, and loneliness. How I lost myself" (83). As an adult she is stripped of her Tiger nature once again when she immigrates to America. Since there is no immigration category for "the Chinese wife of a Caucasian citizen," Ying-ying is declared a "Displaced Person" (104). Then her husband proudly renames her "Betty St. Clair" without seeming to realize he is effacing her Chinese identity in doing so. The final stroke is his mistakenly writing the wrong year of birth on her immigration papers. As Ying-ying's daughter Lena puts it, "With the sweep of a pen, my mother lost her name and became a Dragon instead of a Tiger" (104). Unwittingly, Clifford St. Clair erases all signs of Ying-ying's former identity and, more importantly, symbolically denies her Tiger nature.

The belief that personality and character are determined by zodiacal influences imposes predictable and regular patterns onto what might otherwise seem random and arbitrary, thereby minimizing uncertainty and anxiety. In this light, the anchor for identity that astrology offers Ying-ying is beneficial. Over the years she comes to understand what her mother once explained about her Tiger nature: "She told me why a tiger is gold and black. It has two ways. The gold side leaps with its fierce heart. The black side stands still with cunning, hiding its gold between trees, seeing and not being seen, waiting patiently for things to come" (248). The certainty that these qualities are her birthright eventually guides Ying-ying into renouncing her habitual passivity. The catalyst for this decision is her perception that her daughter Lena needs to have her own "tiger spirit" cut loose. She wants Lena to develop fierceness and cunning so that she will not become a "ghost" like her mother or remain trapped in a marriage to a selfish man who undermines her worth. Ying-ying expects resistance from Lena, but because of the strength of her belief system, she is confident about the outcome: "She will fight me, because this is the nature of two tigers. But I will win and give her my spirit, because this the way a mother loves her daughter" (252). Tan uses the Chinese zodiacal Tiger as a potent emblem of the way culturally determined beliefs and expectations shape personal identity.

Another element of Chinese cosmology that Tan employs in *The Joy Luck Club* is *wu-hsing*, or the Five Elements, mentioned above in conjunction with astrology.[4] The theory of the Five Elements was developed by Tsou Yen about 325 B.C. As Holmes Welch notes, Tsou Yen "believed that the physical processes of the universe were due to the interaction of the five elements of earth, wood, metal, fire, and water" (96). According to eminent French sinologist Henri Maspero, theories such as the Five Elements, the Three Powers, and *yin* and *yang* all sought to "explain how the world proceeded all by itself through the play of transcendental, impersonal forces alone, without any intervention by one or more conscious wills" (55). Derek Walters specifies how the Five Elements are considered to "stimulate and shape all natural and human activity":

> The Wood Element symbolizes all life, femininity, creativity, and organic material; Fire is the Element of energy and intelligence; Earth, the Element of stability, endurance and the earth itself; Metal, in addition to its material sense, also encompasses competitiveness, business acumen, and masculinity; while Water is the Element of all that flows—oil and alcohol as well as water itself, consequently also symbolizing transport and communication. (29)

The Elements correspond to certain organs of the body and physical ailments as well as to particular geometric shapes. An extended array of correspondences includes seasons, directions, numbers, colors, tastes, and smells (Lam 32). In the physical landscape the Elements can be placed in a productive order, in which each Element will generate and stimulate the one succeeding it, or a destructive order, in which Elements in close proximity are considered harmful. To avoid negative effects, a "controlling" Element can mediate between two elements positioned in their destructive order.

Suyuan Woo subscribes to a traditional application of the theory of the Five Elements in what Jing-mei calls her mother's "own version of organic chemistry" (31). As Ben Xu has observed, the Five Elements are "the mystical ingredients that determine every person's character flaw according to one's birth hour." *Wu-hsing* theory posits that "none of us has all the five character elements perfectly balanced, and therefore, every one of us is by nature flawed" (Xu 12). Accordingly, Suyuan believes that too much Fire causes a bad temper while too much Water makes someone flow in too many directions. Too little Wood results in one bending "too quickly to listen to other people's ideas, unable to stand on [one's] own" (31). Jing-mei, who does not understand how Suyuan's pronouncements tie to a larger belief system, associates her mother's theories with displeasure and criticism: "Something was always missing. Something always needed improving. Something was not in balance. This one or that had too much of one element, not enough of another."

According to *wu-hsing* theory, flaws can be amended and balance attained by symbolically adding the element a person lacks. Xu points out that "the 'rose' in Rose Hsu Jordan's name, for example, is supposed to add wood to her character" (12). Conversely, elements can be removed to create an imbalance. When Lindo Jong does not become pregnant in her first marriage, the matchmaker tells her mother-in-law: "A woman can have sons only if she is deficient in one of the elements. Your daughter-in-law was born with enough wood, fire, water, and earth, and she was deficient in metal, which was a good sign. But when she was married, you loaded her down with gold bracelets and decorations and now she has all the elements, including metal. She's too balanced to have babies" (63). Although Lindo knows that the direct cause of her failure to become pregnant is not her having too much metal but rather her husband's refusal to sleep with her, she accepts the matchmaker's reasoning about the Five Elements. Years later Lindo comments: "See the gold metal I can now wear. I gave birth to your brothers and then your father gave me these two bracelets. Then I had you [Waverly]" (66). The implication here is that the gender of Lindo's male children corresponds to her natural deficiency in Metal. Adding Metal back into her composition through the bracelets causes her next child to be female.

More significantly, Lindo, like Suyuan, believes that the Elements affect character traits: "After the gold was removed from my body, I felt lighter, more free. They say this is what happens if you lack metal. You begin to think as an independent person" (63). Tan suggests that Lindo's natural "imbalance" is key to her true identity, the self that she promises never to forget. As a girl she had determined to honor the marriage contract made by her parents, even if it meant sacrificing her sense of identity. But on her wedding day she wonders "why [her] destiny had been decided, why [she] should have an unhappy life so someone else could have a happy one" (58). Once Lindo's gold and jewelry are repossessed by her mother-in-law to help her become fertile, Lindo begins to plot her escape from the marriage. Her feeling lighter and more free without Metal corresponds to her assertion of her true identity. Destiny is not so narrowly determined that she cannot use her natural qualities as a Horse—quickness, eloquence, ruthlessness—to free herself from her false position in the marriage. Because Lindo has secretly blown out the matchmaker's red candle on her wedding night, she has in effect rewritten her fate without breaking her parents' promise. Rather than restricting her identity, her belief in astrology and *wu-hsing* gives her a secure base from which to express it.

As with astrology, Tan uses the theory of the Five Elements not only for characterization but also for the development of conflict in *The Joy Luck Club*. "Without Wood" deals with the disastrous effects of Rose Hsu Jordan's not having enough Wood in her personality, at least according to her mother An-mei's diagnosis. An-mei herself has inspired "a lifelong stream of criticism" from Suyuan Woo, apparently for bending too easily to others' ideas, the flaw of those who lack Wood (30–31). An-mei admits to having listened to too many people when she was young. She almost succumbed to her family's urgings to forget her mother, and later she was nearly seduced by the pearl necklace offered to her by her mother's rival. Experience has shown An-mei that people try to influence others for selfish reasons. To protect her daughter from opportunists, An-mei tells Rose that she must listen to her mother if she wants to grow "strong and straight." If she listens to others she will grow "crooked and weak." But Rose comments, "By the time she told me this, it was too late. I had already begun to bend" (191).

Rose attributes her compliant nature to the strict disciplinary measures of an elementary school teacher and to the influences of American culture: "Chinese people had Chinese opinions. American people had American opinions. And in almost every case, the American version was much better" (191). Not until much later does she realize that in the "American version" there are "too many choices," so that it is "easy to get confused and pick the wrong thing." Rose, emotionally paralyzed at fourteen by a sense that she is responsible for the death of her four-year-old brother, grows into an adult who not only listens to others but lets them take responsibility for her so that she may avoid committing another fatal error. Her husband, Ted, makes all the decisions in their marriage until a mistake of his own brings on a malpractice suit and shakes his self-confidence. When Ted abruptly demands a divorce, Rose's lack of Wood manifests itself: "I had been talking to too many people, my friends, everybody it seems, except Ted" (188). She tells a "different story" about the situation to Waverly, Lena, and her psychiatrist, each of whom offers a different response. An-mei chides Rose for not wanting to discuss Ted with her, but Rose is reluctant to do so because she fears that An-mei will tell her she must preserve her marriage, even though there is "absolutely nothing left to save" (117).

Contrary to Rose's expectations, her mother is less concerned that she stay married than that she deal with her inability to make decisions. An-mei wants her daughter to address the personality deficiencies that are the cause of her circumstances. Believing that Rose needs to assert her identity by acting on her own behalf, An-mei admonishes: "You must think for yourself, what you must do. If someone tells you, then you are not trying" (130). An-mei's advice is embedded in the broader context of her Chinese worldview. When Rose complains that she has no hope, and thus no reason to keep trying to save her marriage, An-mei responds: "This is not hope. Not reason. This is your fate. This is your life, what you must do" (130). An-mei believes life is determined by fate, by immutable celestial forces. But like Lindo Jong, she sees fate as having a participatory element. Earthly matters admit the influence of human agency. Consequently, her admonition to Rose is focused on what Rose must "do."

As a child Rose observes that both her parents believe in their *neng-kan*, the ability to do anything they put their minds to. This belief has not only brought them to America but has "enabled them to have seven children and buy a house in the Sunset district with very little money" (121). Rose notes that by taking into account all the dangers described in *The Twenty-Six Malignant Gates*, An-mei has "absolute faith she could prevent every one of them" (124).

However, An-mei's optimism about her ability to manipulate fate is challenged when her youngest child, Bing, drowns. An-mei does everything she can to recover her son, but she realizes she cannot "use faith to change fate" (130). Tragedy teaches her that forethought is not the same thing as control. Still, she wedges a white Bible—one in which Bing's name is only lightly pencilled in under "Deaths"—beneath a short table leg as a symbolic act, "a way for her to correct the imbalances of life" (116). Although An-mei accepts that her power over fate is limited, she continues to believe that she can positively influence her circumstances. The idea of balance she is enacting is a fundamental element of *yin–yang* philosophy, according to which two complementary forces "govern the universe and make up all aspects of life and matter" (Rossbach 21). As Johndennis Govert notes, "to remove an obstruction to your happiness, regain a state of health, or create a more harmonious household, *yin* and *yang* must be in balance" (7). An-mei may use a Bible to balance the kitchen table, but she rejects the Christian beliefs it represents. Rose notes that her mother loses "her faith in God" after Bing's death (116). The belief system that governs An-mei's actions is Chinese, an amalgam of luck, house gods, ancestors, and all the elements in balance, "the right amount of wind and water" (122).

In contrast to her mother, Rose lacks a means by which she can delineate or systematize her notions of causality and responsibility. Moreover, she eschews any real sense that people can have control over their circumstances. As a teenager Rose is appalled to discover she is powerless to prevent little Bing from falling into the ocean as she watches. Later Rose thinks "that maybe it was fate all along, that faith was just an illusion that somehow you're in control. I found out the most I could have was hope, and with that I was not denying any possibility, good or bad" (121). When her husband Ted wants a divorce, Rose compares the shock she receives to having the wind knocked out of her: "And after you pick yourself up, you realize you can't trust anybody to save you—not your husband, not your mother, not God. So what can you do to stop yourself from tilting and falling all over again?" (121). Added to her sense of helplessness is the suspicion that whenever she is forced into making a decision, she is walking through a minefield: "I never believed there was ever any one right answer, yet there were many wrong ones" (120). Rose's lack of any sort of a belief system fosters a crippling passivity characterized by a fear that whatever she chooses will turn out badly. Her inability to make even the smallest decisions becomes the equivalent, in Ted's mind at least, of her having no identity.

Ironically, once Rose realizes that Ted has taken away all her choices, she begins to fight back. She seizes on the metaphor An-mei has used to explain the lack of Wood in her personality: "If you bend to listen to other people, you will grow crooked and weak. You will fall to the ground with the first strong wind. And then you will be like a weed, growing wild in any direction, running along the ground until someone pulls you out and throws you away" (191). Inspired by the weeds in her own neglected garden that cannot be dislodged from the masonry without "pulling the whole building down" (195), Rose demands that Ted let her keep their house. She explains, "You can't just pull me out of your life and throw me away" (196). For the first time in her life she stands up for what she wants without soliciting the advice of others. After her assertion of selfhood, Rose dreams that her "beaming" mother has planted weeds that are "running wild in every direction" in her planter boxes (196). This image, which suggests that An-mei has finally accepted Rose's nature instead of trying to change her, is consistent with the desires the Joy Luck daughters share regarding their mothers. Each one struggles to feel loved for who she is. In part the younger women's insecurity stems from having a different set of cultural values than their mothers. The older women try to encourage their daughters but do not always know how to cope with the cultural gap that separates them. As Lindo states: "I wanted my children to have the best combination: American circumstances and Chinese character. How could I know these two things do not mix?" (254). But Rose's dream-image submerges the fact that Rose has finally acted on her mother's admonition to speak up for herself. An-mei has guessed that Ted is engaged in "monkey business" with another woman, and it is at the moment when Rose realizes her mother is right that she begins to move intuitively toward standing up for her own needs and desires. As it turns out, An-mei is correct in wanting Rose to listen to her mother rather than to her bored and sleepy-eyed psychiatrist in order to be "strong and straight." Ultimately, An-mei's belief that one's fate involves making choices instead of being paralyzed as a victim is validated by Rose's assertion of her identity.

A third element of traditional belief in *The Joy Luck Club* is *feng shui*, or geomancy. The most opaque yet potentially the most important aspect of Chinese cosmology to Tan's exploration of identity, *feng shui* plays a pivotal role in Lena St. Clair's story "The Voice from the Wall," which chronicles her mother Ying-ying's gradual psychological breakdown and withdrawal from life. Ten-year-old Lena, having no knowledge of her mother's past, becomes convinced that her mother is crazy as she listens to Ying-ying rave after the death of her infant son. Even before Ying-ying loses her baby, however, her behavior appears to be erratic and compulsive. When the family moves to a new apartment, Ying-ying arranges and rearranges the furniture in an effort to put things in balance. Although Lena senses her mother is disturbed, she dismisses Ying-ying's explanations as "Chinese nonsense" (108). What Lena does not understand is that her mother is practicing the ancient Chinese art of *feng shui* (pronounced "fung shway"). Translated literally as "wind" and "water," *feng shui* is alluded to only once in the book as An-mei Hsu's balance of "the right amount of wind and water" (122). Although the term "*feng shui*" is never used overtly in conjunction with Ying-ying St. Clair, its tenets are fundamental to her worldview.

Stephen Skinner defines *feng shui* as "the art of living in harmony with the land, and deriving the greatest benefit, peace and prosperity from being in the right place at the right time" (4). The precepts of *feng shui* were systematized by two different schools in China over a thousand years ago. The Form School, or intuitive approach, was developed by Yang Yün-Sung (c. 840–888 A.D.) and flourished in Kiangsi and Anhui provinces. Practitioners focus on the visible form of the landscape, especially the shapes of mountains and the direction of watercourses. The Compass School, or analytical approach, was developed by Wang Chih in the Sung dynasty (960 A.D.) and spread throughout Fukien and Chekiang provinces as well as Hong Kong and Taiwan (Skinner 26). The analytic approach is concerned with directional orientation in conjunction with Chinese astrology. As Walters notes, Compass School scholars have traditionally "placed greater emphasis on the importance of precise mathematical calculations, and compiled elaborate formulae and schematic diagrams" (10). Geomancers using this approach employ an elaborate compass called the *lo p'an*, astrological charts and horoscopes, numerological data, and special rulers.

According to Susan Hornik, the beliefs encompassed by *feng shui* date back 3,000 years to the first practice of selecting auspicious sites for burial tombs in order to "bring good fortune to heirs" (73). As Skinner explains, "Ancestors are linked with the site of their tombs. As they also have a direct effect on the lives of their descendants, it follows logically that if their tombs are located favourably on the site of a strong concentration of earth energy or *ch'i*, not only will they be happy but they will also derive the power to aid their descendants, from the accumulated *ch'i* of the site" (11). By the Han dynasty (206 B.C.), the use of *feng shui* was extended to the selection of dwellings for the living (Hornik 73). The basic idea is to attract and channel *ch'i*, or beneficial energy, and "accumulate it without allowing it to go stagnant" (Skinner 21). Since *ch'i* encourages growth and prosperity, a wise person will consider how to manipulate it to best effect through *feng shui*, the study of placement with respect to both natural and man-made environments. As a form of geomancy *feng shui* is "the exact complement of astrology, which is divination by signs in the Heavens" (Walters 12), but it is based on a different presupposition. Whereas the course of the stars and planets is fixed, the earthly environment can be altered by human intervention through *feng shui*. The practice of *feng shui* offers yet another variation of the belief that people have the power to affect their destiny.

Thus Ying-ying St. Clair's seemingly idiosyncratic actions and their nonsensical explanations in "The Voice from the Wall" are grounded in a coherent system of beliefs and practices concerned with balancing the environment. Since Ying-ying feels her surroundings are out of balance, she does everything she can to correct them. For instance, she moves "a large round mirror from the wall facing the front door to a wall by the sofa" (108). *Ch'i* is believed to enter a dwelling through the front door, but a mirror hung opposite the entrance may deflect it back outside again. Mirrors require careful placement so as to encourage the flow of *ch'i* around a room. Furniture, too, must be positioned according to guidelines that allow beneficial currents of *ch'i* to circulate without stagnating. Through properly placed furniture "every opportunity can be taken to correct whatever defects may exist, and to enhance whatever positive qualities there are" (Walters 46). Hence, Ying-ying rearranges the sofa, chairs, and end tables, seeking the best possible grouping. Even a "Chinese scroll of goldfish" is moved. When large-scale changes are impossible, *feng shui* practitioners frequently turn to symbolic solutions. Strategically placed aquariums containing goldfish are often prescribed for structural problems that cannot be altered, in part because aquariums symbolically bring all Five Elements together into balance (Collins 21). In Ying-ying's case, a picture is substituted for live goldfish, which represent life and growth.

Ying-ying's attempt to balance the living room follows a *feng shui* tradition: "If beneficial *ch'i* are lacking from the heart of the house, the family will soon drift apart" (Walters 42). But Ying-ying is also compensating for negative environmental and structural features that she cannot modify. The apartment in the new neighborhood is built on a steep hill, a poor site, she explains, because "a bad wind from the top blows all your strength back down the hill. So you can never get ahead. You are always rolling backward" (109). In ancient China the ideal location for a building was in the shelter of hills that would protect it from bitter northerly winds. However, a house at the very base of a sloping road would be vulnerable to torrential rains, mudslides, and crashes caused by runaway carts. Ying-ying's concern with psychic rather than physical danger is consistent with modern applications of *feng shui*, but her notion of an ill wind sweeping downhill is based on traditional lore. In addition to the unfortunate location of the apartment building, its lobby is musty, a sign that it does not favor the circulation of *ch'i*. The door to the St. Clairs' apartment is narrow, "like a neck that has been strangled" (109), further restricting the entrance of beneficial energy. Moreover, as Ying-ying tells Lena, the kitchen faces the toilet room, "so all your worth is flushed away." According to the Bagua map derived from the *I Ching*, the ancient Chinese book of divination, every building and every room has eight positions that correspond to various aspects of life: wealth and prosperity; fame and reputation; love and marriage; creativity and children; helpful people and travel; career; knowledge and self-cultivation; and health and family (Collins 61–62). Heidi Swillinger explains the problem of a dwelling where the bathroom is located in the wealth area: "Because the bathroom is a place where water enters and leaves, and because water is a symbol of wealth, residents in such a home might find that money tends to symbolically go down the drain or be flushed away."[5] Even if the St. Clairs' bathroom is not actually in the wealth area, *feng shui* guidelines dictate that it should not be placed next to the kitchen in order to avoid a clash between two of the symbolic Elements, Fire and Water.

In light of the bad *feng shui* of the apartment, Ying-ying's unhappiness with it is logical. Once she finishes altering the living room, she rearranges Lena's bedroom. The immediate effect of the new configuration is that "the nighttime life" of Lena's imagination changes (109). With her bed against the wall, she begins to listen to the private world of the family next door and to use what she hears as a basis for comparison with her own family. It is not clear whether Lena's bed has been moved to the "children" area of the room, which would enhance her *ch'i*, but certainly the new position is more in keeping with the principles of good *feng shui*, which indicate a bed should be placed against a wall, not a window (Walters 53). From this standpoint, Ying-ying's inauspicious positioning of the crib against the window appears to be inconsistent with her other efforts. Lena notes, "My mother began to bump into things, into table edges as if she forgot her stomach contained a baby, as if she were headed for trouble instead" (109). Since according to *feng shui* theory protruding corners are threatening (Collins 47), Ying-ying's peculiar neglect toward sharp table edges along with her placement of the crib suggest that her efforts at generating good *feng shui* are suspended with regard to her unborn baby.

When the baby dies at birth, apparently from a severe case of hydrocephalus and spina bifida, Ying-ying blames herself: "My fault, my fault. I knew this before it happened. I did nothing to prevent it" (111). To Western ears her self-accusation sounds odd, for birth defects such as spina bifida are congenital, and nothing Ying-ying could have done would have prevented the inevitable. However, her Eastern worldview dictates that fate can be manipulated in order to bring about good effects and to ward off bad ones. Ying-ying believes that her violation of good *feng shui* principles constitutes negligence, causing the baby to die. She is accusing herself not merely of passivity but of deliberate complicity with a malignant fate.

The burden of guilt Ying-ying carries over an abortion from her first marriage is the root of her disturbed mental state during her pregnancy. Her bumping into table edges may even be a form of self-punishment. In any case, whether she has subconsciously tried to harm the fetus or has merely failed to fend off disaster through the use of *feng shui*, in blaming herself for the baby's death Ying-ying is clearly wrestling with her responsibility for the death of her first son. In her mind the two events are connected: "I knew he [the baby] could see everything inside me. How I had given no thought to killing my other son! How I had given no thought to having this baby" (112). Instead of finding any resolution after the baby dies, Ying-ying becomes increasingly withdrawn. She cries unaccountably in the middle of cooking dinner and frequently retreats to her bed to "rest."

The presence of *feng shui* in the story suggests that however displaced, demoralized, and severely depressed Ying-ying may be, she is not "crazy," as Lena fears. Ying-ying's compulsion to rearrange furniture does not presage a psychotic break with reality but rather signals that, transplanted to a foreign country where she must function according to new rules and expectations, Ying-ying relies on familiar practices such as *feng shui* and astrology to interpret and order the world around her, especially when that world is in crisis. Lena, of course, is locked into a ten-year-old's perspective and an American frame of reference. She shares Jing-mei Woo's problem of being able to understand her mother's Chinese words but not their meanings. Whereas Clifford St. Clair's usual practice of "putting words" in his wife's mouth stems from his knowing "only a few canned Chinese expressions" (106), Lena's faulty translation of her mother's distracted speech after the baby dies reflects a lack of sufficient personal and cultural knowledge to make sense of Ying-ying's references to guilt.

Ying-ying's story, "Waiting Between the Trees," traces the origins of her decline to a much earlier time. At sixteen Ying-ying is married to a man who impregnates her, then abandons her for an opera singer. Out of grief and anger, she induces an abortion. However, after this defiant act she loses her strength, becoming "like the ladies of the lake" her mother had warned her about, floating like "a dead leaf on the water" (248–49). Unfortunately, Ying-ying's Tiger characteristic of "waiting patiently for things to come" (248) turns from easy acceptance of whatever is offered into listlessness and acquiescence over a period of fourteen years: "I became pale, ill, and more thin. I let myself become a wounded animal" (251). She confesses, "I willingly gave up my *chi*, the spirit that caused me so much pain" (251). Giving up her vital energy is tantamount to giving up her identity. By the time Clifford St. Clair takes her to America, she has already become "an unseen spirit," with no trace of her former passion and energy. Nevertheless, she retains her ability to see things before they happen. Her prescience stems from her trust in portents, which constitutes another facet of her belief system. When she is young, a flower that falls from its stalk tells her she will marry her first husband. Later on, Clifford St. Clair's appearance in her life is a sign that her "black side" will soon go away. Her husband's death signals that she can marry St. Clair.

Years later, Ying-ying can still see portents of the future. She knows Lena's is "a house that will break into pieces" (243). Ying-ying also continues to think in terms of *feng shui*. She complains that the guest room in Lena's house has sloping walls, a fact which implies the presence of sharp angles that can harbor *sha*, malignant energy signifying death and decay. With walls that close in like a coffin, the room is no place to put a baby, Ying-ying observes. But it is not until Ying-ying sees her daughter's unhappy marriage that she accepts responsibility for the fact that Lena has no *ch'i* and determines to regain her own fierce spirit in order to pass it on to her daughter. Ying-ying knows she must face the pain of her past and communicate it to her daughter so as to supply Lena with the personal and cultural knowledge of her mother's life that she has always lacked. By recounting her life's pain, Ying-ying will in essence reconstruct her lost identity. To set things in motion, she decides to topple the spindly-legged marble table in the guest room so that Lena will come to see what is wrong. In this instance Ying-ying manipulates her environment in a literal as well as a symbolic sense, drawing on her traditional Chinese worldview once more in order to effect the best outcome for her daughter's life.

Unlike her mother, Lena has no consistent belief system of her own. She inherits Ying-ying's ability to see bad things before they happen but does not possess the power to anticipate good things, which suggests that Lena has merely internalized "the unspoken terrors" that plague Ying-ying (103). According to Philip Langdon, "second- or third-generation Chinese-Americans are much less likely to embrace *feng shui* than are those who were born in Asia" (148). Not only is Lena a second-generation Chinese-American, she is half Caucasian, which makes her Chinese heritage even more remote. Nonetheless, Lena is profoundly affected by Ying-ying's way of perceiving the world. As a child Lena is obsessed with knowing the worst possible thing that can happen, but unlike her mother, she has no sense of being able to manipulate fate. Thus, she is terrified when she cannot stop what she supposes to be the nightly "killing" of the girl next door, which she hears through her bedroom wall. Only after Lena realizes that she has been wrong about the neighbor family does she find ways to change the "bad things" in her mind.

Lena's muddled notions of causality and responsibility persist into adulthood. In "Rice Husband," she still views herself as guilty for the death of Arnold Reisman, a former neighbor boy, because she "let one thing result from another" (152). She believes there is a relation between her not having cleaned her plate at meals when she was young and Arnold's development of a rare and fatal complication of measles. She wants to dismiss the link as ridiculous, but she is plagued by doubt because she has no philosophical or religious scheme by which to interpret events and establish parameters for her personal responsibility: "The thought that I could have caused Arnold's death is not so ridiculous. Perhaps he was destined to be my husband. Because I think to myself, even today, how can the world in all its chaos come up with so many coincidences, so many similarities and exact opposites?" (154). Whereas Ying-ying's belief system affords her a sense of certainty about how the world operates, Lena's lack of such a system leaves her in confusion.

It is Lena's uncertainty about causality together with her failure to take purposive action that leads Ying-ying to believe her daughter has no *ch'i*. Lena tells herself, "When I want something to happen—or not happen—I begin to look at all events and all things as relevant, an opportunity to take or avoid" (152). But Ying-ying challenges her, asking why, if Lena knew the marble table was going to fall down, she did not stop it. By analogy she is asking Lena why she does not resolve to save her marriage. Lena muses, "And it's such a simple question" (165). It is unclear whether Lena has already decided not to rescue the marriage or whether she is simply confused about her capacity to act on her own behalf. But the fact that Lena cannot answer her mother's question quietly privileges Ying-ying's perspective on the situation, much as An-mei's viewpoint of Rose's predicament is validated in "Without Wood."

Marina Heung has pointed out that among works which focus on mother–daughter relations, *The Joy Luck Club* is "remarkable for foregrounding the voices of mothers as well as of daughters" (599). However, Tan goes further than "foregrounding" the mothers; she subtly endorses their worldview at strategic points in the text. Whereas Rose, Lena, and Jing-mei are paralyzed and unable to move forward in their relationships and careers and Waverly is haunted by a lingering fear of her mother's disapproval, Suyuan, Lindo, An-mei, and even Ying-ying demonstrate a resilient belief in their power to act despite having suffered the ravages of war and the painful loss of parents, spouses, and children. Out of the vast range of Chinese religious, philosophical, and folkloric beliefs, many of which stress self-effacement and passivity, Tan focuses on practices that allow her characters to make adjustments to their destinies and thereby preserve and perpetuate their identities. Suyuan Woo is most striking in this regard. She goes outside of conventional Chinese beliefs to make up her own means of dealing with fate. Suyuan invents "Joy Luck," whereby she and her friends in Kweilin "choose [their] own happiness" at their weekly mah jong parties instead of passively waiting for their own deaths (25). Joy Luck for them consists of forgetting past wrongs, avoiding bad thoughts, feasting, laughing, playing games, telling stories, and most importantly, hoping to be lucky. The ritualistic set of attitudes and actions that Suyuan and her friends observe keep them from succumbing to despair. When the war is over, Suyuan holds on to the main tenet of her belief system—that "hope was our only joy"—by refusing to assume a passive role in the aftermath of tragedy. She never gives up hope that by persistence she may be able to locate the infant daughters she left in China. When Suyuan says to Jing-mei, "You don't even know little percent of me!" (27), she is referring to the complex interplay among the events of her life, her native culture and language, and her exercise of her mind and will. These things constitute an identity that Jing-mei has only an elusive and fragmentary knowledge of.

The references in *The Joy Luck Club* to traditional beliefs and practices such as astrology, *wu-hsing*, and *feng shui* emphasize the distance between the Chinese mothers and their American-born daughters. Tan hints through the stories of Lindo and Waverly Jong that a degree of reconciliation and understanding is attainable between mothers and daughters, and she indicates through Jing-mei Woo's journey that cultural gaps can be narrowed. In fact, Jing-mei Woo starts "becoming Chinese" as soon as she crosses the border into China (267). But overall, Tan's portrayal of first-generation immigrants attempting to transmit their native culture to their offspring is full of situations where "meanings" are untranslatable. The breakdown in communication between mothers and daughters is poignantly encapsulated in "American Translation," the vignette that introduces the third group of stories in the book. A mother tells her daughter not to put a mirror at the foot of her bed: "'All your marriage happiness will bounce back and turn the opposite way'" (147). Walters notes that mirrors are "regarded as symbols of a long and happy marriage" but also that "care has to be taken that they are not so placed that they are likely to alarm the soul of a sleeper when it rises for nocturnal wanderings" (55). According to *feng shui* principles, a mirror "acts as a constant energy reflector and will be sending [a] stream of intensified power into the space over and around [the] bed, day and night. It will be a perpetual cause of disturbance" during sleep (Lam 105). The daughter in the vignette is "irritated that her mother s[ees] bad omens in everything. She had heard these warnings all her life." Lacking an understanding of the cosmological system to which her mother's omens belong, the daughter simply views them as evidence that her mother has a negative outlook on life.

When the woman offers a second mirror to hang above the headboard of the bed in order to remedy the problem, she is seeking to properly channel the flow of *ch'i* around the room. The mother comments, "this mirror see that mirror—*haule!*—multiply your peach-blossom luck." The daughter, however, does not understand her mother's allusion to peach-blossom luck, which "refers to those who are particularly attractive to the opposite sex" (Rossbach 48). By way of explanation, the mother, "mischief in her eyes," has her daughter look in the mirror to see her future grandchild. She is acting in accordance to the ancient Chinese belief that the "mysterious power of reflection" of mirrors, which reveal "a parallel world beyond the surface," is magical (Walters 55). The daughter, unfortunately, can only grasp literal meanings: "The daughter looked—and *haule!* There it was: her own reflection looking back at her." The mother is incapable of translating her worldview into "perfect American English," so the daughter's comprehension remains flawed, partial, incomplete. Whether or not she apprehends, from her literal reflection, that she herself is the symbol of her mother's own peach-blossom luck is ambiguous. In the same way, the uneasy relations between the older and younger women in *The Joy Luck Club* suggest that the daughters understand only dimly, if at all, that they are the long-cherished expression of their mothers' Joy Luck.

NOTES

1. For a discussion of existential unrepeatability and the role of memory in *The Joy Luck Club*, see Ben Xu, "Memory and the Ethnic Self: Reading Amy Tan's *The Joy Luck Club*," *MELUS* 19.1 (1994): 3–18. An interesting treatment of language, storytelling, and maternal subjectivity in Tan's novel can be found in Marina Heung, "Daughter-Text/Mother-Text: Matrilineage in Amy Tan's *Joy Luck Club*," *Feminist Studies* 19.3 (1993): 597–616.

2. Jing-mei Woo thinks her mother's "telltale Chinese behaviors" are expressly intended to embarrass her, including Suyuan's predilection for yellow, pink, and bright orange (143, 267). When Jing-mei arrives in China, she notices "little children wearing pink and yellow, red and peach," the only spots of bright color amidst drab grays and olive greens (271). Tan seems to suggest through this detail that Suyuan's color preferences reflect not only her personal taste but Chinese patterns and traditions. According to Sarah Rossbach, yellow stands for power, pink represents "love and pure feelings," and orange suggests "happiness and power" (46–47). In this light, Lindo Jong's criticism of Suyuan's red sweater in "Best Quality" is ironic since it is Lindo who provides evidence that red is regarded by the Chinese as an auspicious color connoting "happiness, warmth or fire, strength, and fame" (Rossbach 45). In "The Red Candle" Lindo mentions not only her mother's jade necklace and her mother-in-law's pillars, tables, and chairs but also her own wedding banners, palanquin, dress, scarf, special eggs, and marriage candle as being red.

3. Jing-mei Woo, born in the same year as Waverly (37), is a Metal Rabbit, and like Waverly, she exhibits a "Rabbit-like" sensitivity to criticism, especially when it comes from her mother.

4. The Chinese system of astrology has Buddhist origins, while the theory of the Five Elements derives from Taoist thought. Holmes Welch observes that "there was little distinction—and the most intimate connections—between early Buddhism and Taoism" (119).

5. Similar reasoning obtains in "Rice Husband" when Ying-ying tells Lena that a bank will have all its money drained away after a plumbing and bathroom fixtures store opens across the street from it (149). Lena comments that "one month later, an officer of the bank was arrested for embezzlement."

WORKS CITED

Collins, Terah Kathryn. *The Western Guide to Feng Shui*. Carlsbad, CA: Hay House, 1996.

Govert, Johndennis. *Feng Shui: Art and Harmony of Place*. Phoenix: Daikakuji, 1993.

Heung, Marina. "Daughter-Text/Mother-Text: Matrilineage in Amy Tan's *Joy Luck Club*." *Feminist Studies* 19.3 (1993): 597–616.

Hornik, Susan. "How to Get that Extra Edge on Health and Wealth." *Smithsonian* Aug. 1993: 70–75.

Jackson, Dallas. "Chinese Astrology." *Los Angeles Times* 20 Feb. 1991, Orange County ed.: E2. *News*. Online. Lexis-Nexis. 15 Mar. 1997.

Lam, Kam Chuen. *Feng Shui Handbook*. New York: Henry Holt, 1996.

Langdon, Philip. "Lucky Houses." *Atlantic* Nov. 1991: 146+.

Maspero, Henri. *Taoism and Chinese Religion*. Trans. Frank A. Kierman, Jr. Amherst: U of Massachusetts P, 1981.

Rossbach, Sarah. *Living Color: Master Lin Yun's Guide to Feng Shui and the Art of Color*. New York: Kodansha, 1994.

Scott, Ann. "Chinese New Year: The Year of the Tiger." *United Press International* 5 Feb. 1986, International sec. *News*. Online. Lexis-Nexis. 15 Mar. 1997.

Skinner, Stephen. *The Living Earth Manual of Feng-Shui*. London: Routledge, 1982.

Swillinger, Heidi. "Feng Shui: A Blueprint for Balance." *San Francisco Chronicle* 8 Sept. 1993: Z1. *News*. Online. Lexis-Nexis. 15 Mar. 1997.

Tan, Amy. *The Joy Luck Club*. New York: G.P. Putnam, 1989.

Walters, Derek. *Feng Shui: The Chinese Art of Designing a Harmonious Environment*. New York: Simon & Schuster, 1988.

Welch, Holmes. *Taoism: The Parting of the Way*. Revised ed. Boston: Beacon, 1966.

Xu, Ben. "Memory and the Ethnic Self: Reading Amy Tan's *The Joy Luck Club*." *MELUS* 19.1 (1994): 3–18.

Youngblood, Ruth. "Baby-Poor Singapore Looks to Dragon for Help." *Los Angeles Times* 29 Nov. 1987, sec. 1: 41. *News*. Online. Lexis-Nexis. 15 Mar. 1997.

MARC SINGER

Moving Forward to Reach the Past: The Dialogics of Time in Amy Tan's The Joy Luck Club

History and myth coexist in Amy Tan's *The Joy Luck Club*, but they do not coexist easily. The novel forges connections between two generations of women, traces four family genealogies that span the twentieth century, and stresses the importance of ethnic heritage, suggesting a heavy investment in history and historical representation. Yet the family histories depicted in the novel are profoundly mythical—the tales of the mothers' youth are timeless fables filled with supernatural wonders, presenting a China that seems drawn as much from occidental cliché as from authentic Chinese history. Even events as clearly historical as the Communist revolution become transmuted into heavily allegorical parables such as An-mei Hsu's tale of angry peasants rising up against tyrannical magpies (Tan 272–73).[1]

This fusion of historicity and mythic fabrication is all the more unusual because Tan assigns radically separate cultural and temporal valences to each: the techniques of myth are unilaterally reserved to represent China and the past, while America is narrated with a historical specificity which, for Tan, connotes modernity and the present. Indeed, the split is so extreme that Tan creates two entirely different scripts of cultural identity, a realistically-outlined "American" identity for the daughters and an Orientalized "Chinese" one for their mothers. With such a drastic cultural and temporal divide bifurcating its stories, Tan's work might easily be classified as a mere collection of independent short stories,

From *JNT: Journal of Narrative Theory* 31, no. 3 (Fall 2001): 324–352. © 2001 by *JNT: Journal of Narrative Theory*.

or at best a novel pulled in two different directions by its dissonant components. Indeed, much of the academic criticism of *The Joy Luck Club* presumes that the novel is split into a dialogic divergence of different characters, voices, and cultural settings; some studies go so far as to attribute all of the novel's apparent discontinuities to its dialogic structure.

Yet such readings do not consider the variety and the power of the interconnective tactics Tan deploys to integrate her sixteen short stories into a single overarching narrative. Amy Tan fashions a unifying narrative structure for *The Joy Luck Club* by aligning its sixteen stories into a coherent and deliberate temporal order. This order emerges from advancements and juxtapositions in the timing of each of the stories; the larger, supranarrative plot only becomes apparent when the stories are connected and contrasted with each other, exposing a systematic progression through time. Furthermore, this narrative structure not only connects the past to the present, it also balances the modes of historicity and myth that Tan uses to represent those periods. Thus, the true dialogue in *The Joy Luck Club* is not a cacophony of voices but a convergence of different moments in and methods of representing time.

However, few critics have explored Tan's use of time in *The Joy Luck Club*, despite its centrality to the novel's articulation and negotiation of conflicting modes of gender, generational, and cultural subjectivity. Tan models and previews her manipulation of narrative time in the novel's eponymous opening tale, which suggests that Jing-mei Woo and the other daughters can only attain understanding and rapprochement with their mothers through techniques of temporal juxtaposition and investigations into the familial past. This interaction of past and present replaces any literal dialogue between mothers and daughters, which is actively prevented by the stories' temporal framing. Instead, the stories interact through their superstructural arrangement into a narrative that stresses the importance of returning to the past in order to progress into the future; because Tan almost uniformly associates China with the past and America with the present, she also implies that this polychronic progression can resolve the temporalized contradictions of Chinese American female identity. Tan thus capitalizes on *The Joy Luck Club*'s formal capabilities as a collection of interdependent stories to reconcile the potentially contradictory temporalities, ideologies, and subjectivities that drive her novel.

Temporality, Dialogicity, and the Critics

Many studies of *The Joy Luck Club* preempt any examination of these contradictions, however, by explaining them as mere consequences or indicators of the work's dialogic structure. While the novel's interconnected, multivocal narratives obviously lend themselves to a Bakhtinian theoretical analysis, Tan's complex narrative structure cannot be reduced to a simple scheme of dialogism. Bonnie Braendlin, for example, writes that "Tan's novel depicts the socialization of young women as a dialogical process" between mothers and daughters (Braendlin 114), but does not examine how these dialogic interactions occur. Gloria Shen similarly presumes the characters conduct a literal dialogue through their stories (Shen 240–41), a common conclusion but one that the stories' isolating narrative frames do not support. *The Joy Luck Club* instead displays a far less literal mode of dialogicity, one that moderates between competing historical periods, narrative chronologies, and methods for manipulating the passage of time.

The critical discourse has only fleetingly acknowledged this temporal dialogicity. Braendlin touches on the contradictions between the changes in the characters brought about by their maturation and the similarities that defy these changes (114)—in other words, between the temporally progressive and counter-progressive or atemporal forces at work in *The Joy Luck Club*. Yet Braendlin turns away from this largely unexplored topic, instead classifying the novel and all of its paradoxes within the easily-applied label of dialogics. A perfectly viable interpretive framework of Bakhtinian theory is thus used to close down an area of inquiry which practically demands further exploration by virtue of its centrality to Tan's work.

Stephen Souris conducts a formalistic, narratological analysis of *The Joy Luck Club*, and discovers some of the limits of a narrowly dialogic reading of Tan's novel. Like numerous other *Joy Luck* scholars, Souris views the novel as a heteroglossic collection of voices in dialogue with one another. However, he also detects a potential contradiction between the novel's division into multiple, multivocal narratives and its attempted closure into one univocal ending (114). Souris recognizes that his Bakhtinian, Iserian reading "privileges the flaunting of diverse perspectives that, while dialogized, are never resolved into harmonious agreement or simple synthesis" (115), a reading strategy that stands in stark contrast with the novel's larger narrative structure and particularly with its conclusion. Upon discovering this contradiction, however, Souris shifts his terms of analysis, arguing that Bakhtinian dialogicity dictates the impossibility of a formal closure in *The Joy Luck Club* but that other factors of gender and cultural identity bring it to a thematic resolution. He quite accurately concludes that *The Joy Luck Club* "suggests resolution and reconciliation, but the actual collection of voices cannot with complete accuracy be reduced to a thematic reading" (119), identifying a powerful narrative tension between the work's multivocality and its attempts to assemble those voices into a single novelistic plot. Nevertheless, he focuses almost solely on the literal dialogicity between characters' voices, at the expense of examining the novel's manipulation of chronology and sequence, which overwrites the dialogue between characters with a less visible but no less present dialogicity of time.

Instead Souris, like many other *Joy Luck* critics, suggests the novel's formal dilemmas are resolved by the common subjectivities it inscribes upon its characters. Critics such as Amy Ling, Elaine Kim, and Bonnie TuSmith have all located the novel's structural unity in the similarities it draws between characters through their gender, their culture, and especially their generation; Ling, for example, contends that the mothers "seem interchangeable in that the role of mother supersedes all other roles" (138) and that the novel presents a generalized struggle between mothers and daughters.[2] Other critics begin with a more explicitly narratological focus but arrive at the same basic point. Walter Shear initially suggests that Tan's multiple-narrative form allows her to negotiate the contradictions of representing different generations and different perspectives on Chinese American culture within one text (Shear 193–94). However, when confronted with the novel's ending, Shear too abandons his formal focus and suggests that Tan does the same, arguing that "Tan seems to place more emphasis on the Chinese identity as the healing factor" that reunites the family unit and the fictional narrative (Shear 199). Similarly, Marina Heung argues that Tan's narrative form resolves her novel's temporal contradictions by making the reader an "active constructor of meaning" (Heung 613) who connects the sixteen stories both synchronically and diachronically. Yet even Heung ultimately subordinates this polychronic narrative structure to the matrilineal narrative it creates, suggesting once again that *The Joy Luck Club*'s formal continuity stems from its construction of a unifying mother/daughter plot and not from its form *per se*. Thus, each author maintains that the dialogic diversities of the characters are subsumed by their deeper narrative roles and shared subjectivities as mothers and daughters, Chinese Americans, and women.

Curiously, Malini Johar Schueller makes the same argument in reverse: she maintains that "Tan's decision to have several different mothers and daughters telling their different stories reflects her awareness of ethnicity as a constantly shifting social construct" (80)—in other words, Schueller says, Tan uses her novel's dialogicity to undermine and avoid any unifying, essentialist generalizations about identity. But whether the critics argue that Tan's schemes of collective identity counteract her methods of dialogic divergence or vice versa, they always posit the same split, suggesting that the novel's unifying theme of identity stands in opposition to its diversifying form of dialogicity. Inevitably, any problems in one area (narrative closure for Souris, essentialized identity for Schueller) are solved by Tan's tactics in the other: theme unites form, form alters theme. I will suggest instead that Tan's form and content are complementary rather than counterpoised—that any contradictions or tensions within one area are reflected in the other. Exploring *The Joy Luck Club*'s formal and temporal tensions, rather than seeking to close them down, can reveal serious thematic and ideological discontinuities in Tan's work, and can expose the strategies with which she attempts to balance them.

Sau-ling Cynthia Wong has initiated one such reading of *The Joy Luck Club*, detecting in the novel a deliberate tension among conflicting models of ethnic identity. She acutely criticizes Tan for fabricating a "quasi-ethnographic, Orientalist," heavily mythologized version of Chinese culture (Wong 181)—but rather than claim this portrait is mitigated by any literal dialogue between the stories, Wong notes the novel also presents "counter-Orientalist interpretive possibilities" (Wong 191). Wong perceives a dialogic relationship not among the characters' voices, but between the novel's multiple models of Chinese subjectivity. Although she castigates Tan for privileging the false, exoticized, Oriental identity, her argument credits the novel with sufficient complexity that it no longer requires a literal dialogue to support a multiplicity of meanings; another kind of dialogism, Wong would argue, already exists within Tan's varied ideological statements. However, Wong only briefly considers time and other narrative techniques in her discussion of Tan's delicate ideological balancing act, focusing primarily on an analysis of the reasons for Tan's enormous popular success. Wong points the way to a deeper understanding of the structure of *The Joy Luck Club*, but the need for a full analysis of Tan's use of time and narrative form still remains. Such a formal analysis is especially important because, as critics from Souris to Wong all demonstrate, Tan's use of time and history affect not only the novel's form, but also its figuration of Chinese and Chinese American cultural identity.

Strangely, one aspect of Bakhtinian theory that critics have not applied to *The Joy Luck Club* is the concept of the chronotope, "the intrinsic connectedness of temporal and spatial relationships that are artistically expressed in literature" (Bakhtin 84)—in other words, a narrative's articulation of patterns of time and space. Given that Tan constructs divisions in both space and time—divisions between China and America, the past and the present—the chronotope seems particularly relevant to her work. As Bakhtin suggests in his "Concluding Remarks" to "Forms of Time and of the Chronotope in the Novel," dialogic interactions need not occur solely between literal voices:

> Chronotopes are mutually inclusive, they co-exist, they may be interwoven with, replace or oppose one another, contradict one another or find themselves in ever more complex interrelationships.... The general characteristic of these interactions is that they are *dialogical* (in the broadest use of the word). (252)

Structures of time can also interact dialogically within a novel, as they do in *The Joy Luck Club*. These dialogics of time forge many of the narrative interconnections between Tan's component stories; they also rationalize and harmonize the novel's mutual narrative drives towards divergence and amalgamation, drives that under more literally dialogical readings terminate only in paradox. These dialogics of time even reinforce the novel's ideological claims: Tan complements *The Joy Luck Club*'s mythical, static portrayal of Chinese American women's subjectivity with its framework of historical progress and change by arranging these conflicting narrative structures into a dual temporal order. In this temporal order, progression into the future is dependent upon the characters' return to and acceptance of their mythologized Chinese past.

One final explanatory note must precede the examination of Tan's temporal structure. Throughout this article I frequently refer to *The Joy Luck Club* as a novel, in spite of Tan's own well-documented reluctance to use that term (Huntley 43, Souris 99). Tan's ambivalence notwithstanding, *The Joy Luck Club* contains one crucial novelistic element: an overarching plot which progresses through a carefully-modulated chronological arrangement of events. However, unlike more conventionally telic multiple monologue narratives—such as Faulkner's *As I Lay Dying*, in which the monologues convey different perspectives on the same central plot—*The Joy Luck Club* advances this chronological master-plot through multiple independent stories and sets of stories, few of them ostensibly concerned with the same actions. Tan is not simply depicting one plot through a variety of perspectives, but building a larger master narrative through the arrangement and juxtaposition of smaller, independent short-story narratives. Time and sequence become key syntactical elements in building this master-plot—the grammar by which Tan turns the divergent stories into a unified narrative.

The term "master narrative" can hardly be used lightly in contemporary literary criticism, not only because it conjures images of racial and sexual tyranny in an era of constant theoretical self-examination, but because of the phrase's verbal similarity to Jean-François Lyotard's concept of the *grand récit*, the "grand narrative" through which cultures legitimate knowledge and meaning. In reference to *The Joy Luck Club*, however, neither connotation of "master narrative" is entirely inappropriate. Tan's novel builds a grand narrative of its own, a superstructural story in which the daughters' maturation in the present day leads to a confrontation with and acknowledgment of the distant, mythologized Chinese past that is represented by and transmitted through their mothers. This narrative may be somewhat more limited in philosophical scope than Lyotard's critique of Enlightenment and postmodern knowledge, but it is a *grand récit*, a metanarrative of knowledge acquisition and legitimation, nonetheless.

The more ideologically disturbing connotations of "master narrative" are also quite apt—not because Tan's metanarrative is explicitly invested in the values of slavery, but because for critics such as Ben Xu and Sau-ling Cynthia Wong, *The Joy Luck Club* promotes a shallowly essentialized scheme of ethnic identity in which Chinese American women must find validation from a heavily Orientalized version of their Chinese heritage. For these critics, Tan's novel subjugates both individual subjectivity and historical specificity to the mythologizing ideology of its master narrative. An analysis of *The Joy Luck Club*'s temporal technique can bolster these claims, for the content and structure of the novel's master-plot are key elements in Tan's appeal to the authority of a mythologized past. Furthermore, because this master-plot is formed through the sequencing and interconnection of seemingly independent pieces—formed, in other words, by the reader's assembly of sixteen stories into a novel, just as Heung has argued—Tan has arranged for her audience to participate in the creation of this ideological narrative, although she nevertheless determines its content.

Critical readers therefore have ample reason to examine *The Joy Luck Club*'s supranarrative structure. The same techniques that conjoin the short stories also manage the formal tensions that have most vexed some critics, and reinforce the ideological claims that have most angered others. Furthermore, because Tan builds this master narrative largely by manipulating the timing of the various stories and their narrative frames, any discussion of *The Joy Luck Club*'s overarching narrative design must first look to time—both as the technical means of assembling the master-plot and as the thematic cornerstone that gives it meaning.

Formal and Thematic Preludes in "The Joy Luck Club"

Tan begins her novel with "The Joy Luck Club," the eponymous short story which doubles as an introduction to the thematic concerns and temporal techniques of the entire work. This metanarrative role distinguishes it from the other three stories in "Feathers from a Thousand *Li* Away," the novel's first section. While those stories are childhood tales of An-Mei Hsu, Lindo Jong, and Ying-ying St. Clair, the three surviving mothers, "The Joy Luck Club" does not adhere to this pattern. Tan instead opens the novel with Jing-mei Woo's attempt to replace her late mother, Suyuan, at the Joy Luck Club's mah jong table. Even the flashbacks in "The Joy Luck Club" depict Suyuan Woo's adult life in Kweilin, not her childhood. The story thus defies the common focus in "Feathers from a Thousand *Li* Away" on mothers-as-daughters, before that focus is even established. Yet "The Joy Luck

Club" also serves as a typological model for the entire collection, providing reflections (or rather, precursors) of the subjects and narrative techniques of subsequent episodes—including a demonstration of how a dialogicity of time will supplant a literal dialogue among characters as the chief means of conjoining Tan's individual episodes into a single narrative.

Because it metanarratively anchors the collection, "The Joy Luck Club" is a tale of storytelling. In fact, it is almost an anthology unto itself, encapsulating or alluding to numerous stories in less than thirty pages: the founding of the San Francisco Joy Luck Club, Suyuan's journey to Kweilin, the founding of the Kweilin Joy Luck Club, Suyuan's flight from Kweilin and abandonment of her daughters—a separate story from the previous one, demarcated by Jing-mei's narratorial intercession (12–13)—the Hsus' unfortunate trip to China, Suyuan's rivalry with Lindo Jong, Jing-mei's attendant rivalry with Waverly Jong, the final revelation that Jing-mei must meet her half-sisters, and of course, the frame-story of Jing-mei taking Suyuan's place in the Joy Luck Club, the occasion for all these other revelations and reveries.

This is an incomplete and reductive listing of tales, however; "The Joy Luck Club" also contains a host of other, less fully narrative memories that a more expansive definition might term "stories." The tale begins with one such mnemonic proto-narrative, as Jing-mei recalls her mother's preparations for the latest meeting of the Joy Luck Club. The memory becomes an epigraph for the novel when Jing-mei expresses her confusion over Suyuan's Chinese terms, saying "I can never remember things I didn't understand in the first place" (6). The anecdote establishes a dilemma common to all four *Joy Luck* daughters, who believe they can never understand their mothers and who do not appreciate their heritage. Even if Jing-mei's initial memory is not a proper "story," it still becomes an anticipation, an emblematic reduction of the thematic core of *The Joy Luck Club* as a whole.

"The Joy Luck Club" therefore serves as a prelude on both narrative and metanarrative levels, in its annunciation of the novel's central theme and in its emphasis on stories and storytelling. Because the novel is organized around a common script of using and telling stories to gain self-identity, then in some sense every story in *The Joy Luck Club* is a metanarrative—which is entirely consonant with its multilayered narrative structure, in which nearly every story frames or contains another story. Nevertheless, "The Joy Luck Club" offers the earliest and most explicit reflections on the power and value of narrative. Narrative functions as a social glue between the women, as they trade gossip and generate stories around the mah jong table. Jing-mei, however, detects a more sinister and competitive cast in the gossip, especially when the gossip is about her: "what little we say to one another often comes back in another guise. It's the same old game, everybody talking in circles"

(28). Jing-mei also sees a more personal purpose in the stories the aunties tell about themselves and their families:

> They go back to eating their soft boiled peanuts, saying stories among themselves. They are young girls again, dreaming of good times in the past and good times yet to come. A brother from Ningbo who makes his sister cry with joy when he returns nine thousand dollars plus interest. A youngest son whose stereo and TV repair business is so good he sends leftovers to China. A daughter whose babies are able to swim like fish in a fancy pool in Woodside. Such good stories. The best. They are the lucky ones. (32)

"The Joy Luck Club" ends with these hypothetical stories, each one a dream of wish fulfillment that reverses some predicament in the mothers' families: the greedy and larcenous kinsmen of An-mei Hsu become honest relatives and good sons, while the loveless, childless marriage of Ying-ying St. Clair's daughter Lena turns happy and fertile. Jing-mei perceives that the older women circulate these tales around the mah jong table to comfort themselves, indicating storytelling's power to reshape reality. By exploiting this power, however, these mothers may be further alienating themselves from their times and their families.

The mothers see a different purpose to stories and storytelling. At the end of "The Joy Luck Club," they charge Jing-mei with a mission to tell her long-lost sisters stories of their late mother, hoping Jing-mei can reconstitute the absent Suyuan through narrative. Astonished when Jing-mei says she doesn't know her mother well enough to perform this reconstitution—and hence afraid that their own daughters similarly do not understand them—the aunties nearly drown Jing-mei under a tide of stories they need to see transmitted:

> "Tell them stories of your family here. How she became success," offers Auntie Lin.
> "Tell them stories she told you, lessons she taught, what you know about her mind that has become your mind," says Auntie Ying. "Your mother very smart lady."
> I hear more choruses of "Tell them, tell them," as each auntie frantically tries to think of what should be passed on. (31)

The narrative superabundance in "The Joy Luck Club" becomes far more than a social agent or a cushion of comforting lies; it is the only way Jing-mei can preserve Suyuan's memory. Tan invests narrative with tremendous representational power, presenting it as a means of recovering the past and fostering communication between mothers and daughters. The fifteen tales that follow "The Joy Luck Club," and their arrangement into a collection, are the only way mothers and daughters can understand one another.

This narrative mission might appear to support the critical truism that *The Joy Luck Club* builds a conversation between its characters—yet none of the novel's sixteen tales are ever spoken or delivered to any other character. Without such a dialogue to connect her tales, Tan turns to other, more strictly formal methods to assemble the sixteen short stories into a single novelistic plot. Ironically, however, the strategies Tan deploys to interconnect her narratives sometimes reinforce the disconnection between her characters—particularly when Tan displaces the mothers' Chinese heritage into a distant, mythologized past that is forever denied to the modernized American daughters.

Tan's temporal framing embodies and increases the formal tensions between past and present in *The Joy Luck Club*. The characters' desires for emotional connection in the present would seem to invite a synchronic dialogue among the stories, yet that drive for synchronism conflicts with the novelistic narrative scheme that separates the stories along a diachronic timeline and divides the stories of the past from those of the present. Tan's narrative framing only exacerbates this tension. While she does locate nearly all of the stories within a common frame in mid-1980s San Francisco, this setting never generates a dialogue between the characters or their stories. In fact, as Sau-ling Wong has argued, this framing deliberately dislocates the mothers' Chinese stories from modern-day America by constantly stressing the differences, not only between the two time periods, but between the ways time itself is experienced in those two periods. Tan represents the mothers' youth as occurring solely within a "Typological Time" (Wong 185) that contrasts "the static, ritual-permeated, mythical Time of a China past . . . [with] the unfolding, enlightened, rational, secular Time of contemporary America" (Wong 186). Even the mothers' voices, which frame their stories with narrative openings like "When I was a young girl in China, my grandmother told me my mother was a ghost" (33), assume the qualities of a folktale or oral narrative—the mothers are ambiguous about the stories' exact placement in chronological history but quite unambiguous about their geographical and temporal distance from the present day.

"The Joy Luck Club" begins this pattern of mystification with its first flashback to China. Significantly, this flashback is framed not once but twice, with Jing-mei Woo recounting Suyuan's recollection of her journey to Kweilin; the first glimpse of China is attained at a double remove, as if this past can only be seen through the lifting of many veils. Suyuan tells Jing-mei, "I dreamed about Kweilin before I ever saw it . . . jagged peaks lining a river, with magic moss greening the banks" (7). When Suyuan sees the real Kweilin, her descriptions become even more awestruck:

> And when I arrived, I realized how shabby my dreams were, how poor my thoughts.... The peaks looked like giant fried fish heads.... And then the clouds would move just a little and the hills would suddenly become monstrous elephants marching slowly toward me! Can you see this? And at the root of the hill were secret caves.... These were things so strange and beautiful you can't ever imagine them. (8)

Grisly images of wartime chaos soon follow this account, but do little to demystify Kweilin after Suyuan's spellbound introduction. Tan frames the China of her initial story, and therefore of the rest of the novel, as a land of childlike wonder and innocence. (The other stories of "Feathers from a Thousand *Li* Away," in which the mothers recall their childhood, reinforce this characterization.) The hills themselves are infused with animal energy and sentience, and caves which will soon be hiding desperate war refugees are simply "secret caves." Suyuan describes a China which lies beyond the imagination even of its own residents, let alone the foreign-born children of its emigrants. Her question to Jing-mei, "Can you see this?", proves an impossible challenge—by Suyuan's own declarations her daughter can never imagine this terrain.

But while this distancing of an unrecuperable China privileges the mothers as the only characters who can envision their homeland, it also effects a more subtle privileging of the modern, American viewpoint as the framing perspective for the entire novel. By shrouding China in memory, the novel presumes it is only remembered from the present; by rendering it mysterious and alien, the novel presumes a normative American viewpoint rather than a native Chinese one. This narrative strategy is reinforced by the order and arrangement of the tales. However much critics have observed that the two sections of mother stories surround the two sections of daughter stories—"embrace" is a particularly popular description (Ho 149, Huntley 45)—Tan ultimately denies the mothers the first or last word. Instead, Jing-mei narrates the first story in "Feathers From a Thousand *Li* Away" and receives the last position in every other section, becoming a choral or narratorial figure for the entire novel. Paradoxically, this device narratively recreates the same level of mediation between past and present that the aunties fear will render Jing-mei unable to reconstruct Suyuan's life story. Thus, although the novel's framing establishes a common temporal setting in which the stories are told, it also increases the dislocation between mothers and daughters, and between the historically specific present and the mythologically vague past. This tension between frame and story escalates throughout the novel, into its final section.

Tan must turn to other narrative techniques to resolve this dilemma. If her frames, and her figuration of a mythologized Chinese past, create a widening divide between the mystified past and the immediate present, then her use of temporal juxtaposition attempts to bridge that divide by creating a free interaction between time periods. Once again, while these techniques of juxtaposition are on display throughout the novel—particularly in the fourth and final section, "Queen Mother of the Western Skies," which groups together stories from four different time periods—they are also modeled and previewed in "The Joy Luck Club." The premiere story presents a string of rapid-fire temporal alternations between Jing-mei's present-day initiation into the Joy Luck Club and the countless narratives of the past conjured by that initiation. Sometimes Tan demarcates these temporal interruptions with typographical curlicues (6, 7) or a simple blank space (12, 16), separating the memories from the frame-story and from each other and preserving the division between past and present. But in other instances, and with increasing rapidity as "The Joy Luck Club" progresses, Tan gently elides that division, negotiating between past and present within one story as easily as the rest of the novel does between its four sections.

Jing-mei Woo drifts almost unconsciously from present-day, present-tense narration into past-tense memory, as when she considers playing mah jong with her aunties:

> Auntie Lin looks exasperated, as though I were just a simple child: "How can we play with just three people? Like a table with three legs, no balance. When Auntie Ying's husband died, she asked her brother to join. Your father asked you. So it's decided."
> "What's the difference between Jewish and Chinese mah jong?" I once asked my mother. (22)

This passage exemplifies so much that is central to *The Joy Luck Club*, both in its characters' preoccupations with intergenerational continuity and Chinese identity, and in its temporal technique. Thematically, the Joy Luck Club's empty mah jong seat emblematizes not only a missing maternal authority for Jing-mei, but also an unbridgeable generation gap within all of the families; so long as the daughters cannot understand their mothers, so long as the mothers cannot perpetuate their traditions through their daughters, the families will be as out of balance as the mah jong table.

Yet, in its free interplay of past and present, this same passage slyly suggests a possible resolution to this generation gap. Tan no longer separates memories and flashbacks with typographical devices; having trained her readers to expect temporal alternations, she now signals those alternations with little more than a change in tense. Thus, while Lindo and Jing-mei both worry about their inability to bridge past traditions and the present day, Tan's passage creates just such a temporal union. And Jing-mei's transition out of the mah jong reverie is even more immediate than her slide into it:

> These kinds of explanations made me feel my mother and I spoke two different languages, which we did. I talked to her in English, she answered back in Chinese.
> "So what's the difference between Chinese and Jewish mah jong?" I ask Auntie Lin. (23)

By the end of "The Joy Luck Club," these alternations become so frequent and so effortless that Jing-mei can project herself into Suyuan's past, erasing the division between mother and daughter. She says, "And now I feel as if I were in Kweilin amidst the bombing and I can see these babies lying on the side of the road, their red thumbs popped out of their mouths, screaming to be reclaimed" (29). Jing-mei's description of her mother's history in the present tense, from her own point of view, further erases the division between Chinese past and American present. Despite her fears of generational and cultural disconnection, then, Jing-mei reaches her first tentative understanding with Suyuan through the temporal alternations and elisions of Tan's narrative. In this way, "The Joy Luck Club" foreshadows how the rest of the novel will resolve its thematic dilemmas through the formal arrangement and manipulation of time, particularly through the characters' engagement with their own pasts.

Thus, while Tan's narrative (and ideological) framing of a mystified China creates temporal dissonance and structural tension within the novel, other narrative techniques serve to reunite past and present. However, the temporal juxtapositions Tan forges from story to story are often displaced into the non-narrative gaps between stories and sections; those that are contained entirely within "The Joy Luck Club" become far more immediate and visible, highlighting Tan's technique of temporal alternation. The story thus serves as a blueprint to the novel, a recreation in miniature of its predominant thematic concerns and formal tactics. As both a component in the overall narrative structure and a reflection of that structure, "The Joy Luck Club" proves to be a carefully wrought *mise-en-abyme* representing the novel's formal tensions and their resolutions.

Framing Narrative Isolation: A Dialogic Breakdown

Although Tan places past and present into chronotopic interaction with one another, the stories themselves rarely interact as conversations. Tan's stories are radically isolated from one another, locked into a dialogicity of time that hinders any literal dialogue between mothers and daughters. To some extent this confirms J. Gerald Kennedy's contention in "From Anderson's *Winesburg* to Carver's *Cathedral*" that the genre of the short story sequence "embodies an insistently paradoxical semblance of community in its structural dynamic of connection and disconnection" (195). Characters in short story sequences, and in works like *The Joy Luck Club* which contain more unified and novelistic plots yet still incorporate separate short-story narratives, frequently remain unaware that they share a common narrative; the forging of connections between these frustratingly isolated characters "instead remains the reader's function" (Kennedy 196), though the author often directs the formation of such interconnections. While *The Joy Luck Club*'s more novelistic aspects might preclude it from Kennedy's definition of the short story sequence, his insights on the form are readily applicable to Tan's work in one important respect.[3] For most of the book, the characters do not become conscious of one another's private or past narratives, "and thus remain unaware of the ways in which their situations may be similar" (Kennedy 196). This isolation results both from Tan's diachronic temporal arrangement—in which stories generally depict different moments in time—and from Tan's unusual use of narrative frames.

Tan eschews any global extradiegetic frame in the arrangement and relation of her sixteen stories. "The Joy Luck Club" does function as a thematic frame which introduces the novel's central characters and its preoccupation with narrativity and time, but this tale exists on the same diegetic level as the other fifteen, as one story among many. There is no single space in which all of the tales are told, no dramatic circumstance in which the characters might hear one another's stories. Each story instead bears its own separate narrative frame; most if not all of the tales appear to be internal monologues, rehearsed but never spoken. Sadly, and in keeping with Kennedy's observations on the alienating effects of the short story sequence, few of Tan's characters are even speaking, let alone listening.

Joy Luck critics often assert that the various stories constitute a literal dialogue between characters. Gloria Shen suggests that "the mothers finally discover that storytelling is the best way to reach the hearts and minds of their daughters"; her primary example of a mother sharing her own past is Ying-ying St. Clair's story "Waiting Between the Trees" (Shen 240–41). But "Waiting Between the Trees" is a purely internal monologue, delivered while Lena St. Clair argues with her husband, Harold, in another room; Ying-ying only imagines the dialogue with her daughter, projecting it into the future: "I will use this sharp pain to penetrate my daughter's tough skin" (Tan 286). E. D. Huntley comes closer when she writes, "Addressing their stories to their daughters, the mothers remain aware that their words are falling on indifferent ears" (Huntley 49); the mothers are indeed afraid their words will be unheeded, yet the daughters never hear them at all. Instead, each mother frames her story in isolation, filling the frames with comments *about* their daughters, but never speaking *to* them. Even the willful Lindo Jong, who addresses Waverly directly in her narrative frames, obviously does so either *in absentia* or silently; the story "Double Face," for example, is narrated while Lindo sits beside Waverly in a hair salon, yet it provokes no reaction or conversation. Lindo, like Ying-ying, projects her dialogue with her daughter into an imagined future, saying "I will ask my daughter what she thinks" (305). These dialogues never occur within the scope of *The Joy Luck Club*; Shen and other optimistic readers rarely consider the disturbing possibility that the mothers' narratives of understanding are silent and unshared.

If the mothers fail to voice their thoughts, then the daughters are even more radically self-isolating. As Huntley notes, the daughters never address their mothers; their stories are "shaped as internal monologues" (49) which "give voice to their emotional estrangement from their mothers" (50)—yet the stories also reinforce that estrangement through their own isolation. Thus, the desired flow of understanding in *The Joy Luck Club* is resolutely one-way, with the mothers wishing to speak to their daughters, but rarely doing so, and the daughters hiding their monologues from their mothers. The sole exception is Jing-mei Woo, who attempts to reconstruct her mother through narrative and who eventually listens to her father's story about Suyuan—the final parental tale in the novel, and the only one for which Tan depicts an audience. Significantly, by assigning this climactic parental tale to Canning Woo, Tan sustains the lack of communication between women even as she reverses the novel's consistent displacement of male characters and voices to the narrative periphery. While this reversal arrives at a formally appropriate moment—in "A Pair of Tickets," one of the stories that reverses the novel's pattern of temporal progression and its ahistorical portrayal of China—it also insures that the novel's individual stories never interact in a literal mother–daughter conversation.

Although no such literal dialogue occurs, there is nevertheless a dialogic design to Tan's stories. The unidirectional flow (or potential flow) of information from parent to daughter becomes a corrective to the "one-way assimilation-acculturation process into Anglo-American culture and society" (Ho 170) occurring in the younger generation. The four daughters, having thoroughly acculturated to mainstream (white) American society, are each faintly embarrassed by and dismissive of their Chinese mothers (Shen 239, Ho 165–171).[4] By containing half of her stories within the exclusionary frames of daughters who do not wish to address their mothers, Tan builds this phenomenon of acculturation into the structure of her narrative; by depicting mothers who hope to fight the process by addressing their daughters directly, Tan also constructs her novel (if not the mothers' uncommunicative monologues) as a solution to that phenomenon.

This script of nativism yielding to assimilation suggests a temporal master narrative, a movement from China and the past to America and the present. Lisa Lowe has observed that this cultural shift is often narrativized as a generational struggle, foregrounding the temporal element even further since each generation represents a different age as well as nationality and cultural identity. *The Joy Luck Club* provides ample evidence of this generational narrativization, as noted by many of its critics. However, Lowe also warns that this master narrative often creates a reductive binary opposition between Asian nationalism and Western assimilation, and that critics such as Frank Chin have used this opposition to accuse female writers such as Maxine Hong Kingston and Amy Tan herself of promoting "assimilationist" values (Lowe 75–6). Ironically, then, Tan's use of this generational master narrative perpetuates the nativism-vs.-assimilation dichotomy that enables Chin's "profoundly anti-feminist" (Kim 78) appeal to cultural nationalism to attempt to silence Asian American female writers. This confluence should deter Tan's readers from uncritically reducing *The Joy Luck Club* to a narrative of generational struggle, as should Lowe's and Melani McAlister's claims that the assimilation narrative overshadows other concerns such as gender and class issues. Both types of criticism demonstrate—Lowe and McAlister through analysis, Chin by example—how a generational master narrative can naturalize or efface numerous other components of Asian American female subjectivity.

Typically, however, Tan's polychronic plot structure resists as well as confirms the generational master narrative of assimilation. Tan narratively challenges the purported unidirectionality of assimilation by directing *The Joy Luck Club*'s temporal progress back to the mothers, China, and the past; she thereby raises the possibility that modernization and progress need not sever all connections with native heritage. But because the mothers never voice their stories directly to their daughters, Tan's counterassimilationist narrative strategies function only on the extradiegetic, supra-narrative level of the novel as a whole. The daughters are united with their matrilineal heritage not by conversation but by *The Joy Luck Club*'s narrative form and its interconnective tactics—the recurring characters and themes, the interlocking networks of symbols, and especially the stories' chronological alignment into a supra-narrative master-plot. This diachronic structure governs the novel's narrative interconnections so thoroughly, in fact, that it sometimes prevents any literal, synchronic conversations between the stories and characters. In the novel's fourth section, for example, the mothers vow to end the intergenerational isolation: Ying-ying swears she will "penetrate my daughter's tough skin and ... give her my spirit" (286), while Lindo decides to initiate a two-way dialogue and "ask my daughter what she thinks" (305). But these stories happen during or after the tales of the third section, in which the daughters have already begun to respond to the mothers and their stories of the past. The potential dialogue between story and character suggested by the fourth section is rendered irrelevant, if not impossible, by the novel's temporal structure. The literal dialogue proves unnecessary, however, since a dialogicity of time has already provided the novel's true narrative interactions.

Negotiating the Double Chronology

The techniques of timing and sequencing that impede synchronic dialogue between the stories also provide an alternate, diachronic scheme that orders and connects those stories. Tan fashions this supranarrative trajectory through juxtaposition and alternation, modulating the stories' temporal settings and uniting them into a single historical progression. Over the first three sections of *The Joy Luck Club*, Amy Tan structures the stories into a colonialist narrative of progress from the mythologized Eastern past to the modernized Western present; however, she also inverts and complicates this scheme in the final section, making the pinnacle of her novel's historical and geographical advancement a return to China and to the past.

Tan's narrative progress from China to America first unfolds by section, with each of the first three groups of stories occurring in a consistent and advancing temporal setting. With the exception of "The Joy Luck Club," the stories of the first section, "Feathers from a Thousand *Li* Away," all focus on the mothers as children and daughters in pre-Revolutionary China. The next section, "The Twenty-Six Malignant Gates," leaps forward a generation to offer four stories of the daughters as young girls in postwar America. The third section, "American Translation," moves still further forward to depict the four daughters as adults, although this section too has its exception; the story "Best Quality" eschews the romantic and marital focus of the other three tales to continue examining Jing-mei Woo's relationship with her mother. Just as Suyuan's death distinguished "The Joy Luck Club" from the other stories in its section by forcing Jing-mei to substitute for her mother, Suyuan's absence once again deforms the structure of "American Translation." Jing-mei's attempts to replace, reconstitute, and comprehend her mother take precedence over any other continuities of theme or narration within the individual sections.

Despite this topical discontinuity, "Best Quality" retains the other "American Translation" stories' temporal setting of present-day San Francisco, and thus maintains the novel's steady chronological progression from the mothers' childhood in China to the daughters' adulthood in America. From this pattern, readers might easily infer—as Sau-ling Wong has—that *The Joy Luck Club* fashions and promotes a traditional colonialist master narrative of ostensible progress from the primitive Third World to the advanced West (Wong 199–200). While such a pattern does exist in *The Joy Luck Club*, the novel's fourth and final section, "Queen Mother of the Western Sky," performs a dramatic alteration on this simplistic chronological and cultural scheme. Indeed, the fourth section's drastic deformation of the novel's apparent pattern of progress should suggest that *The Joy Luck Club* also follows another temporal scheme entirely.

The first story in the final section, An-mei Hsu's "Magpies," is a virtual continuation of her story "Scar" in "Feathers from a Thousand *Li* Away," resuming the narrative of An-mei's childhood reunion with her mother in China. Ying-ying St. Clair sets the next story, "Waiting Between the Trees," significantly after her earlier tale; "Waiting" begins with Ying's adolescent marriage and abortion in China, relates her second marriage to Clifford St. Clair and, in the final pages, glosses over her subsequent emigration to America (286). Lindo Jong's "Double Face" recounts Lindo's emigration to America as a young woman and culminates with the birth and naming of Waverly. However, this story also opens and closes with an extended framing sequence depicting Lindo and Waverly in the present day as they prepare to travel to China for Waverly's impending honeymoon. As *The Joy Luck Club*'s final section, then, "Queen Mother of the Western Skies" both ignores the novel's previous temporal and geographic progressions and recapitulates them. The first three stories replicate the novel's progress from the mothers' childhood in China to the daughters' adulthood in America.

The final story, however, runs against this pattern, defying the previous emigrations across time and space. "A Pair of Tickets" depicts a trip to China in which Jing-mei Woo meets her abandoned half-sisters and comes to terms with her mother and her Chinese heritage. The final story apparently reverses the course of the novel, returning the narrative to China and to a rapprochement with the past. Yet this story, too, contains its recapitulations; "A Pair of Tickets" also contains a flashback which spans from wartime China to contemporary America (324–29), replicating the novel's patterns of progression once again. Tan concludes *The Joy Luck Club* with a cascade of multiply-layered, self-reflexive recursions: the novel's temporal progression is re-enacted in its final section, and in its final story, and in the flashback which fills its final pages. Significantly, however, these recursions alter the temporal progression of *The Joy Luck Club* even as they reflect it, since they are not only recapitulations of the novel but also elements in it. As a result, *The Joy Luck Club* concludes in recursion—turning geographically back to China, temporally back to the past, and narratively back to repeat its own structure. In the fourth section, the novel is no longer simply a progress away from China and the past; instead, Tan reveals, it has in fact been a return to Jing-mei's Chinese heritage all along.

However, another chronology complicates this recursive temporal scheme: the timing of the stories' narrative frames. Each character narrates her stories from the same present-day setting in America, a strategy which serves to normalize and centralize the American point of view while distancing the mothers' Chinese background (Wong 185–86). Such a framing is consistent with the progression of the first three sections, which posit a modernized American present as the destination of the novel's temporal progress—and, implicitly, as the pinnacle of cultural progress. Yet this same framing contrasts greatly with the recursive turn of the fourth section. In fact, while the frames of the first three sections are roughly contemporaneous, Tan advances their timing in "Queen Mother of the Western Skies" even as the stories begin reaching backwards in time. Yet despite this structural contradiction, the mutual progression and recursion of the novel's fourth section narratively demonstrates the emotional strategies by which Tan's characters must negotiate the differences between generations and the passage of time.

The stories of the first three, "progressive" sections of *The Joy Luck Club*, in which the daughters demonstrate their estrangement from their familial heritage, are narrated from an immediate and generally unchanging American present that defers the past back into mythological timelessness. Ironically, though, that present is equally timeless due to its relentless immediacy. The constant use of the present tense creates the impression that the frames occur simultaneously, but it does so precisely by rendering everything in them hyper-immediate. Even those events which are only one week old, like Jing-mei's re-tuning of a piano or Lena's realization of her dimming love for Harold (155, 174), are uniformly consigned to the past tense, locking the frames in a narrowly-defined present. But this is a different kind of timelessness from that which marks the mothers' stories; that mystified vagueness consigns the Chinese stories to an undefined but distant *then*, while this narrative immediacy grounds the frames in an instantaneous and highly specified *now*.

The frames in "Queen Mother of the Western Skies" initially inhabit this same timeless but immediate present; the first two stories, An-mei Hsu's and Ying-ying St. Clair's, are framed contemporaneously with their daughters' marital troubles in the previous section. An-mei begins "Magpies" by lamenting her daughter's crumbling marriage and her fruitless trips to the psychiatrist, two situations which begin Rose's previous story, "Without Wood." Ying-Ying's "Waiting Between the Trees" is even more definitively framed within the events of Lena's "Rice Husband": Ying's opening line, "My daughter has put me in the tiniest of rooms in her new house" (274) verifies that she is in the midst of her visit to Lena and Harold's Woodside home during Lena's story. The two St. Clair tales also conclude simultaneously as Ying-ying topples Harold's poorly-made marble table (180, 287). Even within this contemporaneity, however, the frames do advance slightly—moving from a rough concurrence with the initial situation of Rose's story to a precisely-delineated synchronization with the end of Lena's.

Lindo Jong's frame in "Double Face" pushes the novel into new temporal territory by advancing beyond the events of the previous Jong story. In Waverly's story "Four Directions," Lindo persuades Waverly and Rich to postpone their wedding so she can accompany them on a honeymoon trip to China; in "Double Face," the women get their hair styled in anticipation of the imminent wedding and the subsequent travel. While the frame's advancement is small, perhaps only a few months, it is one of the first measurable differentiations registered in the frames. This advancement carries the characters closer to their projected goal of a return to China, a goal which is finally realized in the last story when Jing-mei Woo makes her own long-anticipated trip. Thus, while the chronology of the stories in *The Joy Luck Club* leaps forward from early twentieth-century China into Tan's present, the chronology of their frames also progresses minutely—from the vague and unchanging setting of the first three sections to the slightly later, more time-bound frames in the fourth.

These two progressions—frame and story—comprise a bizarre double chronology in the fourth book of *The Joy Luck Club*. The extradiegetic time of the frames advances into the future even as the stories and characters return to the past. However, the structural parallelism also rationalizes this apparent paradox. The narrative frames advance only when Waverly and Jing-mei take steps to travel to China and bond with their mothers, implying that forging connections to the past is in fact necessary for progression in the present and future; similarly, the advancement of the fourth section's stories from America back to China implies that progression in the present leads inevitably to a re-engagement with the past. The double chronology of frame and story in "Queen Mother of the Western Skies" structurally demonstrates Tan's claims about the interdependence and interactivity of past and present.

Tan has already presented a similar geographical irony at the end of "Four Directions," when Waverly envisions her trip to China with her mother as "moving West to reach the East" (205). This phrase neatly sums up the novel's temporal resolution as well; because Waverly's trip East offers her a chance to reconnect with her mother and her heritage—indeed, because Tan has assigned temporal values of "past" and "present" to "East" and "West" throughout the novel—Waverly's paradox can easily be read in temporal terms. Just as the West leads to the East, so does the future lead to the past, and vice versa. Tan's dual narrative systems of progression and recursion unite the distant past and the immediate present into a dialogic interaction.

Narrative and Temporal Closure in "A Pair of Tickets"

This fusion of past and present, progression and recursion, is nowhere more evident than in the novel's final story, "A Pair of Tickets," which completes and reiterates *The Joy Luck Club*'s narrative superstructure. Just as "The Joy Luck Club" opens the novel with an explosion of stories, the complementary "A Pair of Tickets" closes it with a cascade of recursions that answer questions, fill in narrative gaps, and resolve the mysteries of Suyuan Woo's past. These recursions accumulate so rapidly that they sometimes recirculate back on themselves; Canning Woo, for example, has barely begun telling Jing-mei about Suyuan's life when he initiates a second "flashback" depicting the rescue and upbringing of Suyuan's first daughters (326). By depicting these previously unknown or unrepresented periods, "A Pair of Tickets" completes the chronology of *The Joy Luck Club*—Canning's tales chart the previously undisclosed time between the endings of the mothers' stories and the death of Suyuan, the event which prompts "The Joy Luck Club" and the novel's present-day action. Tan's final tale completes her narrative circuit; the stories advance to an ending which supplies the historical information necessary to connect the narratives of mythologized China with those of modern-day America.

But this interactivity between past and present, and between narrative progress and recursion, still creates a profound structural tension in Tan's work. As the final story, "A Pair of Tickets" most advances the narrative into the future; however, it is also the story most characterized by the return to the past. Marina Heung suggests that "*The Joy Luck Club* demands a reading that is simultaneously diachronic and synchronic" (612), but the novel's scheme is still more complicated than that—even its diachronic readings extend both forward and backward in time. "A Pair of Tickets" is again perhaps the best demonstration of the supple interaction between the novel's temporal structures, because it directly emblematizes and addresses these tensions. The story attempts to balance the novel's progressive impulses with its nostalgic ones by bringing Tan's version of modern, American time to a China which she has previously mythologized.

The notion that America and China could have different types of time, that America could exist in the "present" while China could not, might seem ludicrous if the rest of Tan's novel did not create this very division. However, Tan begins to erode this temporal distancing in "A Pair of Tickets." Wong has observed that Tan figures the 'modern' time of her American stories through "descriptions of high material specificity or informational density ... a high degree of topical and local precision" (Wong 186): modernity is represented through highly specific brand names, locations, television shows and other markers of American life. The Chinese stories, by contrast, are filled with undifferentiated details and unnamed objects, creating a sense of ahistorical vagueness and distance.

Yet the China Jing-mei discovers in "A Pair of Tickets" is described with the techniques Tan reserves for modern, commodified time. Jing-mei remarks that downtown Guangzhou "looks like a major American city, with high rises and construction going on everywhere," although Chinese signifiers linger in the bamboo scaffolding on those high-rises (317). Her father's relatives are enamored of a Polaroid camera and a hotel mini-bar "stocked with Heineken beer, Coke Classic, and Seven-Up, mini-bottles of Johnnie Walker Red, Bacardi rum, and Smirnoff vodka, and packets of M&M's, honey-roasted cashews, and Cadbury chocolate bars" (319). Whether this scene depicts the awe of a 'backwards' Chinese family for modern conveniences or, more likely, the awe of a poor family for the trappings and luxuries of capitalism, it still portrays China with the same historical specificity that Wong argues has been reserved for America. However, this historical specificity has only come to China through the goods and technologies of western capitalism; the process is jarring enough that Jing-mei remarks, "This is communist China?" (319).

Jing-mei's presumption that a barful of Western goods equates to a political transformation seems fatuous; just a few short months after the publication of *The Joy Luck Club*, the Chinese government would demonstrate its dedication to communism with the subjugation of student protesters at Tiananmen Square. The commodity capitalism of Jing-mei's mini-bar, it would seem, is not incompatible with the institutions of totalitarian government. But despite the absence of any real political transformation, "A Pair of Tickets" reveals a dramatic narrative and temporal transformation; its China is no longer the ahistorical, mythical setting of the mothers' tales. By introducing a Western, capitalist, commodified temporality, Tan transforms China into a site of dialogic interaction between different modes of culture and time, in which rising skyscrapers clash semiotically with their bamboo scaffoldings. This interaction, like the interactions wrought by the simultaneous progressions and recursions in "Queen Mother of the Western Skies," brings Tan's conflicting temporalities of myth and modernity back into a careful equilibrium. China becomes a site of both historic specificity and ahistorical heritage, a fitting final destination for a book that trades on the powers of both history and myth. "A Pair of

Tickets" thus serves as a crucial final step in Tan's creation of a dialogism and a continuity of past and present in *The Joy Luck Club*.

Conclusion

This dialogicity serves another, more ideologically laden purpose as well. By connecting the previously separated past and present, Tan does not simply provide a narrative and emotional resolution for her novel—she also brings its fabricated past, and its Orientalized portrait of Chinese identity, into continuity with the novel's more realistically delineated present. These two worlds have previously inhabited separate spheres, with characters in American settings mocking fortune-cookie aphorisms and other Chinese stereotypes even as the Chinese stories promote their own Orientalist clichés of exotic settings and self-sacrificing women. But by connecting these two worlds, Tan holds their radically different temporalities in suspension, justifying the mythologized past within the more demanding and realistic framework of the present; the Chinese myths cannot be unreal, because they are clearly continuous with the "real world" of the present.

Furthermore, because "the reader's construction of interconnections . . . dissolves individualized character and plot and instead collectivizes them into an aggregate meaning" (Heung 612), readers themselves play a role in reuniting Tan's ideological and structural disjunctions. Tan divides her conflicting mythic and historical structures, and her models of gender and ethnic identity, among sixteen stories and seven narrative voices. In separating these conflicts, Tan both defers them and invites readers to help balance them by assembling a narrative and ideological structure that can incorporate all of these oppositions. By participating in Tan's supranarrative composition, readers become active agents in bringing her often-conflicting ideologies into resolution.

Of course, some of Tan's compositional structures are themselves in conflict, such as her progressive and recursive temporal patterns. Yet in Tan's intricate narrative design, even these patterns are thoroughly interrelated. The temporal progression among the stories ultimately directs characters and readers back towards Tan's mythic Chinese past; the recursions in "Queen Mother of the Western Skies" connect that past to Tan's historically specific present. By fragmenting her narrative, Tan is able to intertwine these two structural patterns so thoroughly that, once assembled by the reader, the historical and mythological systems become complementary. This deft narratological manipulation can help expose Tan's own ideological assumptions, but it should also demonstrate that *The Joy Luck Club* possesses a narrative construction of remarkable subtlety and versatility. Scholars should continue to investigate this structure, to better understand how the novel's interdependence of form and ideology reconciles its often-conflicting claims about history, myth, and identity.

Notes

1. Unless otherwise noted, all references are to Amy Tan, *The Joy Luck Club*, Ivy Books, 1989.

2. Not all critics define Tan's characters solely by their generational archetypes, however. In her book *Immigrant Acts* (1996), Lisa Lowe advances the compelling argument that "interpreting Asian American culture exclusively in terms of the master narratives of generational conflict and filial relation essentializes Asian American culture, obscuring the particularities . . . of class, gender, and national diversities" (63). Lowe uses *The Joy Luck Club* as an example, demonstrating how a privileging of the intergenerational trope ignores or conceals other fissures among the characters' "different conceptions of class and gender" (79).

3. *The Joy Luck Club* is to some extent closer to Kennedy's definition of the novel rather than the short story sequence. Tan's work certainly creates "the sense—common to the novel—of a fluid social order in which personalities interact from episode to episode across time" (Kennedy 196). Furthermore, several of the stories fail to depict "separate, completed actions" (196), an incompleteness which Kennedy associates with novel chapters rather than with component short stories in a linked sequence.

4. Melani McAlister has argued that this embarrassment is symptomatic not of cultural assimilation but of class consciousness, and that *The Joy Luck Club* uses cultural difference as a substitute or surrogate for class anxiety. See McAlister, "(Mis)reading *The Joy Luck Club*."

Works Cited

Bakhtin, Mikhail. "Forms of Time and of the Chronotope in the Novel." 1938, 1973. *The Dialogic Imagination*. Austin: U of Texas P, 1981.

Braendlin, Bonnie. "Mother/Daughter Dialog(ic)s in, around, and about Amy Tan's *The Joy Luck Club*." *Private Voices, Public Lives: Women Speak on the Literary Life*. Ed. Nancy Owen Nelson. Denton: University of North Texas Press, 1995. 111–124.

Heung, Marina. "Daughter-text/Mother-text: Matrilineage in Amy Tan's *Joy Luck Club*." *Feminist Studies* 19.3 (Fall 1993): 597–616.

Ho, Wendy. *In Her Mother's House: The Politics of Asian-American Mother–Daughter Writing*. Walnut Creek, CA: AltaMira Press, 1999.

Huntley, E. D. *Amy Tan: A Critical Companion*. Westport, CT: Greenwood Press, 1998.

Kennedy, J. Gerald. "From Anderson's *Winesburg* to Carver's *Cathedral*: The Short Story Sequence and the Semblance of Community." *Modern American Short Story Sequences: Composite Fictions and Fictive Communities*. Ed. J. Gerald Kennedy. New York: Cambridge UP, 1995. 194–215.

Kim, Elaine. "'Such Opposite Creatures': Men and Women in Asian American Literature." *Michigan Quarterly Review* 29 (1990): 68–93.

Ling, Amy. *Between Worlds: Women Writers of Chinese Ancestry*. New York: Pergamon, 1990.

Lowe, Lisa. *Immigrant Acts*. Durham, NC: Duke UP, 1996.

Lyotard, Jean-François. *The Postmodern Condition: A Report on Knowledge*. 1979. Trans. G. Bennington and B. Massumi. Manchester: Manchester UP, 1984.

McAlister, Melani. "(Mis)reading *The Joy Luck Club*." *Asian America: Journal of Culture and the Arts* 1 (Winter 1992): 102–18.

Schueller, Malini Johar. "Theorizing Ethnicity and Subjectivity: Maxine Hong Kingston's *Tripmaster Monkey* and Amy Tan's *The Joy Luck Club*." *Genders* 15 (Winter 1992): 72–85.

Shear, Walter. "Generational Differences and the Diaspora in *The Joy Luck Club*." *Critique* 34.3 (Spring 1993): 193–199.

Shen, Gloria. "Born of a Stranger: Mother–Daughter Relationships and Storytelling in Amy Tan's *The Joy Luck Club*." *International Women's Writing: New Landscapes of Identity*. Ed. Anne E. Brown and Marjorie Goozé. Westport, CT: Greenwood Press, 1995. 233–244.

Souris, Stephen. "'Only Two Kinds of Daughters': Inter-Monologue Dialogicity in *The Joy Luck Club*." *MELUS* 19.2 (Summer 1994): 99–123.

Tan, Amy. *The Joy Luck Club*. New York: Ivy Books, 1989.

TuSmith, Bonnie. *All My Relatives: Community in Contemporary Ethnic Literatures*. Ann Arbor: U of Michigan P, 1993.

Wong, Sau-ling Cynthia. "'Sugar Sisterhood': Situating the Amy Tan Phenomenon." *The Ethnic Canon: Histories, Institutions, and Interventions*. Ed. David Palumbo-Liu. Minneapolis: U of Minnesota P, 1995. 174–210.

Xu, Ben. "Memory and the Ethnic Self: Reading Amy Tan's *The Joy Luck Club*." *Memory, Narrative, and Identity: New Essays in Ethnic American Literatures*. Ed. Amritjit Singh, Joseph T. Skerrett, Jr., and Robert E. Hogan. Boston: Northeastern UP, 1994. 261–277.

YUAN YUAN

Mothers' "China Narrative": Recollection and Translation in Amy Tan's The Joy Luck Club and The Kitchen God's Wife

Many critics, including Amy Ling and Sau-ling Cynthia Wong, have previously addressed the issue of authenticity in Chinese American narratives and specifically focused on interrogating the authenticity of "Chineseness" in the novels produced by Chinese American writers. Apparently, this issue of "nativeness," or the representation of the native Chinese in Chinese American literature, is both intriguing and perplexing. However, I have noticed that to date critics tend to engage issues of authenticity in these ethnic narratives without taking into full consideration the intricate role played by the narrative in configuring nativeness, especially in terms of narrative agencies and narrative strategies. That is to say, the whole issue of nativeness in ethnic literature requires careful examination in the context of the historical and cultural displacement of the narrative subject, and in relation to the function of narration in literary representation. In this chapter, I will explore the complicated nature and complex structure of the mother figures' narratives of their experiences in China in terms of "China narratives" within the context of Amy Tan's novels *The Joy Luck Club* and *The Kitchen God's Wife*.

In both *The Joy Luck Club* and *The Kitchen God's Wife*, Tan tells us the stories of the mothers of daughters in America and the daughters of mothers in China, that is, the mother–daughter relationship across three generations

From *The Chinese in America: A History from Gold Mountain to the New Millennium*, edited by Susie Lan Cassel, pp. 351–364. © 2002 by AltaMira Press.

and two continents. In this context, I will only focus on the hermeneutic space, which I call the "China narratives," that emerges in a dialectical process between the Chinese mothers' recollection of their past experiences in China and the American-born daughters' translations of their mothers' stories of China. Therefore, it is not the purpose of this chapter to investigate the authenticity of those mother figures' accounts of China in reference to China; instead, this chapter attempts to explore the nature, the constitution, the theme, and the function of China narratives in relation to the current position and strategies of narrative agency in American society. Specifically, I will examine the following issues in regard to mothers' China narratives: how they are created by the mothers' recollections of past memory and reconstituted by their daughters' translations; the purpose of this reflective process for marginal characters—immigrants—in American society; the central theme of loss, which forms the essential "plot"; and the function of China narratives for the mothers as either defensive instruments for self-empowerment or discourse strategies with which to dominate their daughters. In the last part, I will analyze China narratives as the bicultural and bilingual site of contention between dominating mothers and their rebellious daughters.

First of all, the mothers' China narratives involve an intricate process of the recollection of past memory. To a certain extent, the narrative structures of both *The Joy Luck Club* and *The Kitchen God's Wife* are partly based on the mothers' recollections of their past experiences. Therefore, in Tan's novels, the mothers' experiences in China all emerge as narratives of reflection—which means, in Tan's novels, different mother figures reconstruct various narratives of their experiences in China against the background of American society and within the context of American culture. For immigrants, recollection is an important strategy used to negotiate a marginal position in an alien society. Specifically for Amy Tan, by retelling her mother's story of the past, she is able to explore the nature and the function of memory and recollection, especially how recollection functions in a bicultural context and how it affects the re-creation of individual identities.

Generally speaking, all recollection entails one's conscious negotiation with and active reconstitution of the memory of the past. Put another way, all memories are socially and culturally reconstituted within a specific historical and cultural context and emerge in the form of narratives. This self-reflexive narrative initiates a process of construction of new stories and new histories in search of new identities. Thus, all memory exists in a form of narrative—recollection—and this narrative recollects by preserving, revising, erasing, and recovering past memories, involving both reproduction and repression, inclusion and exclusion. Hence, recollection is a complicated reading of and way of coming to terms with the past, depending on the specific purposes of recollection and the present position of the recollecting subject. Generally, it is through a self-reflexive narrative that memory, especially the repressed memory of the past, finds its way to articulate itself, like in dreams or fables or fiction. Possibly it is only through fables, fictions, or dreams that repressed memories can be expressed. Therefore, the mothers' China narratives, that is, their recollections of past experiences in China, are necessarily constituted partly through the collective cultural history (i.e., myth, folklore, and legends) and partly through personal memories of the past.

For instance, *The Joy Luck Club* begins with a mother's recollection. Tan writes: "the old woman remembers a swan she had bought many years ago in Shanghai for a foolish sum. . . . Then the woman and the swan sailed across an ocean many thousands of Li wide, stretching their necks toward America. . . . Now the woman was old. And she had a daughter who grew up speaking only English and swallowing more Coca-Cola than sorrow."[1] Clearly, memory here involves a cultural reproduction within the American context instead of pointing to the real past in China. So, the mother's China narrative emerges in the United States, the "other" cultural territory, informed by a complex process of translation, translocation, and transfiguration via fairy tales, imaginations, and fictionalization of the original experiences in China. In this retelling/recollecting, the memories of past experiences are recast in the form of a fable or folktale and the real-life experiences in China have been transfigured into a mythical narrative.

In fact, mothers' experiences in China are generally transfigured into China narratives only after they have lost their reference to China; thus they are related more to the present American situation than to the original context of Chinese society. Hence, recollection becomes a dialectical process in which the past and the present engage each other in a continuous dialogue, each revising and configuring the other endlessly. Perhaps, only under such circumstances of loss of origin can experiences in China emerge as a China narrative—a text reconfigured within other contexts. Said differently, it is not so much the reality of the past that is crucial to the formation of China narratives. Instead, it is the present American context that provides meaning and determines the content of the mothers' stories of China. China narratives, therefore, differ from the experiences in China because they signify a specific kind of self-reflexive discourse that is reinscribed within another cultural context to serve specific goals: self-affirmation or self-negation, remembrance or repression. Eventually, China as the memory of personal experiences is translated into a semiotic space of recollection, and China as a geographical location is reconfigured into a variety of discourses: myth, legend, history, and fantasy. No wonder in their China narratives that the mothers themselves turn into mythical figures who forever haunt the lives of their daughters.

China is recollected or re-created somewhere between memory and imagination. That is why the daughters tend to dismiss the tales of their mothers' past experiences in China as either unreal fairy tales or didactic fables or impossible and incomprehensible stories conjured up to control them. That is why Pearl, the daughter in *The Kitchen God's Wife*, is confused and frustrated about her mother's China narratives. As she observes, "To this day it drives me crazy, listening to her various hypotheses, the way religion, medicine, and superstition all merge with her own beliefs."[2] So the mothers communicate to the daughters in a specific form of discourse that is both real and unreal, both personal and cultural; it sounds like, in Pearl's terms, "a Chinese version of Freud."[3]

Furthermore, sometimes the mothers' China narratives are based on the recollections through other narrative agencies that further complicate the credibility of the mothers' personal stories. For instance, Suyuan, a mother in *The Joy Luck Club*, does not directly tell her daughter June about her past. The mother's China narrative is not passed on to the daughter until after the mother's death. Put another way, Suyuan's personal narratives of her past experiences in China are re-collected by her daughter, June, who gathers her mother's fragmented and varied stories partly from her mother, partly from her Joy Luck aunties, and partly from her father who, in turn, learns many of the stories from his wife's friends and family in China years later. Personal stories, when mediated by various narrative agencies, tend to develop into legends. Such is the case with Winnie, the mother in *The Kitchen God's Wife*. Winnie reveals to her daughter Pearl the essential part of her hidden past only after Winnie is convinced she is going to die. Part of her China narrative is further complicated by a dialogical structure maintained by Winnie's recollection and her friend Helen's remembrance—the two versions of the same past experiences in China, for various reasons, not only complement, but also contradict each other. So in both novels, the mothers' China narratives are linked to the death of the mothers; otherwise both mothers' tales of China would reside in silence, the unspeakable silence that points to a horrible memory of the past. Apparently, recollection through various agencies eventually lends the memory a status of folk tale or legend.

According to Hayden White in *Metahistory*, all historical narratives are "emplotted." That is to say, all histories are written (recollected) around specific themes or plots, depending on the narrator's point of view or the purpose of narration. History as a form of cultural recollection can be written in the genres of comedy, tragedy, farce, or romance and using certain moral justifications or utopian desires as main themes. In both *The Joy Luck Club* and *The Kitchen God's Wife*, the mothers' recollections are also organized around certain recurring tropes, to use Hayden White's term, or certain plots. I believe that the plot at the center of the mothers' recollection is loss—a tragedy of loss.

In both *The Joy Luck Club* and *The Kitchen God's Wife*, loss functions as the dominant metaphor and the recurring theme for the mothers' China narratives. It is also the central code through which to decipher their existence. Each mother's story of her experiences in China eventually develops into a story of loss. Hence, moving to America means to them a loss of identity, center, home, and the reality of existence—they feel themselves being reduced to "ghosts," as in an alien territory. Even though mothers and daughters interpret China with different codes and from different positions, they are all overshadowed by a prevalent sense of loss. To quote Ying-Ying St. Clair in *The Joy Luck Club*, "We are lost."[4] The daughters seem to be lost between cultures, whereas the mothers appear to have lost everything. As June says about her mother, "She had come here in 1949 after losing everything in China: her mother and her father, her family home, her first husband, and two daughters, twin baby girls."[5] Lena St. Clair shares June's position regarding her own mother: "My mother never talked about her life in China, but my father said he saved her from a terrible life there, some tragedies she could not speak about. My father proudly named her in her immigration papers: Betty St. Clair, crossing out her given name of Gu Ying-ying. And then he put down the wrong birthyear, 1916 instead of 1914. So, with the sweep of a pen, my mother lost her name and became a Dragon instead of a Tiger."[6] Their previous identities are deleted with immigration: the mothers become the others.

In *The Kitchen God's Wife*, the mother's China narratives are based on Winnie's recollection of her horrible experiences in China. In fact, the pain and suffering that are central to Winnie's recollection of her past invite repression rather than recall. The recollection process becomes extremely painful because it resurrects a traumatic past that has been buried and muted in Winnie's memory. Due to the repression of the past memory, Winnie's China narrative is subject to constant postponement, revision, and erasure in order to conceal the unspeakable pain. As Winnie says, "Now I can forget my tragedies, put all my secrets behind a door that will never be opened, never seen by American eyes. I was thinking my past was closed forever."[7] Memory for Winnie embodies loss or pain; her China narrative requires concealing instead of unfolding. Remembering inevitably entails pain and, eventually, desires for repression transform into the necessity of repression. In short, Winnie's experience in China is transfigured into a discourse of repression and her recollection of experiences in China is translated into a narrative of loss.

It is interesting to note that most mothers in Tan's novels share a similar form of speech about their past—a silence that attempts to repress the painful memory of the past. Generally speaking, the mothers in Tan's novels do not want to share their past memories with their daughters and the past is simply something they are not able to talk about to their daughters directly, as both June and Pearl are made aware. Hence, narrative and silence, seemingly opposed to each other, actually tell the same story—the repressed memory of the past. If narrative is one strategy of dealing with the past via recollection, silence is the other via repression: one attempts to affirm the present self and the other tries to negate the past memory. Recollection functions as a defensive contraction of the self, as Beng Xu observes: "The memory itself has become a psychic defense."[8] A coherent memory reconstituted through the process of recollection ensures the continuity of identity in the alien environment.

However, despite the fact that recollection of one's past has been reconfigured as a discourse strategy for self-affirmation and self-construction, it is interesting to note that mothers' recollections of their past experiences in Tan's novels sometimes demonstrate more loss of memory rather than recall of the past. Ironically enough, forgetting plays an important role in the process of recollection. In *The Joy Luck Club*, June complains of her mother repeating the same Kweilin story to her in various versions and with different endings. She says: "I never thought my mother's Kweilin story was anything but a Chinese fairy tale. The endings always changed. . . . The story always grew and grew."[9] Eventually Suyuan's Kweilin story becomes a fairy tale, more connected to imagination than remembrance. In *The Kitchen God's Wife*, Winnie, failing to recall her mother, provides us with contradictory versions of her mother's image. Winnie believes her mother is pretty, strong, educated, and comes from a good family. But later she admits that "maybe my mother was not pretty at all, and I only want to believe that she was."[10] Winnie's mother becomes a fairy tale figure, conjured up by her imagination, rather than her memory: she becomes a beautiful mother she never sees nor remembers in the first place. That is why Winnie keeps repeating to herself: "Now I no longer know which story is the truth, what was the real reason why she left. They are all the same, all true, all false. So much pain in everyone. I tried to tell myself. The past is gone, nothing to be done, just forget it. That's what I tried to believe."[11] Because of loss of memory, there is simply no prior text present in her mind to be re-collected. Hence, recollection transforms into a creative process. In short, mothers' China as a historical reality lies at a remote distance from their present remembrance, irretrievably lost beyond recall; it is made present only through a narrative that involves forgetting instead of remembering. The mothers' recollection of China signifies nothing less than the lost memories of the past. It is inevitable that their accounts of the past are multiple and contradictory, imaginative and illusive.

Ironically, China, lost or otherwise, functions as the locus that more or less defines the mothers' sense of present reality. American experiences, by contrast, only characterize their marginal existence and alien position. They feel themselves to be out of place, exotic if not outlandish, from their daughters' points of view. Mothers tend to have their homes and identities centered elsewhere—in China. If life in America is too disappointing to be real, their experiences in China, at least, can be transliterated into a body of ideas and vocabulary that give them a unique sense of reality and presence. In the preface to *Memory, Narrative, and Identity: New Essays in Ethnic American Literature*, the authors write, "Memory in this context shapes narrative forms and strategies toward reclaiming a suppressed past and helps the process of re-visioning that is essential to gaining control over one's life and future."[12] Hence, China narratives retroactively create multiple imaginary texts of China that are both defining and defined by the mothers, with their displaced mentality and exile consciousness, conditioned by a paradoxical desire of both repression and nostalgia.

In "Daughter-Text/Mother-Text: Matrilineage in Amy Tan's *The Joy Luck Club*," Marina Heung remarks, "Storytelling heals past experiences of loss and separation; it is also a medium for rewriting stories of oppression and victimization into parables of self-affirmation and individual empowerment."[13] Hence, recollection turns into an active process of negotiation with the past, constantly translating and revising the past into a narrative that grants reality to present situations. In a displaced context, the mothers have imaginatively constructed various China narratives out of their experiences in China for themselves and for each other. One mother, Helen, in *The Kitchen God's Wife*, comments on the past to Winnie: "She and I have changed the past many times, for many reasons. And sometimes she changes it for me and does not even know what she has done."[14] It is indeed ironic that at the end of the novel both of them are compelled to tell the truth that they no longer remember, and continue to "recollect" the stories, even though they have lost the memory. That is why Pearl, Winnie's daughter, complains: "I laughed, confused, caught in endless circles of lies. Or perhaps they are not lies but their own form of loyalty, a devotion beyond anything that can ever be spoken, anything that I will ever understand."[15] The past, paradoxically, is lost in the process of recollection. I agree with Debra Shostak when she says: "In general, memory is about absence. It concerns itself with the pastness of time past and with filling gaps in the known continuum of experience. The imaginative capacity of memory to recover and reinvent images and ideas of absent places bridges the locales, supplying a crucial sense of self."[16] Recollection becomes an imaginative process of self-creation despite a "loss of memory."

China is, so to speak, a "mother land," a repository of history with haunting memories and extraordinary experiences—a repository positioned for reproduction. The mothers constantly revise their China narratives in terms of their present conscious needs and unconscious desires, asserting them in the context of American culture for self-empowerment. Tan made the following remark regarding her own mother's China narrative: "It was a way for her to exorcise her demons, and for me to finally listen and empathize and learn what memory means, and what you can change about the past."[17] The experiences in China, or the past in general, even though forgotten to a certain extent, have always been reconstituted by mothers into narratives that carry out a special mission: to control the fate of their "American-made" daughters. Thus, the loss narrative is transformed into a discourse of control. In *The Kitchen God's Wife*, Winnie says to her daughter Pearl: "In China back then, you were always responsible to somebody else. It's not like here in the United States—freedom, independence, individual thinking, do what you want, disobey your mother. No such thing."[18] In this case, she has transformed an imaginary text of China into a powerful narrative for the purpose of domination. She uses China narratives to establish and reinforce her present authoritative position in America. At least she believes she has the entire knowledge of China, an alternative cultural space to which only she has access.

Lacking ontological stability and lost in constant recollection, China narratives are fabricated and manipulated in various forms. Possibly, the power of China narratives resides precisely in their "loss of reality." The mothers in Tan's novels, assuming the absolute authority of the culture of China, transform China into a semiotic space wherein they can continue to exercise the power that they have lost in the American society. Collectively, they have constructed another cultural territory, actually an alternative cultural space within American society. Eventually, the experiences in China that are channeled through the mothers' narratives are translated into a mode of discourse, a style of domineering, a tongue for control, and a posture for having authority over their daughters' lives. China becomes less a geographical location than a cultural extraterritory that the mothers have created in order to construct or deconstruct the subjectivity of their "American-made" daughters. Collectively, mothers construct this alternative history with their China narratives to empower marginalized positions and combat and control their rebellious daughters.

The mothers' experiences in China become a cultural repository of potential power from which the mothers reproduce excessive China narratives for the purpose of control. As Wendy Ann Ho correctly points out, "The personal stories of the Joy Luck Club mothers do battle through gossip, circular talking, cryptic messages/caveats, dream images, bilingual language, and talk-story tradition."[19] Through various discourse strategies, the mothers employ many different China narratives to redeem, if not to combat, their American-made daughters. Ying Ying St. Clair, in *The Joy Luck Club*, has the following observation about her daughter Lena: "All her life, I have watched her as though from another shore. And now I must tell her everything about my past. It is the only way to penetrate her skin and pull her to where she can be saved."[20] Sometimes, they turn their China experiences in o a disciplinary lesson that reinforces restrictive cultural values (An-Mei Hsu's story of recognition of one's worth and value); sometimes they translate their personal memory into a fantastic tale with powerful seduction (Suyuan Woo's Kweilin story of the beautiful Kweilin ladies in an exotic wonderland); and sometimes they transliterate China into a secret text where daughters are excluded, and to which only the mothers themselves have direct access (Winnie's story of the horror of betrayal and abuse by her husband in China).

Lena St. Clair also says: "When we were alone, my mother would speak in Chinese, saying things my father could not possibly imagine. I could understand the words perfectly, but not the meaning."[21] That is, only the mothers possess the keys to decode the meaning of their China narratives. Hence, Chinese, a secondary language to the daughters, becomes the mothers' primary discourse strategy to manipulate their daughters. As one mother in *The Joy Luck Club* reminds her daughter about *The Book of the Twenty-Six Malignant Gates*, which is written in Chinese: "You cannot understand it. That is why you must listen to me."[22] Daughters, for their part, resist their mothers' China narratives by reminding their mothers that their stories are out of context because, as June asserts, "this wasn't China."[23] It is not surprising that June has the following remark about her mother's China narrative: "Over the years, she told me the same story, except for the ending, which grew darker, casting long shadows into her life, and eventually into mine."[24] Even after the death of her mother, those stories continue to haunt June throughout her life.

Marie B. Foster remarks: "Tan's characters are of necessity story tellers and even historians, empowered by relating what they know about their beginnings and the insufficiencies of their present lives.... The storytelling, however, is inundated with ambivalences and contradictions which ... often [take] the form of blame in mother–daughter relationships."[25] So, the daughters, not good listeners in the first place, have to translate their mothers' China narratives within the American context. As Rose Jordan complains of her mother: "More than thirty years later, my mother was still trying to make me listen."[26] The daughter's reception or reconstitution of the China narratives informs a process of translation into a different linguistic system and cultural space. That is to say, the daughter's cognition of China seems to be always already structured, mediated, and overdetermined by the semiotics of the (m)other tongue that serves as the first order symbolic signification. Clearly, the ambiguous nature and intricate structure of the mothers' China narratives make it impossible for the daughters to identify what is Chinese and what is not. Just as Lindo Jong says to her daughter in *The Joy Luck Club*: "How do you know what is Chinese and what is not Chinese?"[27] And it seems that the mothers often enjoy the narrative ambiguity they have created in order to maintain a superior position as the authorities on China.

Therefore, the daughters' reconstructions of their mothers' China narratives are based on the signifier of the first linguistic order (mothers' stories), which assumes somewhat of a historical reference to China. The mothers' China narratives function as the ultimate interpretive frames of the daughters' reconceptualizations of China. It is actually the absolute horizon of the daughters' cognition of China. That is to say, not only do the mothers' stories of their experiences in China provide the daughters with China narratives, but the mothers themselves function as the China narratives to a certain extent, marking the limit of their daughters' perceptions and conceptions of China. Hence, China narratives inform a process of displacement, transformation, and absence in regard to the representation of China. In the (m)others' tales, this China narrative is inevitably a translation, a displacement, and a transformation of the past for present usage. That is exactly why when June, in *The Joy Luck Club*, compares her own observation of Chinese activities with her mother's China narratives, she finds a revealing difference between her mother's fascinating China narratives and her direct social reality at home: "Eating is not a gracious event here. It's as though every body had been starving. They push large forkfuls into their mouths, jab at more pieces of pork, one right after the other. They are not like the ladies of Kweilin, who I always imagined savored their food with a certain detached delicacy."[28]

I argue that the China narrative in Tan's novels serves as an undercurrent but central text that structures the present relationship between mothers and daughters because of the specific roles this narrative plays in their lives. Therefore, the cross-cultural hermeneutics of China are conducted within this domestic space, generally between two generations and, more specifically, between the Chinese mothers and their American-born. Here is Lindo's comment on her daughter Waverly in *The Joy Luck Club*: "she didn't look Chinese. She had a sour American look on her face."[29] "Only her skin and her hair are Chinese. Inside—she is all American-made."[30] As products of different cultures and histories, mothers and daughters abide by different cultural values and possess different codes of interpretation. In fact, they speak entirely different languages whenever they talk about China: "My mother and I spoke two different languages, which we did," June says in *The Joy Luck Club*, "I talked to her in English, she answered back in Chinese."[31] The bilingual conversion turns into a game of translation, and in this translation meaning is transfigured, displaced, and occasionally, lost. June remarks, "We translated each other's meanings and I seemed to hear less than what was said, while my mother heard more."[32] With the power of China narratives, the mothers hope to ensure some continuity of their cultural heritage with their daughters, as Huntley notes: "Tan's Chinese mothers have a sense of generational continuity; they feel connected with their own mothers and their mother's mothers, and they feel equally linked with their daughters."[33] Nevertheless, their daughters feel differently about this connection or disconnection. In a bicultural context, the generational dialogue turns into a site of contention between the diasporic mothers and the culturally displaced daughters in this mother–daughter dyad.

Both mothers and daughters have to constantly reevaluate their respective versions of China narratives that are grounded in entirely different cultural contexts, with different historical references and subject positions. For the mothers, China narratives inform a process of recollection (history or loss of it) whereas for the daughters, who have never been to China, China narratives become a text of culture. In other words, experiences in China become semiotic texts that are reconstituted through two different modes of discourse: historical recollection and cultural reproduction. And this dichotomy is dramatized essentially through the dialectic structure between mothers' historical recollection and daughters' cultural reproduction (translation). China narratives, eventually, become a semiotic site where culture and identity are fought over, negotiated, displaced, and transformed. Instead of the static ontological presence of a unitary category, the China narrative becomes a hermeneutic space for articulating identity and difference, a dialectical process that initiates the cultural and historical reconstitution of the subjects.

China in mothers' stories resides in a domain of memory based on the personal recollection of a social reality in China, whereas China for the daughters indicates a territory of dream and fantasy. The daughters' experiences of China are entirely based on the tales of China via the narratives of their mothers, which have already been translated in a new cultural context and with reference to their American experiences.

Notes

1. Tan (1989, 3).
2. Tan (1991, 27).
3. Tan (1991, 27).
4. Tan (1989, 64).
5. Tan (1989, 141).
6. Tan (1989, 107).
7. Tan (1991, 81).
8. Xu (1994, 263).
9. Tan (1989, 12).
10. Tan (1991, 120).
11. Tan (1991, 130).
12. Singh et al. (1994, 2).
13. Heung (1993, 607).

14. Tan (1991, 69).
15. Tan (1991, 524).
16. Shostak (1994, 234).
17. Lyall (1995, C6).
18. Tan (1991, 162).
19. Ho (1996, 339).
20. Tan (1989, 274).
21. Tan (1989, 109).
22. Tan (1989, 87).
23. Tan (1989, 152).
24. Tan (1989, 7).
25. Foster (1996, 210).
26. Tan (1989, 208).
27. Tan (1989, 228).
28. Tan (1989, 21).
29. Tan (1989, 288).
30. Tan (1989, 289).
31. Tan (1989, 23).
32. Tan (1989, 27).
33. Huntley (1988, 62).

Works Cited

Foster, M. Marie Booth. 1996. "Voice, Mind, Self: Mother–Daughter Relationships in Amy Tan's *The Joy Luck Club* and *The Kitchen God's Wife*." In *Women of Color: Mother–Daughter Relationships in 20th Century Literature*, ed. Elizabeth Brown-Guillory, 209–27. Austin: University of Texas Press.

Heung, Marina. 1993. "Daughter-Text/Mother-Text: Matrilineage in Amy Tan's *The Joy Luck Club*." *Feminist Studies* 19 (fall): 597–608.

Ho, Wendy Ann. 1996. "Swan-Feather Mothers and Coca-Cola Daughters: Teaching Tan's *The Joy Luck Club*." In *Teaching American Ethnic Literature: Nineteen Essays*, ed. John R. Maitino and David R. Peck, 327–45. Albuquerque: University of New Mexico Press.

Hune, Shirley, Hyung-Cha Kim, Stephen S. Fugita, and Amy Ling. 1991. *Asian Americans: Comparative and Global Perspectives*. Pullman, Wash.: Washington State University Press.

Huntley, E. D. 1988. *Amy Tan: A Critical Companion*. Westport, Conn.: Greenwood.

Ling, Amy. 1990. *Between Worlds: Woman Writers of Chinese Ancestry*. New York: Pergamon.

———. 1991. "'Emerging Canons' of Asian American Literature and Art." In *Asian Americans: Comparative and Global Perspectives*, ed. Shirley Hune, Hyung-Cha Kim, Stephen S. Fugita, and Amy Ling, 191–98. Pullman, Wash.: Washington State University Press.

Lyall, Sarah. 1995. "In the Country of the Spirits: At Home with Amy Tan." *New York Times*, 28 December, C1, C6–C7.

Rubenstein, Roberta. 1987. *Boundaries of the Self: Gender, Culture, Fiction*. Chicago: University of Illinois Press.

Shostak, Debra. 1994. "Maxine Hong Kingston's Fake Books." In *Memory, Narrative, and Identity: New Essays in Ethnic American Literature*, ed. Amritjit Singh, Joseph Skerrett Jr., and Robert Hogan, 233–60. Boston: Northeastern University Press.

Singh, Amritjit, Joseph Skerrett Jr., and Robert Hogan. 1994. *Memory, Narrative, and Identity: New Essays in Ethnic American Literature*. Boston: Northeastern University Press.

Tan, Amy. 1989. *The Joy Luck Club*. New York: Ballantine Books.

———. 1991. *The Kitchen God's Wife*. New York: Ballantine Books.

White, Hayden. 1973. *Metahistory: The Historical Imagination in Nineteenth-Century Europe*. Baltimore: Johns Hopkins University Press.

Wong, Sau-ling Cynthia. 1993. *Reading Asian American Literature: From Necessity to Extravagance*. Princeton, N.J.: Princeton University Press.

Xu, Beng. 1994. "Memory and the Ethnic Self: Reading Amy Tan's *The Joy Luck Club*." In *Memory, Narrative, and Identity: New Essays in Ethnic American Literature*, ed. Amritjit Singh, Joseph Skerrett Jr., and Robert Hogan, 261–77. Boston: Northeastern University Press.

BELLA ADAMS

Identity-in-Difference: Re-generating Debate about Intergenerational Relationships in Amy Tan's The Joy Luck Club

Recently, Gary Pak asserted that "the test" for a new generation of Asian-American writers, now in their third period,[1] "is to transcend 'your typical Asian American mother/daughter sweet stories, your cross-generational stuff, your intercultural relationship jive'" (qtd. in Sarna 22). In light of this assertion, the possibility of regenerating debate on a sixteen-year-old novel widely regarded as one of the "sweetest," Amy Tan's *The Joy Luck Club*, seems difficult. Pak and his masculinist peers in Asian America and beyond "can't get on with" such a novel, especially not its first-person narratives by three Chinese immigrant mothers and four American-born daughters that, according to British critic Nicci Gerrard, "draw" female readers "in close" (2). Apparently, *The Joy Luck Club* takes them "from loss to gain, desire to fulfillment, loneliness to community. . . . It has a happy sad ending, the kind of sweet melancholy ever after we want and can't get from real life" (2).

On either side of the masculinist/feminist divide on both sides of the Atlantic, the consensus seems to be that *The Joy Luck Club* offers particular readers emotional closure in part brought about by the presumed formal closure of its "happily-ever-after" ending as the two generations of narrators apparently close the gap that has generated so much "irritat[ion] . . . upset [and] silence" between them (*Joy* 183).[2] Even the small number of critics who are not persuaded by the novel's "sweetness," among them David Leiwei Li, Sau-ling

From *Studies in the Literary Imagination* 39, no. 2 (Fall 2006): 79–94. © 2006 by Georgia State University.

Cynthia Wong, and Sinkwan Cheng, as they respectively proclaim the novel's and, at times, Tan's suspect ideological commitments to neo-conservatism (112), neo-Orientalism (197), and neo-racism (95), base their arguments in part on the presumption of formal closure. In the context of Asian-American literary history and, for that matter, the wider context of the western literary canon as it shifts from modernism to postmodernism, *The Joy Luck Club* is to them closer to the second period and identity politics, if not the first period of "sentimental fiction" and "'ambassador[ial]'" autobiography. Both periods, despite their ideological asymmetry, fail to problematize radically stereotypes and essences. Thus contextualized, *The Joy Luck Club* seems far removed from the third period and a politics of difference (Wong and Santa Ana 185–86).

Or, so it seems. While sentimentalized readings and readings critical of this sentimentalism powerfully dominate the Tan critical canon, *The Joy Luck Club* arguably promotes another more critical reading. This latter reading is generated through, interestingly enough, the very same detail—the intergenerational relationships—that has persuaded so many of the novel's readers to marginalize or even ignore its literariness and forge an identification between it and the world compatible with "the anthropomorphic or humanistic realism" in which "multicultural" literature is so regularly interpreted (Chow, "Women" 214). Significantly, this novel/world identification, along with its colonial underpinnings, and the identification between the novel and the ("neo") meaning(s), depend on an ideological understanding of literariness that *The Joy Luck Club* problematizes, albeit figuratively via its complex negotiation of intergenerational relationships.

Crucial to this complexity and to the novel's postmodernity is the Woos' frequently overlooked asymmetrical mother–daughter relationship, which serves "to create," as Tan asserts in *The Opposite of Fate*, "a sense of imbalance, a feeling that someone or something is missing" (302). Suyuan Woo's absence through death interrupts the novel's *almost* symmetrical structure of sixteen stories, by seven, not eight, narrators, in four parts divided more or less evenly between two generations. It also interrupts the novel's *almost* "happily-ever-after" ending, and, by extension, criticism based on the assumption of mother–daughter reconciliation and other "identitarian" terms to do with closure: oneness, togetherness, wholeness, and a generally "sweet" rhetoric privileging intergenerational harmony (Spivak, "Poststructuralism" 199).

On one level, Suyuan's American-born daughter, Jing-mei "June" Woo, does desire reconciliation. To this extent, her desires are in keeping with the other narrators who participate in symmetrical relations, if only because An-mei and Rose Hsu (Jordan), Lindo and Waverly Jong, and Ying-ying and Lena St. Clair are all "alive" at the time of the novel's narration. On another arguably political level, however, Jing-mei's narrative and *The Joy Luck Club* in general highlight the benefits *and* the limitations *and* the impossibility of reconciliation in a way that serves to regenerate debate on intergenerational relationships: from "sweet" harmony and its opposite, "un-sweet" conflict, as well as anthropomorphic or humanistic realism, towards a critical, if not deconstructive negotiation of relationships in accordance with Gayatri Chakravorty Spivak's notion of "identity-in-difference" as it empowers a feminist postcolonial critique ("Subaltern" 277).

In "Can the Subaltern Speak?" and elsewhere, Spivak uses this hyphenated notion to discuss the relationship between aesthetic and political representation, and, following this, the gendered/raced relationship between self and other. Her acknowledgement of the fact that self and other identifications are "sustained by irreducible difference" (*Other* 254), understood apart from the unexamined sentimentalism of the conflict/harmony hierarchy and other totalizing and totalitarian structures, provides the basis for an ethical relationship. Rather than constructing "Other as the Self's shadow" ("Subaltern" 280), even in so-called radical critiques that permit others to represent themselves in a way that ultimately privileges the self, an ethical relationship questions this privilege, principally by deconstructing the self/other hierarchy. For Spivak, this privilege constitutes a loss in that it erroneously presumes an undivided subjectivity, and mistakenly presumes a reliable relationship between representation and referent. Questioning this reliability, deconstruction, at least as Spivak (ethico-)politicizes it, draws attention to the linguistic and ideological construction of "Other" or, more specifically, "the Chinese woman" in and around representation.

The possibility of developing ethical relationships or, as Spivak puts it, of relating "to other women, retaining their specificity, their difference, while not giving up our own" (*Post-colonial* 9), preoccupies *The Joy Luck Club*'s seven narrators, particularly Jing-mei in her relationships with her missing Chinese (m)other and her missing Chinese sisters after they were abandoned by Suyuan at the end of the Sino Japanese War (1937–45). More than enabling complex theorization on intergenerational and intercultural relationships, *The Joy Luck Club* furthers this feminist postcolonial critique by also addressing the novel/world relationship. Again, Jing-mei's narrative is instructive as it negotiates an ethics of representing that which is (m)other consistent with "identity-in-difference." By making an issue of representation and its part in the de/construction of the (m)other's identity, *The Joy Luck Club* problematizes radically its essentialism and ("neo") arguments presuming formal, thematic, and ideological closure.

Before regenerating debate on various relationships in and around *The Joy Luck Club* via the deconstructive notion of "identity-in-difference," it is first necessary to clarify briefly the debate as it stands. From Pak's recent call for transcendence, it would appear, if only by implication, that the Tan critical canon is still dominated by an "un/sweet" rhetoric privileging inter-generational/intercultural harmony. In short, *The Joy Luck Club* is typically analyzed in "identitarian" terms, particularly the narrators, who, in addition to apparently offering a point of identification between novel and world, are also considered similar, if not interchangeable.

Amy Ling suggests why this is the case, specifically in relation to the mothers who "seem interchangeable in that the role of mother supersedes all other roles and is performed with the utmost seriousness and determination." "All the mothers," she continues, "are strong, powerful women" (138), a point endorsed and developed by Gloria Shen who also argues that intragenera-tional similarity is based on "mysterious power" (235). So "mysterious" are the mothers that one reviewer, Orville Schell, becomes confused about which mother is actually speaking, and mistakenly puts An-mei's words into Suyu-an's mouth (3).[3] Other critics also proclaim interchangeability, more often, as it happens, between the two generations. For example, Bonnie TuSmith con-tends that "mother and daughter are one and the same" (67), as does Elaine Kim: "daughters and mothers are each other" (82). In all these instances, then, interchangeability both within and between generations is emphasized, even celebrated: "one of the triumphs of this book," remarks Kim, "is that it is easy to lose track of the individual women's voices: the reader might turn distract-edly to the table of contents, trying to pair the mothers and daughters or to differentiate among them, only to discover the point that none of this matters in the least" (82). Perhaps none of this matters because intergenerational rela-tionships promise, in Patricia Gately's words, "peace, understanding, comfort, union, and wholeness" (53).

In some respects, *The Joy Luck Club* lends support to this argument about interchangeability because its complex form—sixteen stories, four parts, and two generations of narrators, when coupled with narratives that move back and forth in time and across continents without any apparent concern for order—"make it difficult to know . . . the specifics of who's who" (McAlister 109). Content-wise, intergenerational similarity is frequently highlighted via references to shared physical features (255), as well as to shared psychologies and behaviors (252, 199, 209). The uncanny resemblance between mother and daughter is noted by An-mei in particular, a resemblance that she extends to all Chinese and Chinese American women: "All of us are like stairs, one step after another, going up and down, but all going the same way" (215).

Furthermore, the narrators suggest, albeit negatively, the benefits of intergenerational identification as a way of averting the "irritat[ion] . . . upset [and] silence" engendered particularly when the daughters defy maternal expectations with their "new thoughts, willful thoughts, or rather thoughts filled with lots of won'ts" (183, 134). For example, Waverly's defiance leaves her "othered": "'We no concerning this girl. This girl not have concerning for us.' Nobody looked at me . . . and I was alone" (100–01). Similarly Lena, Rose, and Jing-mei comment on the "unbearable . . . pain of not being seen" (115) by mothers who appear to be on and for the other side.[4] Apparently unseen by their mothers, and not seeing their mothers, as the latter painfully realize when their "gifts," particularly criticism, fail to signify maternal affection, the daughters seem unable/unwilling to see that, as TuSmith (and others[5]) observes, "Chinese mothers never pay a direct compliment but, instead, express their support and love indirectly" (68).

This direct/indirect opposition is vividly reconfigured as skin/bone or surface/depth in An-mei's story, "Scar": "My mother took her flesh and put it in the soup. She cooked magic in the ancient tradition to try to cure her mother this one last time" (48). Although literally failing to enliven, cannibalism conveys the idea that a mother's identity depends on that of her daughter's, to the point that fleshly differences seem inconsequential. Without skin, the two generations of women are rendered identical: "Your mother is in your bones!" (40), and, as Jing-mei later proclaims, "in our blood" (288). A proclamation of this kind leads TuSmith to conclude "that underneath the skin, we (mother/daughter, Chinese/American, etc.) are all one" (68).

This "oneness" is apparently borne out at the end of The Joy Luck Club when Jing-mei finally meets her Chinese sisters. Their meeting is captured on camera, the Polaroid photograph apparently reflecting a unity not only between siblings but also between them and their Chinese mother: "Together we look like our mother" (289). "This composite image," remarks TuSmith, "reflects the novel's communal subtext, which works as a counterpoint to the textual surface of individualistic strife" (68). However, The Joy Luck Club problematizes these surface/depth and individuality/communality hierarchies when, on first seeing her sisters, Jing-mei says that she "see[s] no trace of [her] mother in them" (287–88). This problem is quickly passed over, and Jing-mei, together with her sisters, quietly and eagerly focuses on the developing photograph: "The gray-green surface changes to the bright colors of our three images, sharpening and deepening all at once" (288). The fact that the images in or, more properly, *on* the photograph develop all at once, and that they do so *before* Jing-mei's unspoken proclamation of togetherness outside the photograph, would seem to suggest that the textual surface effects the communal subtext. TuSmith's hierarchy is thus reversed: an analogy on the textual surface unites image and referent, and, crucially, it is this apparent unity that (almost) *effects*, rather than reflects, Jing-mei's sense of togetherness. Clearly, then, intra/intergenerational identification benefits the narrators both personally and politically in that it gives (some of) them a powerful sense of family-based communality across often "irritating" and "upsetting" linguistic and cultural differences more or less consistent with identity politics. More than this, it problematizes, as Elaine Kim argues, "the tiresome East–West binarisms of the colonial imagination.... The lines between 'Chinese,' 'American,' and 'Chinese American' are blurred" (82), as are the equally "tiresome" personal–political binarisms of the patriarchal imagination.[6] Such blurring does problematize colonial or, more specifically, Orientalist binary logic, whereby "the East" is imagined as "an unchanging topos ... identically constructed through time" via tropes that, to continue quoting Lowe, represent "racial Others [as] different from the dominant majority" (6, 26). At the same time, however, the blurring of differences is open to appropriation. In addition to this trope of difference is the equally objectifying trope of sameness: "racial others are *like* the majority" (26–27), "the Asian American" in particular, who, in contrast to "the African American," is stereotyped as America's "model minority" on the basis of shared white middle-class aspirations. This stereotype is also underpinned by the dominant assumption that Asian Americans are all alike.[7] In this context, marked by yet another "tiresome" and "static dualism of identity and difference" (Lowe 7), the blurred lines between Chinese, American, and Chinese American do not reliably problematize the colonial imagination.

For Melanie McAlister, Schell's review of *The Joy Luck Club* in which he not only blurs the lines between mothers but also between families and Joy Luck clubs[8] exemplifies the colonial imagination, albeit in its apparently benevolent form since he praises the novel, particularly the "*recherches* to old China [that] are so beautifully written that one should just allow oneself to be borne along as if in a dream" (28). While *The Joy Luck Club*'s representation of China has to be "dreamy" or, better, generic in that it is remembered by the Chinese mothers and imagined by the American-born daughters, Tan included, Schell's (mis)reading cannot simply be attributed to the novel and "the confusing mental journey Chinese emigrants [therein] had to make" (28). More than an aesthetic effect, his confusion of mothers, families, and Joy Luck clubs suggests, at least to McAlister, that his colonial imagination is not alert to the specificity of Chinese difference, nor, as it turns out, to "*The Joy Luck Club*['s specific] demands that the ... reader counter [his or] her tendency to see 'one' Chinese American voice" (110), most directly via the character of Mrs. Jordan.

Concerned about the developing relationship between her son, Ted, and Rose, Mrs. Jordan "warmly" greets his "Oriental" girlfriend and a surreptitious conversation ensues:

> She assured me she had nothing against minorities; she and her
> husband, who owned a chain of office-supply stores, personally

knew many fine people who were Oriental, Spanish, and even black. But Ted was going to be in one of those professions where he would be judged by a different standard, by patients and doctors who might not be as understanding as the Jordans were. She said it was so unfortunate the way the rest of the world was, how unpopular the Vietnam War was.

"Mrs. Jordan, I am not Vietnamese," I said softly, even though I was on the verge of shouting. (118)

To Mrs. Jordan, then, "minorities" are all alike, "Orientals," in this case, Chinese and Vietnamese especially, although their interchangeability is not based on their "Americanness." Rose's "I'm American" (117), admittedly articulated to her mother, not her mother-in-law, would in all likelihood be wasted on Mrs. Jordan and, for that matter, Schell, in that both racist character and Orientalist critic presume "the sameness of Chinese difference" (McAlister 109–10).

The implications of "sameness," particularly in relation to stereotyping and essentialism, are also addressed, albeit less directly than the scene involving Mrs. Jordan, in Jing-mei's story, "The Joy Luck Club." Before the meeting of the Joy Luck club begins, the first since Suyuan's death, the Jongs distribute "nondescript picture[s]" of their recent trip to China. "There is nothing in this picture," Jing-mei observes, "that shows it was taken in China rather than San Francisco, or any other city for that matter" (27). Indistinguishable cities in nondescript pictures, along with dispensable calendars, free from the Bank of Canton (28), potentially function as tropes for a general indifference not only to Suyuan but also to Jing-mei, and, for that matter, to the difference between them: "what's the Chinese word that means indifferent because you can't *see* any differences?" (27).

Jing-mei's question underscores the point that the club's members cannot see any differences that are, at least to her, so obvious they make intergenerational interchangeability impossible, if not undesirable and harmful. Indeed, how can Jing-mei replace Suyuan when they are two different women, one too emotionally weak, the other, too emotionally strong, a difference emphasized to Jing-mei as a child? "A friend once told me that my mother and I were alike. . . . When I shyly told my mother this, she seemed insulted and said, 'You don't even know little percent of me! How can you be me?' And she's right. How can I be my mother at Joy Luck?" (27). Their difference is insurmountable, as insurmountable as the life/death opposition that renders them irreconcilable and arguably serves as a reminder of the difference between all the mothers and the daughters in *The Joy Luck Club*. Nothing, then, not even "the same wispy hand gestures, the same girlish laugh and sideways look," nor, for that matter, the "blood" they share, can make Suyuan and Jing-mei "indifferent" (27, 288).

Indeed, blood-based "togetherness" relies on a photographic effect that is not absolute in its affect on Jing-mei, and she is forced to admit that she could "never pass for true Chinese," particularly not when "true" Chinese "betray ... expectations of what Communist 'ethnic specimens' ought to be" (Chow, *Diaspora* 28) by indulging in "hamburgers, French fries, and apple pie à la mode" (272, 278).

Moreover, why would Jing-mei want to pass for Suyuan given that she is dead? Perhaps Jing-mei's references to things such as cities, pictures, and calendars also convey the idea that to replace Suyuan involves a deadening objectification. From this perspective, then, intergenerational identification celebrated by so many of Tan's mainstream critics is also harmful because it obliterates identity, objectifying and essentializing women to such an extent that they become things, if not, as Tan puts it in *The Opposite of Fate*, "those little dolls sold in Chinatown tourist shops, heads bobbing up and down in complacent agreement to anything said!" (281).

With such an "agreeable" figure dominating American culture, not just now, but at least since the 1830s and the arrival of the first "Doll" from China,[9] it is hardly surprising that narrators in *The Joy Luck Club* utilize a violent rhetoric of fighting tigers and women armed with kitchen utensils (252, 183–84) as a way of reversing this stereotype. Yet, the representation of stereotypes, even when they are reversed, proves risky, most obviously when Tan is charged with neo-conservatism, neo-Orientalism, and neo-racism for these and the other stereotypes that are so common in *The Joy Luck Club*: from Waverly's, "he is gay. . . . He could have AIDS" (204), and Rose's, "I was victim to his [white] hero" (118), to An-mei's assumption that M&Ms and sweatshirts "would make her brother very rich and happy by communist standards" (36), never mind the Orientalist/Occidentalist stereotyping as performed by both generations. All of Tan's narrators are at one point or another represented as having "closed ... minds" (41), making them "co-conspirator[s] ... turned traitor[s]" (118).

Clearly, then, Chinese and Chinese American women in *The Joy Luck Club* are not beyond prejudice, rendering Tan a functionary of dominant ideologies in the opinion of her more critical commentators on both sides of the masculinist/feminist divide. But to represent Chinese mothers and American-born daughters as necessarily epistemologically advantaged or, as Wong puts it about the Chinese mother(land), "a locus of truth" (196), is to leave their suspect ideological remarks unchallenged ultimately in keeping with the ideological notion of "The Native as ... the Non-Duped" (Chow, *Diaspora* 52). Whether Chinese and Chinese American women, including Tan, are duped or non-duped, China dolls or fighting tigers, they are caught in a double bind in part constituted by an inside/outside model of ideology, not just dominant ideologies. This model presumes that ideology is escapable, although, following Louis Althusser and others, "one of the effects of ideology is this practical *denial* of the ideological character of ideology by ideology" (301).

The fact that Tan's narrators can neither escape nor deny ideology, a fact that *The Joy Luck Club* resists "sweetening," even if it risks the charge of neo-conservatism, neo-Orientalism, and neo-racism, does not have to be interpreted negatively. Granted, the persistence of various essences and stereotypes denies the narrators their (and the novel's) "happily-ever-after" ending, although, at the same time, the resistance to such an ending ensures a future for debate in and around *The Joy Luck Club*. The general movement of the narrative and the relationships therein, from "malignancy" (85) to a situation whereby Chinese mothers are seen teaching their American-born daughters about how to "*multiply* [their] *peach-blossom luck*" and "*How to laugh forever*" (147, 213), would seem to confirm the possibility of debate for six of the narrators. Indeed, the fact that the Hsus, Jongs, and St. Clairs are "alive" means that they can potentially participate in symmetrical, even ethical intergenerational/intercultural relationships consistent with "joy luck" and its openness not only to the future but also to the other (41). Not surprisingly, this openness depends on each narrator acknowledging her "closed mind" and subsequent tendency for (mis)representation, which all six do, more or less, typically via intergenerational/intercultural debate. Even the most outspoken narrators of all, namely Lindo and Waverly, as the former criticizes American "thinking" and the latter, Chinese "nurturing," achieve "joy luck," albeit uneasily as they "peer . . . over the barriers" and affirm each other's differences (173, 254, 183, 197).

According to Jing-mei, the Hsus, Jongs, and St. Clairs are "the lucky ones" (41); no such "joy luck" is available to her because Suyuan is dead. Significantly, however, Jing-mei cannot end her narrative here, with death, since the logic of the novel, as well as her mother's "long-cherished wish" (288) and the obligation she has to her sisters who, as Ying-ying insists, "'must now know . . . the mother they did not know'" (40), compels Jing-mei to negotiate a relationship "beyond" death. Much depends on how she goes about this negotiation, not least her own identity and her relationships with others. As the dominant narrator, in so far as she narrates in all four parts of the novel, thereby crossing the generational/cultural lines, Jing-mei is in a position of power over others—her mother and her sisters. This power effectively prevents her forming ethical relationships, were it not for the fact that she repeatedly draws attention to her own ontological, epistemological, and, ultimately, ideological limitations arguably in the context of a wider debate about the ethics of representing that which is (m)other compatible with "identity-in-difference."

More precisely, the fact that Jing-mei cannot be and cannot know Suyuan because of the difference between them, reinforced by the life/death opposition, allows her to address arguably more radically than the other narrators the implications of representation with regard to both self/other. Granted, representation involves a deadening objectification, if not of herself, then of her mother, but Jing-mei has to speak for Suyuan, reducing both their identities in this essentially political process to "the representative" and "the constituent" respectively. As Spivak highlights in her discussion of political representation in *The Post-colonial Critic* and elsewhere: "no *Vertretung* [or political representation] . . . can take place without essentialism." Spivak goes on to point out that "in the act of representing politically, you actually represent yourself and your constituency in . . . the sense of *Darstellung* [or aesthetic representation]" (108–09).

Crucial to Spivak's feminist postcolonial critique of essentialism is the "identity-in-difference" relationship between these two senses of representation: *Darstellung* at once de/constructs *Vertretung* to the extent that it is marked by literariness resistant to the essentialism it promotes. In other words, "essences," including "the representative," "the constituent," and, moreover, the literary referents (Jing-mei and Suyuan), if not the literal referents ("the American-born daughter" and "the Chinese mother") to which they apparently refer, depend for their construction on a literary effect. This effect is as likely to keep apart as bring together such different entities, unless, of course, this effect is "ideologized" and made to mean and reference reliably. Yet, as Spivak highlights, this ideologization, although inescapable, is impossible since it privileges political representation over aesthetic representation, *Vertretung* over *Darstellung*, regardless of the "identity-in-difference" relationship between them.

More so than the other relationships in *The Joy Luck Club*, it is arguably the Woos' asymmetrical intergenerational/intercultural relationship that interrupts this ideologization—not in terms of an inside/outside model of ideology critique since all the narrators are, as already highlighted, inescapably in ideology, but by drawing attention to its impossibility. Not "merely" a formal interruption to this *almost* symmetrical novel that *almost* ends "happily ever after," the Woos' relationship also interrupts an ideological understanding of literariness based on its presumed capacity to reconcile reliably different entities—from Chinese mothers *and* American-born daughters to novel *and* meaning/referent. This capacity for reconciliation and other terms to do with closure are at issue in *The Joy Luck Club*, particularly when Jing-mei tries unsuccessfully to represent Suyuan. Crucially, however, Jing-mei's "failure" proves her and by extension the novel's "success" in that it highlights *how* an essence, which, in this case, "is" Suyuan, is de/constructed linguistically and ideologically in a way that opens up the debate about essentialism in and around *The Joy Luck Club*.

Perhaps more so than the other "women" since she, unlike them, is "dead" and so is unable to participate in intergenerational/intercultural debate, Suyuan is most vulnerable to essentialism because Jing-mei speaks for her (*Vertretung*). At the same time, however, her "death" also functions to draw attention to the fact that she is and, indeed, *has to* be an effect—a literary effect (as are the other "women")—in the sense of *Darstellung*. And, no amount of essentializing and ideologizing on the part of Jing-mei and, for that matter, (some of) Tan's readers, even if done for sentimental reasons, can alter this fact. As a literary effect, not a woman subject to life, death, and resurrection, Suyuan is at once identical and non-identical to her daughter's representation in the sense that her identity in the novel is dependent on the power of representation to overcome the difference that sustains it. This over-coming is only possible in ideology, and then not absolutely since it privileges identity, if not "identitarianism," over difference and, by extension, political representation over aesthetic representation ultimately made impossible by the "identity-in-difference" relationship between them.

Jing-mei is understandably upset by the fact that she cannot overcome the difference of Suyuan's "death" and, for that matter, "life," especially when her mother, she recalls, "always said things that didn't make any sense, that sounded both good and bad at the same time" (208). In other words, it is upsetting for Jing-mei not to know her mother's meaning. Suyuan's gift of "life's importance," a jade pendant, proves similarly confusing to Jing-mei: "What if . . . this curving line branching into three oval shapes is a pomegranate tree and that my mother was . . . wishing me fertility and posterity? What if my mother really meant the carvings were a branch of pears to give me purity and honesty? Or ten-thousand-year droplets from the magic mountain, giving me my life's direction and a thousand years of fame and immortality?" (197–98). Crucially, Jing-mei's questions go unanswered, even though she wears the pendant close to her skin like Suyuan wore it close to hers, this closeness obviously not being close enough to finalize the meaning of either the pendant or the (m)other (208).

Although upsetting, Jing-mei's inability to identify (with) Suyuan('s meaning) does nevertheless provide the basis for an ethical relationship between mother/daughter, self/other and, ultimately, novel/reader. Understood in this wider context, Suyuan's gift is not only bequeathed to her daughter but also to the reader in that it offers a way of "reading" that which is radically (m)other in terms of an affirmation rather than a mere appropriation. The importance of "life's importance" and by extension *The Joy Luck Club* lies with the questions they generate, and their resistance to the final, even epiphanic meaning that the "name" of the pendant in particular seems to promote. The literariness that marks pendant and novel opens both up to different readings;

and, it is this difference that ensures a "joy luck" future resistant to essentialism in and around *The Joy Luck Club*.

However, dominant readings of *The Joy Luck Club*, by privileging identity over difference, risk this "joy luck" future in favor of a "happily-ever-after" ending. This ending demands that the missing (m)other is missed out, so that the novel coheres formally, thematically, and ideologically. In Shen's words: "the unconnected fragments of life … unfold in a meaningful continuous whole" (233). Whether "wholeness" is regarded as "sweet" or "un-sweet," conciliatory or totalitarian, misses a point made throughout *The Joy Luck Club* about the ultimate impossibility and, indeed, undesirability of intergenerational/intercultural reconciliation by virtue of the fact that identities and relationships are sustained by difference. Not only does difference allow the narrators to become their "own person[s]" (254) in a context *still* marked by "irritation" and "upset," *not* "silence," but it also helps to ensure that self and other identifications do not end with a harmful objectification.

This harm also extends to literature, not just "multicultural" literature. As Tan notes in an interview: objectification turns it "into very limited rhetoric" (Stanton 8) of anthropomorphic or humanistic realism by privileging political representation over aesthetic representation, *Vertretung* over *Darstellung*, ultimately in terms compatible with "a colonialist theory of the most efficient information retrieval" (Spivak, *Post-colonial* 9). Information retrieval or "read[ing] for … role models, cultural explanation, historical point of view" is, as Tan notes, "not bad in and of itself" (Stanton 7). It has to happen. After all, meaning depends on the capacity of tropes and figures to promote such reconciliations. "By itself," however, informational retrieval "does something to literature" by missing the point that tropes and figures are just as likely to keep novel and meaning/referent apart as bring them together (Stanton 7). Rendering literature everything but literary, information retrieval risks not only conflating the two different forms of representation but also marginalizing the unreliable movement of literariness and, with it, the de/construction of essences and stereotypes so fundamental to feminist postcolonial critique.

In the final analysis, then, it should be clear that much depends on how *The Joy Luck Club* is read, specifically the Woos' relationship. Perhaps the significance of this asymmetrical relationship has been overestimated: it interrupts formal, thematic, and ideological closure, and, by extension, the "un-sweet" readings that celebrate and/or criticize the closing of the intergenerational/intercultural gap. More than this, it represents a way of relating to the other, in this case, the mother('s gift), that affirms difference. But, then again, the Woos' asymmetry is difficult not to overestimate since it is sustained by difference or, in Tan's terms, a missing someone or something that, by virtue of its irreducibility, makes impossible one final meaning. Granted, this essay has ventured a meaning that responds to this difference, and, to this extent, participates in that which it criticizes. At the same time, however, it does not presume to overcome this difference and by extension to end debate, only to regenerate debate by reading the intergenerational/intercultural relationships in the novel differently and apart from the conflict/harmony hierarchy, as well as the anthropomorphic or humanistic realism of the colonial/patriarchal imagination. When read as resisting the kind of imagination that presumes to reconcile novel and meaning/referent reliably, by virtue of the emphasis it gives to the "identity-in-difference" relationship between Jing-mei and Suyuan, and by extension self/other, *The Joy Luck Club* arguably articulates a postmodern preoccupation with a politics of difference that radically problematizes essences and stereotypes.

NOTES

1. According to Sau-ling Cynthia Wong and Jeffrey J. Santa Ana, in "Gender and Sexuality in Asian American Literature," (171–226), the three periods of Asian-American literature are generally regarded as the 1850s–1950s, a period of "violence and 'deviance'", the 1960s–1980s, a period of "self-definition and self-representation" associated with identity politics, and the late 1980s–present. Quoting from King-kok Cheung, Wong and Santa Ana argue that the emphasis in the third period is on "heterogeneity and diaspora," and a politics of difference.

2. Hereafter references to *The Joy Luck Club* appear in parentheses in the text.

3. An-mei says, "I was raised the Chinese way" (215).

4. The death of her baby leaves Ying-ying "a living ghost." "My mother," comments Lena, "was now always 'resting' and it was as if she had died. . . . I saw a girl complaining that the pain of not being seen was unbearable. I saw the mother lying in bed in her long flowing robes" (113, 115). While Ying-ying seems to be on the other side in death, An-mei and Suyuan appear to be for the other side through their respective alliances. In Rose's case, her mother forms an anti-Rose alliance with the guardian of (bad) dreams, Old Mr. Chou (186). Similarly, Suyuan sides with Waverly, the child genius and, later, the self-proclaimed style guru for a successful accounting firm that rejects Jing-mei's brochure copy on its tax services: "I heard my mother saying to Waverly: 'True, cannot teach style. June not sophisticate like you. Must be born this way.' I was surprised at myself, how humiliated I felt. I had been outsmarted by Waverly once again, and now betrayed by my own mother" (206).

5. See Amy Ling, *Between Worlds*, 136, as well as Victoria Chen, "Chinese American Women, Language and Moving Subjectivity": "Seeking the motivation behind a hurtful remark . . . leads Tan to an understanding of and sympathy for the mother whose seeming rejection is but a self-defensive mask for her own vulnerability and love"; and, "in the mother's language, 'truth' is characterized by the logic of the opposite; this 'indirect' approach works only if one knows how to hear the statement within the context of a certain kind of relationship. Saying the opposite is what the mother felt obligated to perform; in fact, it was the only language that she could use in order to demonstrate her affection and care for her daughter" (6).

6. Asian-American feminists argue that the personal is political. See Shirley Geok-lin Lim, "Semiotics, Experience, and the Material Self: An Inquiry into the

Subject of the Contemporary Asian Woman Writer": "For Asian [and, presumably, Asian American] women . . . not only is the personal political, but sex is often the field in which the political is waged. In the absence of a tradition of political engagement in the world, they articulate political engagement of their most private encounters with the Male Other" in both Asia and America (444).

7. See Angelo N. Ancheta, *Race, Rights, and the Asian American Experience*: "The 'model minority' stereotype of Asian Americans is a two-edged sword, breeding not only incomplete and inaccurate images of Asian-American success but resentment and hostility on the part of other racial groups" (12). This incompleteness and inaccuracy does not only apply to different Asian-American groups but also to different members of the same group. For instance, "Asian American success" is more readily available to those with diasporic as opposed to immigrant identities.

8. In addition to putting An-mei's words into Suyuan's mouth, Schell makes Jing-mei Woo and Lena St. Clair "sister[s]." He also claims that the "older women . . . still wear" the Chinese dresses of earlier Joy Luck Clubs (3), and thus ignores Jing-mei's comment: "tonight, there's no mystery. The Joy Luck aunties are all wearing slacks, bright print blouses, and different versions of sturdy walking shoes" (28).

9. See Sucheta Mazumdar, "Through Western Eyes": "The first known Chinese woman in the United States was Afong Moy, who was displayed sitting amid Chinese paraphernalia at the American Museum, the Brooklyn Institute, and various other New York locations between 1834 and 1847. In the latter year she shared the star billing with Tom Thumb. When Afong Moy left for Boston, Barnum's Chinese Museum catered to the New Yorker's curiosity by producing Pwan-ye-koo and her maidservant in 1850. The small bound feet of both women were a prime feature of the advertisements announcing their displays. In both these cases the allure of the women was heightened by the suggestion that they were upper class; the illustrations of the women showing them sitting demurely, their contours obscured by brocades and silk clothing" (159).

WORKS CITED

Ancheta, Angelo N. *Race, Rights, and the Asian American Experience*. New Brunswick: Rutgers UP, 1998.

Chen, Victoria. "Chinese American Women, Language and Moving Subjectivity." *Women and Language* 18.1 (1995): 3–7.

Cheng, Sinkwan. "Fantasizing the *Jouissance* of the Chinese Mother: *The Joy Luck Club* and Amy Tan's Quest for Stardom in the Market of Neo-Racism." *Savoir: Psychoanalyse Et Analyse Culturelle* 3.1–2 (February 1997): 95–133.

Chow, Rey. "Women in the Holocene: Ethnicity, Fantasy, and the Film *The Joy Luck Club*." *Feminism and the Pedagogics of Everyday Life*. Ed. Carmen Luke. New York: SUNY P, 1995. 204–21.

———. *Writing Diaspora: Tactics of Intervention in Contemporary Cultural Studies*. Bloomington: Indiana UP, 1993.

Gately, Patricia. "Ten Thousand Different Ways: Inventing Mothers, Inventing Hope." *Paintbrush: A Journal of Multicultural Literature* 12 (Autumn 1995): 51–55.

Gerrard, Nicci, and Sean French. "Sexual Reading." *Observer* (27 September 1998): 2.

Kim, Elaine H. "'Such Opposite Creatures': Men and Women in Asian American Literature." *Michigan Quarterly Review* 29 (1990): 68–93.

Li, David Leiwei. *Imagining the Nation: Asian American Literature and Cultural Consent*. Stanford: Stanford UP, 1998.

Lim, Shirley Geok-lin. "Semiotics, Experience, and the Material Self: An Inquiry into the Subject of the Contemporary Asian Woman Writer." *Women, Autobiography, Theory: A Reader*. Ed. Sidonie Smith and Julia Watson. Madison: Wisconsin UP, 1998. 441–52.

Ling, Amy. *Between Worlds: Women Writers of Chinese Ancestry*. New York: Pergamon, 1990.

Lowe, Lisa. *Critical Terrains: French and British Orientalisms*. Ithaca: Cornell UP, 1991.

Mazumdar, Sucheta. "Through Western Eyes: Discovering Chinese Women in America." *A New Significance: Re-envisioning the History of the American West*. Ed. Clyde A. Milner II. Oxford: Oxford UP, 1996. 158–68.

McAlister, Melanie. "(Mis)Reading *The Joy Luck Club*." *Asian America: Journal of Culture and the Arts* 1 (1992): 102–18.

Sarna, Navtej. "From the Far Corners: Review of Rajini Srikanth and Esther Y. Iwanaga's *Bold Words: A Century of Asian American Writing*." *TLS* (22 March 2002): 22.

Schell, Orville. "Your Mother is in Your Bones: *The Joy Luck Club*." *The New York Times Book Review* (19 March 1989): 3, 28.

Shen, Gloria. "Born of a Stranger: Mother–Daughter Relationships and Storytelling in Amy Tan's *The Joy Luck Club*." *International Women's Writing: New Landscapes of Identity*. Ed. Anne E. Browne and Marjanne E. Goozé. Westport, CT: Greenwood, 1995. 233–44.

Spivak, Gayatri Chakravorty "Can the Subaltern Speak?" *Marxism and the Interpretation of Culture*. Ed. Cary Nelson and Lawrence Grossberg. London: Macmillan, 1988. 271–313.

———. *In Other Worlds: Essays in Cultural Politics*. London: Routledge, 1987.

———. *The Postcolonial Critic: Interviews, Strategies, Dialogues*. Ed. Sarah Harasym. New York: Routledge, 1990.

———. "Poststructuralism, Marginality, Postcoloniality and Value." *Contemporary Postcolonial Theory: A Reader*. Ed. Padmini Mongia. London: Arnold, 1996. 198–222.

Tan, Amy. *The Joy Luck Club*. London: Minerva, 1989.

———. *The Opposite of Fate*. London: Flamingo, 2003.

TuSmith, Bonnie. *All My Relatives: Community in Contemporary Ethnic American Literatures*. Ann Arbor: U of Michigan P, 1993.

Stanton, David. "Breakfast with Amy Tan." *Paintbrush: A Journal of Multicultural Literature* 12 (Autumn 1995): 5–19.

Wong, Sau-ling Cynthia. "'Sugar Sisterhood': The Amy Tan Phenomenon." *The Ethnic Canon: Histories, Institutions, and Interventions*. Ed. David Palumbo-Liu. Minneapolis: U of Minnesota P, 1995. 174–210.

Wong, Sau-ling Cynthia and Jeffrey Santa Ana. "Gender and Sexuality in Asian American Literature." *Signs: Journal of Women in Culture and Society* 25.1 (Autumn 1999): 171–226.

MAGALI CORNIER MICHAEL

Choosing Hope and Remaking Kinship: *Amy Tan's* The Joy Luck Club

Focusing on Amy Tan's incredibly popular *The Joy Luck Club* (1989), this chapter turns to a specific analysis of contemporary American fiction by women who draw from particular ethnic American traditions to reimagine dynamic forms of community and coalition building within the landscape of late twentieth-century America. While the first highly acclaimed and widely read text by a Chinese American woman in the wake of the civil rights and women's movements is arguably Maxine Hong Kingston's *Woman Warrior* (1976), a book that addresses the challenges of developing an identity and sense of self for Chinese American women, I have chosen Tan's novel because of its much more developed and prominent engagement with notions of community. Most specifically, Tan's novel offers a vision of individual agency that gestures away from American adherence to a self-interested, market-driven notion of individualism and anchors itself firmly in interdependence and community derived from a specifically female Chinese American perspective—constructed within the particular hybrid sociocultural context and lived experiences of Chinese women immigrants and the daughters they bear and raise in the United States.

By rejecting both the opposition between the individual and the community and the equation of the individual and individualism that typically underlie conceptualizations of agency within the American context, Tan's novel opens up a space for thinking about agency in Chinese American-inflected

From *New Visions of Community in Contemporary American Fiction: Tan, Kingsolver, Castillo, Morrison*, pp. 39–71. © 2006 by the University of Iowa Press.

terms that value and, indeed, assert the necessity of the material and psychic support that communities and families provide.[1] The novel builds upon what Daniel Shanahan describes as the general tendency within Asian cultures in general to "exhibit patterns of behavior, goals, and norms that contrast sharply with the individualistic heritage of the West," particularly in the emphasis they place "on *affect*—the emotions and attachments that tie one to people, entities, and institutions."[2] In addition, *The Joy Luck Club* explores the ways in which the more specific Confucian-derived Chinese valuing of "collective well-being [. . .] over self-interests"[3] are translated and revised by Chinese American women.

Through its focus on four mothers born in China (Suyuan Woo, An-mei Hsu, Lindo Jong, Ying-ying St. Clair) and their four American-born daughters (Jing-mei "June" Woo, Rose Hsu Jordan, Waverly Jong, Lena St. Clair), the novel negotiates an alternative model of agency inflected by the particular experiences of first- and second-generation Chinese women immigrants to the United States and the ways in which they have negotiated aspects of Chinese and American culture to create their own hybridized cultural traditions. Bringing together the mothers' imported traditional Chinese beliefs and values, especially with respect to family and filial responsibility; the American dream upon which the United States' status as an immigrant nation depends; the realities of contemporary American existence for its racially marked immigrants; and the specific forms of sexism structured into the Chinese, American, and Chinese American cultural contexts allows for the construction of a new notion of agency that revises all these elements in terms of their interactions with each other.

Working simultaneously at the levels of form and content, Tan's novel offers its own fragmented but carefully organized structure as one means to illustrate the interdependence of the individual and the community and thus the communal aspects of agency. Indeed, the novel takes the form of individual stories that enter into dialogue with and depend on each other on the basis of spatial proximity and that together present a whole that is greater than its parts but that nevertheless depends on those parts.[4] The bulk of my discussion, however, focuses on how the San Francisco Joy Luck Club—created by the mothers but also experienced by the daughters—serves as a model for the innovative form of individual agency dependent on community that the novel offers. More than a mere club, the Joy Luck Club becomes an emblem of the mothers' fierce will to survive physically and psychically in a land that is foreign to them, of their recognition that their individual survival and control over their destinies in America requires communal support, and of their need to retain a sense of hope for the future. Moreover, the Joy Luck Club provides for both mothers and daughters a communal space within which to negotiate hybrid individual identities that will enable agency.

Tan's novel is not just a simplistic feel-good novel as some critics have claimed, however. Such a reading requires overvalidating the resolution that the last story offers and seemingly erasing the novel's emphasis on culturally specific forms of oppression. Indeed, as Melanie McAlister argues, such a reading derives at least in part from many readers' and reviewers' wish to insist that "Tan's novel offers a 'universal' narrative, despite its seemingly exotic content."[5] In contrast, I want to focus on how the novel presents the construction and maintenance of a positive form of community as fraught with difficulties and at the same time of vital importance for the women's survival and growth as racially marked women negotiating two radically different cultural traditions. Not only does Tan's novel portray communities as potentially oppressive, but the novel also depicts the characters' abilities to build and sustain a supportive culturally hybrid community as remarkable, given the deep wounds they each carry but cannot voice and the bitter conflicts between the mothers and their daughters. As Wendy Ho succinctly explains, because all the stories "confront personal and communal oppression," they accordingly involve "painful, complicated excavatory work" so that the novel is just as much about "ruptures and contradictions" as about forming links and bonds.[6]

Of particular interest is the novel's highlighting of the ways in which communities of women, typically associated with the realm of the home, are all too often complicit with patriarchal systems of power—particularly within the context of Chinese culture. Many of the mothers' past traumatic experiences in China derive from the actions of women upholding the Chinese male-dominated status quo. In "traditional Chinese society," as Ho notes, women were "confined to the private sphere where their virtue, honor, and chastity could be controlled and preserved" through means that "permitted the psychic and social abuse of women, an abuse in which women sometimes took part."[7] For example, when Lindo is only two years old, she is promised in marriage to the son of a wealthier family and, consequently, her family begins to treat her as if she "belonged to somebody else."[8] After her family is forced to leave the area following severe flooding, at the age of twelve Lindo moves in with her in-laws, who treated her like a servant as she is taught to be an "obedient wife" under the strict tutelage of her future mother-in-law (50). An-mei's beautiful mother, who was married to a scholar but widowed at a young age, is dishonored after a wealthy man's second wife, in an effort to pacify his sexual appetites, tricks An-mei's mother into sleeping in his bed. There he rapes her, after which her family disowns her and bars her from their home; she is thus forced to become one of the man's concubines (266–267). In both cases, women collude with the Chinese patriarchal system by asserting the only power they have—the power to regulate other women—so that in these cases communities of women function as a means of upholding a system that is oppressive to women. Given the mothers' traumatic experiences in China at the hand of a deeply misogynist culture, the difficulties they face dealing with their Americanized independent-minded daughters are not surprising. What is surprising, however, given their harsh experiences in China, is the mothers' understanding that other forms of nonmisogynist and nonpatriarchal communities are possible and their insistence on working to create such an alternative.

That the locus for *The Joy Luck Club*'s revaluing of human interdependence—which grounds the novel's revision of agency—lies in the life stories of eight Chinese American women and thus in realms that have traditionally been silenced and devalued is indicative of the radical nature of the novel's exploration. Indeed, the focus on the four mothers' difficult life experiences in China and then as immigrants to the United States and on the four daughters' experiences as second-generation Chinese American girls and then women places attention upon areas of life conventionally associated with the private side of the Western binary opposition between public and private life, in which the public holds greater status because of its association with politics and with white upper-class men in the United States, and in which the private is often devalued because of its association with women and the realm of nurturing and emotions.[9] However, in the wake of the women's and civil rights movements, the realm of the political has expanded to include experiences previously associated with private life. The 1970s feminist slogan "The personal is political" exemplifies the sea change that has since reverberated in every corner of American culture, whether in the form of questioning, transformation, or resistance.

Not only does Tan's novel focus on women's so-called private lives, but it also pays particular attention to the positive possibilities that inhere within familial structures and relationships and the cultural traditions that govern them. This attention to familial structures is crucial to the novel's development of an alternative model of agency. Although the text makes clear that familial structures can be restrictive, as the mothers' China experiences demonstrate, Tan's novel also makes visible and places value on the potential of the interdependence that is the hallmark of family life and that women have learned to value as a consequence of the nurturing work they have tended to be assigned within the family in patriarchal cultures. As Joan Tronto notes, humans are clearly "interdependent beings," given that "all humans need care"—which she defines as encompassing "attentiveness, responsibility, nurturance, compassion, meeting others' needs"—at various points in their lives. Consequently, care not only is "a central but devalued aspect of human life" but also very much needs to be understood "as a political ideal," as a value that should be made more central in our constellation of political concerns."[10]

One means of doing so, as Alison Jaggar explains, is to reformulate care as simultaneously "critical" and "nurturant."[11] In order to gain public currency, care needs to be reconceptualized in terms that refute and move beyond the classic hierarchical oppositions between public and private, reason and emotion, individualism and dependence, and men and women in which the latter term has consistently been relegated to a position of inferiority. By foregrounding the processes of caring with which families tend to be involved, *The Joy Luck Club* marks interdependence as necessary to the survival of its women characters and to their development as fully fledged agents within a contemporary American cultural landscape in which they are marginalized on several counts.

The intricately orchestrated, fragmented form of the novel illustrates the interdependence that the novel as a whole champions. *The Joy Luck Club*'s structure includes four named sections, each of which contains an italicized introduction that resembles a fable, as well as four stories narrated in the first person. A character's name and a title label each story. The first and final sections focus on the four mothers' stories and the second and third sections focus on the four daughters' stories. With the exception of Jing-mei Woo, whose mother has died and who thus narrates her mother's as well as her own stories, all the women narrate two stories. While each story exists independently, in the sense that it is self-sufficient and readable on its own, the arrangement of the stories next to each other and in groups within sections and their overlaps in terms of characters, situations, and thematic elements create a dialogic relationship among the stories that demonstrates in structural terms the interdependence between the individual (the individual story) and the collective (the collection or, in this case, the novel as a collection of stories).[12] The novel's dialogism thus derives from the spatial positioning and proximity of the stories to one another and not from the literal telling of a story by one character to another—as Marc Singer notes, "None of the novel's sixteen tales are ever spoken or delivered to any other character."[13] Furthermore, this dialogism highlights the oral quality of the women's life stories—in the sense that they are lived but never recorded in written form—and thus links their stories to the myriad stories internationally that have been effaced because they belonged to those on the margins of the dominant group and have thus never been deemed important enough to record by the dominant group, which historically has had greater access to and control over writing and publishing.[14]

By making space for seven distinct narrators and the life stories of eight women, Tan's novel gives voice to a number of Chinese American women characters in two different generations, whose voices and individual histories represent ones that have until very recently remained untold. Indeed, "the long neglect and invisibility of Chinese women's diverse experiences, histories, and standpoints"[15] globally has its own particular history within the context of Chinese immigration to the United States. Given the various "Chinese Exclusion Acts, which were in force between 1882 and 1943" and which "banned the entry of certain groups of Chinese immigrants to America (notably women),"[16] relatively few Chinese American women entered the United States. Because "the number of Chinese women in the United States did not approach equality with Chinese men until 1954" and because of the entrenched racism and sexism of American culture that went virtually unchallenged on a national level until the 1960s and 1970s, the relative paucity of Chinese American women's voices or writing in the United States until relatively recently is not surprising[17]—indeed, as previously noted, Maxine Hong Kingston's 1976 *The Woman Warrior* is arguably the first best-selling text by a Chinese American author. Within the context of this relative absence or silence of Chinese American women's voices until the mid-1970s, the stories offered by Tan's novel also become acts of "self-assertion" and "defiance."[18] The stories function as "a claiming of political and social agency"[19] by and for its multiple Chinese American narrators. In addition, by using multiple narrators whose life stories remain distinct, the novel ensures that the individual women and their particular experiences are not collapsed into some sort of stereotypical or *true* Chinese American woman—indeed, many differences surface among the women in each generation and among the women of different generations—and yet allows for the narratives to enter into dialogue with each other on the level of form and to illustrate the varied texture of Chinese American women's lives.[20] Moreover, *The Joy Luck Club*'s splintered narration provides its narrators with a form of agency grounded in the collective, in the sense that each voice and life story is strengthened by all the others, so that the novel's form reinforces the kind of agency it explores and offers to its readers.[21]

The novel's emphasis on the value and necessity of interdependence in order to envision a form of individual agency that is attainable by all Americans who do not fit the dominant white upper-class male profile and yet who make up an ever-growing segment of the U.S. population goes far beyond the text's structure and is particularly evident in its presentation of the American incarnation of the Joy Luck Club. Although Suyuan Woo creates the Joy Luck Club in China and, after immigrating to the United States, bases the San Francisco version of the Joy Luck Club on the earlier one, so that the two share certain characteristics, the latter club is constructed differently and serves different functions. With her husband away fighting in the war and finding herself in the difficult and potentially traumatic position of being alone with two small children in Kweilin before the Japanese overrun the city,

Suyuan initiates the first Joy Luck Club, inviting three other young women to join her in a ritual of weekly gatherings aimed at raising their depressed spirits (10). The women eat delicacies and play mah jong to ward off the "despair" (11) that inflects their lives as a consequence of the war. The four women choose to cultivate luck through their weekly mah-jong game as a way of holding on to hope and creating joy out of that hope: "That hope was our only joy" (12).[22] By choosing hope, the women assert themselves as active agents rather than passive victims, indicating not only that hope is necessary for survival but also that hope is a *choice*. Rather than focusing on the negative aspects of their lives in the face of war, the women choose to look forward by constructing for themselves a communal space within which for a limited time they allow themselves hope and the joy that comes with it. The Kweilin club is short-lived, however, in that the Japanese soon overrun the city as expected; Suyuan is forced to escape the city in order to avoid execution as the wife of an officer and she never again sees the other three women.

In contrast to the Kweilin club's temporary status, the San Francisco Joy Luck Club is established in 1949, two years prior to Jing-Mei's birth (6), and is still going strong in the present of the novel, set in the late 1980s—with Jing-Mei now thirty-six years old (14). Not only has the United States-based club lasted thirty-eight years, but it also includes many more participants than did its antecedent in China. Although the San Francisco Joy Luck Club also begins with four women, it includes their families from the start. Moreover, it takes on characteristics and functions that correspond to its location in the United States and that address its participants' positioning within American culture. As she had done in Kweilin, Suyuan chooses the other three women who make up the Joy Luck Club on the basis of affinity and empathy. All four women are experiencing similar situations and life trajectories as recent Chinese immigrants. Although the four women's lives in China differed in many ways, they all come from middle- to upperclass backgrounds and have been thrust into the lower class in the American context because of their lack of language skills and their alien cultural and racial status as Asians. What binds these four particular Chinese immigrant women most strongly, however, are the "unspeakable tragedies" they suffered in China, as well as the "hopes they couldn't begin to express in their fragile English" that Suyuan immediately recognizes in "the numbness" she reads in their faces (6). Empathy, "the ability to 'feel into' someone else's experience,"[23] draws them together and creates a connection between them. These women are thus brought together in part by the painful histories of oppression they share but cannot voice—their unspeakable pasts link them—and in part by their shared hopes for the future in their adopted country. Indeed, given the traumas they have all endured in China, the four women's ability to shape a new form of community for themselves in their adopted country speaks to their remarkable resiliency and to their need to imagine a future for themselves and their children.

The formation of the Joy Luck Club in America thus functions as a vehicle for these women not only to survive but also to control their fates in the foreign land they have chosen as the place to secure their hopes for the future. One of the chief attractions of the United States for immigrants is its dominant national myth of the American dream, with its assurances that social mobility is possible, that individual hard work and perseverance will result in material success; and the novel's four mothers pin their hopes for the future of their families, and in particular their daughters, on an American culture in which, as the italicized introduction to the novel's first section proclaims, "*nobody will look down*" on their daughters (3). Although the mothers very quickly understand that access to the American dream is difficult for Chinese immigrants like themselves, they nevertheless refuse to adopt the skepticism of their daughters and to different degrees continue to defiantly choose hope. As Jing-mei asserts, her "mother believed you could be anything you wanted to be in America," always optimistic about the future (141). In contrast, Jing-mei admits that she herself has no such illusions (154). The gap between the hope of the first-generation immigrant Suyuan and the lack of hope of her second-generation daughter appears odd at first glance, especially given the harshness of Suyuan's past in China in comparison to Jing-mei's American life. Given the novel's association of hope with choice, however, Suyuan's choice of immigrating to America and thus of America as the locus for her hopes exists in contrast to Jing-mei's status as an American-born Chinese American who did not have to make the kinds of choices her mother had to make but who as a result does not have the kinds of hopes her mother has. In light of this difference between the two generations, which is present in some form in all four mother–daughter pairs, the Joy Luck Club performs different functions for the mothers and the daughters. For the mothers, it serves as a familial space devoid of the restrictions imposed on such spaces in China in which they can freely enact and revise their (American inflected) Chinese customs without their being considered foreign, whereas for the daughters it is a place that is simultaneously foreign and familial.

The Joy Luck Club as a familial entity is of particular interest, in that it retains the traditional Chinese emphasis on the family and kinship but in a significantly revised form. As Peter Ching-Yung Lee notes, traditional Chinese "social organization centered around family and kinship" and thereby placed a "great emphasis on mutual dependence rather than individual independence."[24] However, this mutual dependence was imbedded at least since "the first century B.C." within "patriarchal power."[25] Most scholars agree that the centrality of the family within Chinese culture derives from the incredible influence of Confucian principles upon Chinese society for over two millenniums.[26] Confucianism places great value on "the principle of mutuality."[27] Of key import is the "affectionate concern with the well-being of others," as well as the family as the locus or foundation for the enactment and development of that mutuality and concern.[28] Indeed, "the supreme virtue of *jen*, meaning 'humaneness' and 'benevolence,'" is central to Confucianism and "enkindles the interrelated values of filial piety, respect and loyalty."[29] However, Confucianism is also a "rigidly authoritarian," "totalitarian," and "hierarchical system," with "filial piety" as "the principle instrument through which it was established and maintained."[30] Until the eruption of revolutionary movements during the late nineteenth century and into the twentieth century shook China's very foundations and "overturned centuries-old feudal structures," Chinese culture remained for centuries based upon the Confucian ideals of "loyalty and subordination," including that of wife to husband.[31] As a result, "class structure was rigidly set" and the "rights of women and children were minimal" at best.[32] Women's inferior status within traditional Chinese culture is particularly evident in the historically prevalent misogynistic "practices of footbinding, concubinage, female slavery, and female infanticide." However, the "establishment of a Republic in 1911–1912" not only dissolved the emperor's "absolute authority at the state level" but also "was accompanied by a displacement of patriarchal authority on the familial level," which in turn led to the establishment of schools for girls and of "women's suffrage societies."[33]

Nonetheless, despite progressive legal reforms and public acknowledgments concerning women, change within Chinese familial and ideological structures has been slow. As Amy Ling notes, "In practice, backed by centuries of history and tradition, the old ways die hard."[34] Moreover, according to Wei-Ming Tu, even "the modern intelligentsia has maintained unacknowledged, sometimes unconscious, continuities with the Confucian tradition at every level of life."[35] As a consequence, aspects of the traditional subordination of women within the family continued and arguably still continue to survive within Chinese culture despite the shift first to a republic and then in 1949 to a Communist system. The mothers' stories in Tan's novel indicate such a persistence of the old customs, leaving critics like Patricia Chu frustrated with the mothers' depictions of the China of their youth in terms that seem to hark back to a prerevolutionary China rather than to what was at that time "a country in which modern and traditional elements co-exist[ed]" and in which "the oppressive family system Tan describes in her novel was being questioned on a national level by Chinese reformers."[36] As I will subsequently argue, part of this discrepancy has to do with the Americanization of the mothers, which heavily colors the stories they tell about their pasts in China.

In addition, I would argue that the changes brought about by the revolutions and shift to a republic do indeed appear in the mothers' stories but on a more implicit level. That each of the mothers in different ways challenges and escapes her oppressive situation indicates an atmosphere conducive to such assertions by women even if the stories paint their families as steeped in tradition. Arguably, the mothers depict themselves as revolutionaries in their refusal to play by the rules that condone women's oppression and in their choices to walk away from the families and structures oppressing them. Moreover, as Eddie Kuo argues, "Geographical and social mobility tend to weaken kinship ties" and, along with "new economic structures" that create jobs for women, result in more "symmetrical and reciprocal" relationships between family members.[37] In the case of the four Chinese mothers, immigration to the United States cuts them off not only from their biological extended families but also from the sociocultural constraints attached to those genealogical ties. In addition, their immigrant status as low-paid workers right alongside their husbands, while problematic in terms of the economic exploitation both the women and the men have to endure, has the potentially positive side effect of loosening the gender hierarchies that delimited their lives in China.

The Joy Luck Club itself can be read as a potential outgrowth of the revolutionary atmosphere and spirit that characterized the China of the mothers' childhood and early adulthood. For the Chinese immigrant mothers and their families, the Joy Luck Club performs a revolutionary function as it becomes a mechanism for enabling a negotiation of Chinese and American cultural structures—both of which the novel depicts as *in process*—as well as the creation of altogether new ones.[38] Indeed, the Joy Luck Club allows for a radical reformulation of the family that continues to value the family and thus does not break totally from certain Confucian ideals but moves away from authoritarianism and dependence on genealogy. To a certain extent, then, the novel supports Walter Slote's contention that "the Confucian family is gradually modifying and adapting itself to an increasingly egalitarian perspective" even as "the substance of Confucianism, particularly in terms of interpersonal relationships and ethical values, is still alive and flourishing."[39] While the four families that make up the Joy Luck Club have no biological relationships to each other, consisting instead of what Ho calls an "extra-familial social network,"[40] they construct an alternative extended family in which kinship derives from similar circumstances, proximity, friendship, support, and nurturance rather than merely from genealogy and in which gender roles deviate from the particular patriarchal structure that dominated the mothers' lives in China. Marina Heung notes that the mothers' stories of their pasts in China indicate a system in which "blood ties" are often "replaced by a network of alternate affiliations"[41]—for example, Lindo is sent to live with her future in-laws when her family is forced to move as a result of massive flooding; An-mei's mother is banished by her family after she is tricked into becoming a wealthy man's concubine; and An-mei chooses to break with her family in order to go live with her mother. But the Joy Luck Club does more than sever ties to genealogy in that it also severs ties to a hierarchical and patriarchal power structure by imagining an alternative family structure that all of its participants help to shape and that distributes power more symmetrically. Although a number of scholars have criticized Tan's novel for relying on biologism, as exemplified by statements like "Your mother is in your bones!" (31), I would argue that the dominant role that the Joy Luck Club plays in the lives of all four Chinese American families indicates that Tan's novel complicates and attempts to move beyond any absolutist dependence on biological kinship.[42] That the children refer to the Joy Luck Club adults other than their own parents as Auntie and Uncle, for example, reinforces the notion that the club functions as an extended family that does not depend solely on biological ties. Perhaps the most overt illustration of how the Joy Luck Club members function as family, as a collective of people who share and foster each other's hopes—even beyond death—lies in the plan hatched by Jing-mei's three aunties after her mother Suyuan's death to send Jing-mei to China to meet her twin half-sisters, whom her mother searched for all her life after last seeing them on the road out of Kweilin during the Japanese invasion.

The mothers' sense of hope appears to be a hybridized version of hope that combines aspects of a traditional Chinese belief in fate and of the hope on which the notion of the American dream depends. According to Patricia Hamilton, an "Eastern worldview dictates that fate can be manipulated in order to bring about good effects and to ward off bad ones," so that fate contains "a participatory element."[43] Moreover, this participatory element arguably found validation in the turn-of-the-century revolutions that led to the establishment of a republic. Once in the United States, the mothers further revise the Chinese notion of fate they have internalized by emphasizing its participatory element in accordance with the more individualistic underpinnings of the American dream. For example, when Lindo tells of how she escaped an arranged marriage in China without shaming her family, the story takes the form of an Americanized assertion of individual identity that makes possible an intricate manipulation of her fate. Lindo reports that, upon looking at herself in a mirror, she saw her strength and understood that she had her own "thoughts inside" that others could neither see nor "ever take away" from her (51). Although, as Chu notes, the novel provides no sense of how Lindo would have developed this strong individual identity or how she could have "survived the sudden independence for which she had never been prepared," given the depiction of "a fictional Chinese world where both individual justice and systemic social change seem impossible,"[44] this need not denote an inherent weakness of Tan's novel. Instead, I read Lindo's story as demonstrating how she as a Chinese American has constructed a sense of hope that borrows from both her Chinese heritage—the traditional notion of fate and the postrevolutionary belief in change—and her new American culture and that she utilizes to translate her past to herself and to her daughter as they both work to construct Chinese American identities with agency.

Structurally, as Sau-Ling Cynthia Wong notes, the mothers' "stories about old China are 'framed' by reference to the present time of America," which overtly points to the retrospective aspect of the stories.[45] Indeed, generally speaking, according to Yuan Yuan, "all memories are [necessarily] socially and culturally reconstituted within a specific historical and cultural context" and entail "preserving, revising, erasing, and recovering past memories [...] depending on the specific purposes of recollection and the present position of the recollecting subject."[46] To some extent, all the mothers' stories about their harsh lives in China are colored by a revised, retrospectively imposed notion of hope, particularly in their positioning of the mothers as heroines of their destinies, albeit to different degrees in each story, and thus as agents manipulating difficult circumstances to their own advantages rather than as victims of those circumstances. As Heung puts it, the mothers engage in "re-writing stories of oppression and victimization into parables of self-affirmation and individual empowerment."[47] Recognizing the stories as parables rather than as realistic renderings makes clearer the ways in which the mothers strategically alter their stories in order to give voice within the context of their relocation to the United States not only to the oppressive and at times tragic events of their pasts in China but also to their trajectory away from those oppressive conditions. These stories in many ways are designed to justify their immigration to the United States and their positions as Chinese Americans. That this process of strategic translation of the past through a present Chinese American lens is taken up to some degree by all four mothers further indicates the ways in which their individual agencies are products of the community they have built for themselves in the form of the Joy Luck Club, a community that continually negotiates aspects of the cultures of their birth and adopted nations.

While many critics and readers focus on the Americanization of the daughters, I am thus arguing that the mothers' stories also indicate that they themselves have become Americanized.[48] Indeed, first-generation immigrant Asian women in general have little choice but to engage in "renegotiating their identities as women, wives and mothers" if they are to survive in America, given that the cultural and social landscape they find upon arrival differs from the one in which they have functioned up to that point.[49] In

Tan's novel, the Joy Luck Club performs the dual role of providing for the mothers a place to hold on to elements of Chinese culture and of allowing a safe space to negotiate between the Chinese and American cultures. Many aspects of the workings of the San Francisco Joy Luck Club provide evidence of such an active process of negotiation. That the club involves the women's husbands and children attests to their positions as immigrants with no biological extended family in the United States and thus with the possibility to reformulate the family in terms other than what they experienced in China. Not only is it practical to bring husbands and children along when the club meets, since there are no relatives to keep the children and feed the husbands, but also, for psychic and practical reasons, each family needs an alternative form of extended family in order to survive successfully within a country in which ethnic and racial minorities tend to be marginalized. Indeed, men and women alike must engage in the "daily negotiations of psychosocial and cultural life" made necessary by their positions as Chinese immigrants and the "inequitable political and economic systems they face" as a consequence.[50] As Yen Le Espiritu argues, within a "hostile environment, the act of maintaining families is itself a form of resistance";[51] but Tan's novel takes this notion a step further by depicting how the Chinese immigrant mothers actively and creatively reconfigure the family itself to meet their own needs and those of their families given their particular situation.

Although Joy Luck Club evenings include lots of Chinese food, the women playing mah jong for small sums of money, and early on, as Jing-mei recalls, the women wearing "funny Chinese dresses" (16), the weekly rituals also increasingly include American elements. Most overtly, the four women and their husbands turn to investing in the stock market as a means to achieve *joy luck*. As An-mei explains, Jing Mei's mother was too skilled at mah jong, which took the element of luck out of the game, so instead they decided to play the stock market so that every one could "win and lose equally" (18). While the notion that the stock market is a game of luck rather than skill serves as a humorous jab at contemporary American capitalism, the characters' decision to play the stock market is nevertheless a *choice* to participate in the American economy in a distinctly Western, American way and thus to become American at the same time they seek to hold on to elements of their Chinese culture—bearing in mind the earlier discussion of the participatory element contained in Eastern notions of fate. Moreover, the link they establish between the stock market and a sense of hope situates that hope firmly in the United States and its promise to immigrants that they can make a better life for themselves and their families if they believe in and work hard enough within the context of its capitalistic economic system—of which the stock market is such a powerful symbol. That they all meet to review the stocks they own and to vote on which stocks they should buy and sell each week before the women play mah jong and the men play cards further situates the Joy Luck Club within the American context of democratic decision making. The use of the American stock market and democratic voting as vehicles to the Chinese concept of *joy luck* thus exemplifies the cultural negotiations that take place within the Joy Luck Club, which exists as a dynamic entity that makes such negotiations possible.

That both wives and husbands play the stock market together indicates that the need for *joy luck* is no longer relegated to the women as it was in the Chinese version of the club. As ethnic immigrants to the United States, the women and men are on equal ground in terms of their precarious positions as racialized aliens in a foreign land and of their need for hope in order to survive both physically and psychically—thus breaking down "traditional Asian patriarchal authority."[52] Indeed, the fathers are no longer "omniscient, omnipotent, and protective" or "feared and distant."[53] Although the mothers still cook while their husbands discuss stocks, indicating a division of tasks at club meetings, the fathers and mothers nevertheless hold more symmetrical positions in terms of power within the club—as becomes evident when they all vote on the stocks, with men and women alike each having one vote and thus sharing equal power over the voting (17–18). Playing the stock market as a group provides the wives and husbands with a form of equalizing *collective joy luck*. Indeed, the collective aspects of the Joy Luck Club derive from its members' specific situation as Chinese Americans, which necessitates the construction of new ways of approaching their lives since the beliefs and customs neither of China nor of the United States speak directly to their circumstances as Chinese immigrants to America. In response, they revise both the traditional Chinese emphasis on "the group rather than the individual," particularly its notion of "mutual obligation within a vertical power hierarchy,"[54] and American notions of democracy and individualism to create a form of democratic community that emphasizes the group without denying the individual and mutual obligation without a context of vertical power hierarchy.

That this increased power symmetry among the men and women occurs within the context of the Joy Luck Club as an extended family but not necessarily within the individual nuclear families—for example, the novel depicts Ying-ying as silenced by her white Irish American husband who consistently speaks for her (108)[55]—positions the club itself as enabling an alternative power structure at least in part because it eschews the patriarchal logic of both Eastern and Western forms of the family. The Joy Luck Club functions as a mechanism for producing something new, for "the making of Chinese American culture—the ways in which it is imagined, practiced, and continued," which Lisa Lowe argues "is worked out as much 'horizontally' among communities as it is transmitted 'vertically' in unchanging forms from one generation to the next."[56] Indeed, in contrast to many critics' reading of Tan's novel in terms of vertical or generational cultural transmission, my discussion emphasizes the novel's depiction of the horizontal or communal creation of a dynamic Chinese American culture through the Joy Luck Club.

While the Joy Luck Club is a dynamic entity in that it revises its own rituals to fit the circumstances of its participants, it also provides a sense of stability in that the same adult members stay at its core throughout the thirty-eight years of its existence, and the *pattern* of its rituals stays virtually intact even as the children come and go and the specifics of the rituals alter over time. Rituals are vital elements of community, according to Michel Maffesoli, in that it is "through the variety of routine or everyday gestures [that] the community is reminded that it is a whole."[57] The ritualistic aspects of the Joy Luck Club are clearly inflected by its members' Chinese heritage, in that these aspects demonstrate a holding on to the Confucian valuing of "social harmony" derived from "ritual performance," in the sense that "to perform ritual is to take part in a communal act to promote mutual understanding."[58] When at the age of thirty-six Jing-mei goes to a Joy Luck Club gathering following her mother's death, she is taken aback initially that no one talks about her mother (17). Indeed, the others, including her father, observe their usual rituals, which anchor all of them in a realm that is both familiar and familial. However, Jing-mei also notices that the rituals contain a certain flexibility, adapting to changes that circumstances bring forth. Although the women play mah jong as they always have, for example, Jing-mei now sits in her mother's seat at the table (21). Rather than the Chinese style dresses they wore when they first arrived from China, now the women wear "slacks" and "bright print dresses" (16). This idea of sameness coexisting with difference marks the success of the Joy Luck Club as a model of community that offers a space for difference and change at the same time its continued presence and adherence to ritualized processes allow for stability.

Not only do the women adapt to the loss of one of their members by accepting Jing-mei in lieu of Suyuan, but they have also from the start adapted to their differences from each other. As they play mah jong, for instance, the women speak "half in broken English, half in their own Chinese dialect" (23–24). Although the different Chinese dialects separate the women, English allows them to communicate; and, more crucially, the existence of a space in which they all accept that combination of what differentiates them and what brings them together creates an environment based on affinity and caring that nevertheless embraces differences and changes. Although technically the club is a construction that exists only insofar as its members continue to meet and to view the club as an entity, the Joy Luck Club's function as an alternative extended family structure provides it with a psychological and cultural *being* for all its participants, parents and children alike. Indeed, all family and community structures are constructed, and their status as stable entities exists in relation to recognition by the dominant cultural apparatuses. Denied substantial recognition by the dominant American culture, the Joy Luck Club's founding members assert a communal form of agency by mutually constructing and validating a familial structure that meets their specific needs, particularly in terms of accepting their differences deriving from their lives and positions in China and of joining forces on the basis of the present similarity of their positions as Chinese immigrants to the United States. By anchoring a familial, communal structure in affinity and friendship rather than in biological ties, the club functions as a distinct example of Ray Pahl's argument that friendship is becoming "an increasingly important form of social glue" that is "taking over the social tasks, duties and functions from [traditionally, biologically defined] family and kin."[59] By forming the Joy Luck Club and then keeping it going, its members choose to orient themselves toward the future; they choose both the dynamism and the joy that comes with such hope.

For the daughters, the Joy Luck Club functions differently, although it is also central to their lives. Essentially born into the Joy Luck Club as an already established entity, the daughters take for granted the community and extended family that the club provides for them as well as its existence as a bridge to their Chinese heritage. As second-generation immigrants and consequently more Americanized than their parents, the daughters view the club from the perspective of both outsiders and insiders. In slightly different ways than their first-generation immigrant parents, the daughters "find themselves caught between two worlds. Their racial features proclaim one fact—their Asian ethnicity—but by education, choice, or birth they are American."[60] As outsiders vis-à-vis the Joy Luck Club, the daughters position themselves within the dominant American culture and see their elders and their rituals as foreign, as *other*, thus indicating their internalization of the Western self–other binary in which the Western is privileged over all other cultures. More specifically, as Ho notes, "Embedded in American mainstream discourses and institutions" are "certain stereotypical and racist views of the Chinese" that the daughters have internalized and that lead them to want to "assimilate into white America." This assimilation process includes the daughters' tendency to view their mothers "in terms of an 'American mindset'" that positions their immigrant mothers "as 'other,' as 'outsider,' as 'intruder,'"[61] which leads to bitter conflicts between the mothers and daughters.

Indeed, the daughters often assert themselves as Americans (and implicitly as superior) in contradistinction to their parents, whom they view in racialized terms. For example, when Rose's mother notes that her daughter's new boyfriend, Ted, is American rather than Chinese, Rose responds sharply, "I'm American too" (124). Moreover, Jing-mei admits that as a child she "imagined Joy Luck was a shameful Chinese custom" (16), thus highlighting not only her internalization of American xenophobia but also her distance from her Chinese heritage. As Lindo puts it most succinctly, what the mothers want for their children is "the best combination: American circumstances and Chinese character," not realizing that "these two things do not mix" (289). Indeed, the mothers find themselves unable to create "an American version of the ideal Chinese daughter,"[62] given that material and cultural circumstances are intricately tied to cultural character. Immersed in American culture and having never lived in China, the daughters cannot help but adopt American attitudes: Ying-ying refers to her daughter Lena's "proud American way" (274) and Lindo notes that on the "inside" her daughter Waverly "is all American-made" (289). Moreover, the mothers' own characters slowly evolve as a function of their new lives in America, as becomes evident in the Americanization of the stories they tell about their pasts in China (as discussed earlier in this chapter). As much as the daughters claim themselves to be American, however, their "physiologically marked bodies" mean that they are nevertheless forced to negotiate "the hybrid, contingent operations of race and ethnicity in daily life."[63] Moreover, their life circumstances include a Chinese American immediate and extended family—the latter in the form of the Joy Luck Club—that surrounds them with Chinese customs, foods, stories, and points of view even though they at times try to escape it.

Indeed, the Joy Luck Club provides the daughters with a community steeped in Chinese traditions, although these are inflected by its members' situation as immigrants to the United States. A gap does exist between the Chinese-born mothers and their American-born daughters with respect to Chinese language and culture—as evidenced by the mothers' recognition that their Americanized daughters do not understand joy luck (31). More insidious is the daughters' tendency to view their mothers as more Chinese and less educated than themselves on the basis of their own mastery of English in contradistinction to their mothers' difficulties with the language, thereby instantiating Ho's claim that "the English language can become a race and class signifier."[64] As they develop into adulthood, however, the daughters come to understand and internalize elements of Chinese tradition. For example, when Waverly brings her fiancé, Rich, to dinner at her parents' home, she sees clearly the faux pas he makes as a function of his ignorance of Chinese customs: not only does Rich take large first helpings of each dish and refuse seconds, but he also inadvertently criticizes Waverly's mother's cooking by adding soy sauce to the serving dish she has claimed has "no flavor" (197). Waverly cringes because she understands the complex "Chinese

cook's custom" of making "disparaging remarks" about the food she has prepared (197), which everyone is supposed to counter vehemently. Moreover,
she feels the insult to her parents when Rich not only addresses them by
their first names but also mispronounces their names, calling them Linda
and Tim rather than Lindo and Tin (198). Similarly, Jing-mei understands
that Chinese mothers like her own show their love differently than do most
American mothers, for example, through "stern offerings of steamed dump-
lings, duck's gizzards, and crab" (227); and, when Rose asserts that she feels
"*hulihudu*" and that things around her are "*heimongmong,*" she acknowledges that these words are untranslatable, referring to "sensation[s] that only
Chinese people have" (210)—thus counting herself among Chinese people.
As these examples demonstrate, the daughters' position vis-à-vis the Chinese
culture in which they participate via their parents and the Joy Luck Club
is not only that of outsider but also that of insider. Raised in America but
also in the midst of the Chinese customs that the Joy Luck Club enables
the four families to keep alive, these grown daughters have had to create a
new, dynamic Chinese American character that acknowledges, negotiates,
and builds from both American and Chinese cultural traditions and perspectives—and, to a certain extent, so have their mothers.

    I stress the role of the Joy Luck Club rather than simply that of the
individual mothers or parents because, whereas the novel foregrounds the tensions between mother–daughter pairings that in many ways lead the daughters
to reject their Chinese heritage, the Joy Luck Club is presented in a positive light as an enabling presence throughout the text. As a communal entity
and force, it distances the Chinese traditions in which its members engage as
a group from individual mother–daughter struggles. Not only does the Joy
Luck Club immerse the daughters in Chinese cultural practices, albeit adapted
to the American context, but it also provides the daughters with Chinese-
born elders (except for Ying-ying's husband, who is Irish American) and with
American-born friends whose circumstances are similar to their own, all of
whom can help the daughters negotiate identities since they all live to a certain
extent caught between two worlds. Although in time the daughters are careful
about what they tell each other so that it does not come back to haunt them
(28), since their mothers talk and brag about their children to each other, the
daughters nevertheless share aspects of their lives with each other based on
their similar positions as second-generation Chinese American girls and then
women. Indeed, the intersection between gender, ethnicity, and race becomes
a locus of difficulties for all the daughters, and the Joy Luck Club gatherings
become a space within which they begin as young girls to discuss their various
problems from the specific position they share while their mothers play mah
jong and their fathers play cards. Although the specifics differ drastically, the

bond between the daughters, like that between their mothers, revolves around unspeakable experiences and feelings connected to their positions as women marked by a Chinese heritage.

While the daughters' lives in America seem liberated in contrast to the ghastly experiences of their mothers in what they depict as a more overtly hierarchical and paternalistic China, the daughters nevertheless experience subtle forms of sexism inflected by racism, as well as inferiority complexes—to the extent of "internalized self-hatred"[65]—that derive from those experiences. Although Lena seems pleased that women often tell her they find her "'exotic'" (170), she also verbalizes all of the daughters' insecurities when she admits to worrying that her American boyfriend—later her husband—"would tell me I smelled bad," to which Rose responds that "thoughts" like those are "commonplace in women like us" (169). Even Waverly, the most assertive and outwardly successful of the daughters, admits to "self-loathing" (194). In all these instances, the daughters demonstrate that they have internalized the dominant American culture's racist equation of physiological difference with inferiority. Indeed, according to Sue Hum, Western forms of racism involve a process of positing "racial and ethnic bodies" as "not just different" but specifically "*different from* white bodies" and consequently inferior.[66] Perhaps in order to better assimilate into the dominant white culture and to move away from their Chineseness, which they seem to imagine in static terms and to associate with their mothers, some of the daughters choose to date and marry white American men. Their fears of their mothers' reactions further signal these daughters' tendency to posit Chinese and American as irreconcilable opposites, again as a result of internalizing the Western tendency to think in terms of fixed binaries. Rose recalls, for instance, her mother's disappointment when she dated and then married the non-Chinese Ted (123). For her part, Waverly fears telling her mother that she and Rich have decided to marry, because Rich is a redhead and she believes she can predict her mother's negative comments (193). The uncertainty and fear that suffuse the daughters' experiences with love relationships are thus inextricable from their complex racial, ethnic, gendered positioning; but, as a counterbalance, the Joy Luck Club offers them a familial, familiar, nurturing space within which they can negotiate their difficult positions as Chinese American women.

As adults, however, the daughters no longer actively participate in the Joy Luck Club gatherings; and, consequently, they not only see each other infrequently but also make little use of this community with which they grew up and with whom they share so much. Indeed, the novel depicts the adult daughters as overly individualistic, keeping to themselves and eschewing the community that the Joy Luck Club offers, and as suffering from a lack of confidence and self-worth. In their efforts to claim themselves to be Americans, they have embraced the American valuing of a self-interested, anticommunal form of individualism in their daily lives and have separated themselves too much from the community of Chinese Americans with whom they share strong affinities. Alone outside this community, and the support and possibilities it offers, the daughters tend to exist in a kind of stasis. They are stuck in positions of ambivalence with little hope for movement forward and development as individuals with agency. Part of the problem is that the daughters mistakenly equate their Chinese heritage with their mothers. Consequently, their American-style rebellions against their mothers include a rejection of their Chinese heritage and thus of part of their own identity.

The daughters do not understand that their mothers have internalized the traditional Chinese Confucian belief in "education as character building"[67] and act accordingly. The mothers in Tan's novel rule the home forcefully and take seriously their duty to bring up their children with a strong Chinese character at the same time they work to give them all that America has to offer.[68] For the daughters, however, this emphasis on a Chinese cultural character they do not understand feels like authoritarianism, one of the things their own mothers had themselves rebelled against in China. Indeed, as previously discussed, communication between the mothers and daughters is difficult not only because of generational conflicts but also because of an interlinked cultural and language gap: as Jing-mei recalls, her mother's explanations of Chinese customs or even games like mah jong did not make much sense, as each literally spoke a different language (23). Moreover, as a child, Jing-mei misunderstands and finally rebels against her mother's attempts to turn her into a child prodigy. Suyuan's belief that Jing-mei could become a prodigy derives from a combination of the Chinese/Confucian faith in educability and the American belief in the self-made person, which Jing-mei does not share. Rather than attempt to negotiate an understanding with her mother, however, Jing-mei decides to stop trying, justifying herself by claiming, "I won't be what I'm not" (144). Similarly, Waverly quits playing chess, even though she excels at the game, in order to punish her mother for supposedly taking credit for her wins and showing her off (187); when she begins to play again, however, Waverly loses the "feeling of supreme confidence" (189) with which she had always played and which she does not understand derived in part from her mother's unshakeable belief in her.

Neither Jing-mei nor Waverly can bear the kind of hope their mothers carry for them, which translates into the mothers' huge time and emotional investment in their daughters' accomplishments. In contrast to the traditional Chinese/Confucian family in which "the primary emotional tie was between mother and son,"[69] Tan's novel depicts a gendered shift in the mother's primary attachment from son to daughter. This shift is in keeping with the mothers' movement away from a patriarchal, hierarchical familial model in their shaping of the Joy Luck Club and their hopes for their daughters away from the particular oppressions they were made to suffer as women in China. Unable to analyze or understand the cultural bases of their mothers' actions and of the tension between themselves and their mothers, however, both Jing-mei and Waverly choose to separate themselves from both their mothers and the Chinese heritage they associate with their mothers. Sadly, the result is that they choose to isolate themselves from the community of Chinese Americans that make up the Joy Luck Club and the nurturing space from which they could negotiate Chinese American forms of identity and agency.

With the other two daughters, Lena and Rose, this double rejection of their mothers and Chinese culture takes the form of marrying white American men, although ironically this move actually links them to their mothers in terms of the patriarchal oppression the daughters experience in their marriages—albeit in a fashion different from their mothers' experiences in China. Lena's marriage to Harold is based outwardly on equality, which they put into practice by splitting all of their expenses evenly, but Lena slowly recognizes that this so-called equality masks a very real form of patriarchal oppression. Although they both work long hours at the architectural firm she encourages him to launch shortly after they become involved and although he successfully uses her ideas for the firm, he does not make her a partner and so continues to make much more money than she does (172–173). Harold's notion that keeping their finances separate will ensure their love thus proves a sham, since he has engineered a relationship in which he has the economic power in the household, given his significantly larger salary, which he then uses to procure other forms of power. For example, while it initially appears fair that Lena should pay a smaller percentage of the mortgage on the house they buy, given her lower earnings, as a result she owns a smaller percentage of it and, on the basis of his larger share, Harold has greater say in decisions about the house (175–176). Consequently, Lena is thrust into a more dependent position. She justifies her tacit acceptance of this position by attributing it to love (174). In many ways, this surrendering to him plays into the stereotype of the submissive Chinese woman, which is ironic given Lena's choice to distance herself from her Chinese heritage and which thus points to similarities between Chinese and American constructions of femininity.

The inequity of the situation comes to a head when Lena's mother, Ying-ying, comes to visit and points to the word "'ice cream'" on the list affixed to the refrigerator of purchases Harold has made during the week. Since Harold and Lena have agreed to split expenses only of the items they share, Ying-ying stands up for her daughter when she asserts that Lena neither likes nor ever eats ice cream (177)—something that Harold seems not to know about her.

Ying-ying's experience with patriarchal inequities back in China, where she was married to a man who cheated on her, enables her both to recognize the oppressive aspects of Lena's marriage and to push Lena into asserting herself, into acting on her own behalf. Indeed, after her mother goes up to bed, Lena finally speaks up and tells Harold that she hates the way they "account for everything" (179) and wants a change. When shortly thereafter the wobbly guest-room bedside table collapses, sending a vase of flowers crashing to the floor, Lena asserts that she "knew it would happen." Ying-ying's response, "Then why you don't stop it?" (180–181), clearly addresses Lena's failure to do something about not only the table but also, more importantly, the aspects of her marriage that prove oppressive and thus affirms support for Lena's new-found voice within her marriage.

Rose's marriage is more overtly inequitable from its inception. In response to their parents' disapproval of their interracial relationship, not only had Rose and Ted clung to each other but also Rose admits to playing "victim to his hero" (125). Neither seems to notice the Orientalist aspect of positioning Rose as the weak, victimized woman; indeed, Ted places Rose within one of the prevalent American stereotypes of Chinese women, which Ling refers to as the fragile "China Doll: demure, diminutive, and deferential [. . .] devoted body and soul to serving ['her man']."[70] As Rose understands in retrospect, they become addicted to the roles they have chosen. Their whole relationship thus relies on her dependence on Ted and his making all the decisions (125–126). Ted holds power within American culture based on his position as a successful white doctor with a wife who depends on him completely. After Ted loses a big malpractice suit and no longer feels all-powerful, however, he begins to blame Rose for never making decisions and, thus, taking no responsibility or blame for anything (126); eventually, he demands a divorce. Accepting the position of victim and dependent thus backfires on Rose when Ted can no longer play the hero. Years of living in her husband's shadow leaves her with no sense of self and thus points to the oppressive quality of her marriage.

Moreover, having never made decisions, Rose becomes overwhelmed when faced with "too many choices" (214). When she talks about her impending divorce with her Joy Luck Club peers, her confusion is reflected in the "different story" (210) she tells each person. Although Waverly and Lena stick up for her and blame Ted, Rose initially chooses to isolate herself rather than make use of the supportive community that these women represent. Unable to make a decision with regard to signing the divorce papers Ted has sent her, Rose again chooses the passive victim position by staying in bed and taking sleeping pills (215). After learning from Ted that he needs the divorce papers signed immediately because he wants to remarry, however, Rose finally chooses to face the situation head on. Moreover, she unconsciously heeds her mother An-mei's advice to "speak up for yourself" (216), something An-mei understands only too well, given that her own mother had no voice—as third concubine to a man who initially raped her as a means of obtaining her as a concubine—and could assert herself only through suicide. Having experienced patriarchal oppression themselves, Waverly, Lena, and An-mei all recognize it when they see it; and they function here to collectively provide Rose a supportive space within which to assert herself as a subject capable of constructive agency.[71] Facing up to Ted, Rose refuses to sign the divorce papers and instructs him to wait for the papers her own lawyer will serve him; asserts that she intends to keep the house she loves; and justifies herself by telling him in person that he cannot just discard her. Rose thus forces Ted to view her as a subject with agency rather than as a victim or a shadow and thereby drastically changes the power dynamics between them. Indeed, she reads the power that her words have in his "confused, then scared" eyes (219).

In the case of all four daughters, movement forward involves an assertion of agency dependent on some reconnection to the Chinese American community—although the degree to which this happens differs. Since arguably Lena and Rose have distanced themselves most fully from their Chinese American extended family and from their Chinese heritage, the reconnections that the novel depicts for them remain small, limited instances. Consequently, their acts of assertion remain first steps that open up possibilities for further agency. For Lena, her mother's visit provides such an instance of reconnection. During the episode in which Lena defends her mother's claim that she (Lena) has never liked ice cream, for instance, Lena reports that Harold looks taken aback as if she "too, were speaking Chinese" (177), thus linking herself not only with her mother but also with the Chinese part of her identity. Moreover, the collective claim by mother and daughter about the ice cream creates a bond between the two that in and of itself serves as an act of assertion and, subsequently, emboldens Lena not only to "cross out 'ice cream'" on Harold's list of purchases but also to question openly the basis of their marriage (179–180).

For Rose, the reconnection with her Chinese American family and heritage comes from conversations with Waverly and Lena about her marital problems and from her mother's encouragement that she express herself, as well as her thinking of herself as Chinese when she makes use of Chinese words to describe her condition (210), all of which allow her to assert herself as agent rather than victim when discussing the divorce with Ted. The novel thus presents Lena and Rose as beginning to assert themselves as agents in order to deal in different ways with marriages that have included structures of patriarchal oppression, which in turn offers hope for their futures as agents;

in both cases, agency is triggered by the support they receive from members of their immediate and extended Chinese American family.

In the cases of Waverly and Jing-mei, who have retained closer ties to their Chinese American families, the novel depicts much stronger reconnections to these families and their heritage and a higher degree of agency—but, in the cases of all four daughters, individual agency is overtly linked to the individual's position within and dependence on a nurturing community. The only one to remain unmarried and working close to her parents' home, Jing-mei has more contact with her immediate family and consequently with members of her extended Joy Luck Club family (223). Marrying a Chinese American and then raising a Chinese American child as a single mother similarly keeps Waverly in closer contact with her immediate and extended family. For example, Jing-mei and Waverly both attend the Chinese New Year dinner that Suyuan hosts, which brings together a number of members of each of their immediate families and thus also of their extended Joy Luck Club family.

Although Waverly has remained more connected to her Chinese American family and heritage because of her personal circumstances, the friction between herself and her mother creates an unease toward her Chinese heritage that parallels that of the other daughters. Consequently, as with the other daughters, the novel depicts the rapprochement between Waverly and her mother and between Waverly and her Chinese heritage as intertwined. Arriving one day to vent her anger at her mother but finding her asleep on a couch, Waverly is stunned to see her formidable mother-opponent looking not only "frail, guileless, and innocent" (199) but also "powerless" (200). Although when Lindo awakes, the mother–daughter battle resumes, Waverly begins to understand what she "had been fighting for: It was for me" (203)— for an identity separate from and yet accepted by her mother. This recognition allows Waverly to separate her Chinese heritage from her mother. Indeed, Waverly and her white fiancé, Rich, choose China as the destination for their upcoming honeymoon (204), indicating Waverly's wish to connect more firmly with the part of her that is Chinese. This choice to go to China denotes not only Waverly's assertion of herself as a subject with agency but also hope with regard to the future. Tan's text even hints that Lindo may accompany the couple to China, a likelihood that Waverly envisions simultaneously as a disaster waiting to happen and as a utopian resolution allowing them—Chinese-born Chinese American mother, American-born Chinese American daughter, and white American son-in-law and husband—to leave their "differences behind" (205). This double vision of her trip to China if her mother were to come along demonstrates Waverly's recognition that her individual relationship with her mother is not synonymous with her Chinese identity. She now can separate out how she would hate spending three weeks with her mother from how "perfect" it would be to sit "side by side, [...], moving West to reach the East" (205). The novel here emphasizes China and its heritage rather than genealogy as establishing a positive, forward-looking link between Waverly and her mother.

Both mother and daughter work actively to negotiate a space not only for a better mother–daughter relationship but also for each to help the other engage in the ongoing work of identity formation. When Waverly insists that her mother have her hair done for the wedding at the chic boutique she frequents, she is stunned by the hairdresser's assertion that they look so much alike. Although Lindo notes to herself in a critical tone that Americans tend to talk to their reflections rather than to each other, her American side surfaces when she and Waverly examine their images in the mirror to judge the hairdresser's claim (290–291). Lindo sees that Waverly has "the same eyes, the same cheeks, the same chin" (303) as herself, thus reinforcing their genealogical tie, but she also knows that Waverly does not look completely Chinese. Even more striking is Lindo's admission that, when she went back to China after many years, the people there "knew my face was not one hundred percent Chinese" (305). This acknowledgment that neither mother nor daughter can pass as Chinese in China highlights not only that there is no such thing as an authentic Chineseness but also that Chineseness is a fluid construct that is contextual and at the same time connected to certain physiological characteristics. As Hum argues, "Embodied enactments of Chineseness shift according to locale" at least in part because "physiologically marked bodies exhibit posture and movement that are environment specific."[72] What connects mother and daughter is thus not merely genealogy but more crucially their positions as Chinese American women who must continuously negotiate identities for themselves that are neither Chinese nor American but, rather, necessarily hybrid.

This process—moving past individual mother–daughter conflicts and thus severing for the daughter the linkage of mother and Chinese heritage in order to negotiate a healthy Chinese American identity that enables agency—is complicated for Jing-mei by her mother's death. Made to take her mother's place at the Joy Luck Club mah-jong table after her death only amplifies Jing-mei's equation of her mother with Chinese culture. Indeed, the cultural gap that separates her from her mother becomes overt when she talks with her three Joy Luck Club aunties about the trip they want her to take to China to meet her half sisters, for which they have handed her a check for $1,200; indeed, Jing-mei notes the parallels between her aunties and her mother, as well as between herself and her aunties' daughters. Most forcefully, Jing-mei sees not only her aunties' "generosity" and "loyalty" (30) but also their fear when she acknowledges she does not know very much about her mother: she reminds them of "their own daughters, just as ignorant, just as unmindful of all the truths and hopes they have brought to America" (31). Despite her fears however, Jing-mei chooses to do her part in the Joy Luck Club aunties' plan to complete their friend's "unfinished business" (5), a plan based upon a notion of and made possible by the women's collective agency.[73] That this plan feeds off and continues the hope that has sustained the mothers indicates that Jing-mei is also choosing hope in its Chinese American inflected form constructed by these immigrant mothers.

Jing-mei's trip to China with her father to meet her mother's twin daughters from a previous marriage not only brings to fruition Suyuan's dream of finding the twin girls but also functions as a means for Jing-mei to explore the Chinese side of her Chinese American identity, which she has suppressed for years. This suppression is rooted at least in part in her own reductive association of Chineseness with things her mother did to embarrass her—such as haggling in stores or wearing strange combinations of colors (307)—suggesting that she has internalized a static notion of an authentic Chineseness with clear Eurocentric and, indeed, racist overtones. Her trip to China educates her into a broader and more fluid notion of Chineseness.

Although she recalls her mother's assertions that being Chinese "is in your blood," Jing-mei's feeling upon her arrival in China that she is "becoming Chinese" appears connected not to some biological imperative but rather to an emotional reaction to her cultural surroundings, to the place itself (306).[74] Moreover, Jing-mei's notion of *becoming* Chinese indicates a *process* rather than a *being* and thus reinforces the novel's overall insistence on identity as always in process and as necessarily culturally mediated rather than dependent solely on genealogy or biology. Jing-mei feels more connections with her Chinese heritage when physically in China and at the same time remains aware of her foreignness despite her direct genealogical ties to China, including overt racial markers imprinted on her physique. As Hum argues, "Chineseness cannot be delineated neatly within biological origins or geographical borders" and "is not a natural, static condition"; rather race and ethnicity are always "dependent on temporal and spatial contingencies."[75] That Jing-mei remembers her mother telling her that she was tall like her grandfather, who was said to have "Mongol blood" (312), further highlights the hybrid quality of Chineseness even before Americanness is thrown into the equation. By demonstrating that there is no such thing as an authentic Chineseness, Tan's novel makes space for her women characters to take control of the construction of their own hybrid Chinese American identities.

In addition, the novel presents China itself as a dynamic rather than a static entity. The China Jing-mei encounters on her trip differs in many ways from the China depicted to her by her parents, which was based on their memories of pre–World War II China and colored by various revisionist impulses. Most significantly, since her parents' emigration, China has experienced a political shift to communism, has developed technologically, and has had to develop trade with the West in order to participate in an increasingly global economy. Consequently, Jing-mei must readjust her simplistic notions of China as the antithesis of the United States when she notes that the city of Guangzhou does not look much different from many American cities—which does not coincide with her American-inflected idea of "communist China" (318). Her subsequent discovery that the high rises coexist with tiny shops and bamboo scaffolding and that her hotel room offers both a minibar containing American sodas and shampoo with "the consistency and color of hoisin sauce" (319–320) forces her to view China as a dynamic culture that is itself negotiating—much like Jing-mei herself—its own cultural traditions with those it has inherited from the West.

When Jing-mei finally meets her twin sisters, she is initially startled that they do not look like their mother. However, she notes in them something familiar, which triggers a recognition of the part of her that is Chinese: "It is so obvious. It is my family" (331). When minutes later she examines the Polaroid picture her father takes of her with the twins, Jing-mei notes that "together we look like our mother" (332). Although many scholars have criticized the ending of *The Joy Luck Club* for depending on what David Li calls a kind of "chromosomal trope of cultural reproduction,"[76] I would argue that Tan's novel as a whole presents a more complex picture of cultural reproduction that places emphasis on the family over and above genetics. Indeed, the entire novel stresses not only the role of the family in cultural production and reproduction but also the dynamic possibilities of conceptions of the extended family with ties based on friendship, empathy, and care. Jing-mei's recognition that her family—and not just her mother—represents the part of her that is Chinese indicates a more inclusive notion of family that pushes beyond mere genealogy despite her subsequent reference to blood ties. What connects Jing-mei to her half sisters is not just a common genetic pool but, more crucially, their shared pain of having lost a loving mother. Furthermore, they share their mother's Chinese-inflected valuing of family, which she put into practice as she raised her Chinese American family in the United States and, simultaneously, continued to search via letters for her twin daughters in China. That their resemblance to their mother occurs only when they appear together on the Polaroid is a function not so much of genetics but rather of their meeting's representing Suyuan's dream of bringing together the children of her two different marriages and lives in different geographical spaces and cultural traditions. For Jing-mei, meeting her half sisters provides her with a closer connection not only to her mother, about whose past life and pains she knew so little, but also to her Chinese cultural heritage.[77] Having flown halfway around the globe to China, Jing-mei locates the part of her that is Chinese in her family; but, as the novel makes clear throughout its pages, her family includes not only her immediate nuclear family but also an extended family: her two half sisters in China and the members of the Joy Luck Club at home in San Francisco. Moreover, her extended family connects her to the part of her that is Chinese precisely because it is the site of the production and reproduction of ever-evolving Chinese cultural traditions.

Tan's novel depicts all four mothers and daughters as actively negotiating their identities as Chinese Americans in order to assert themselves as subjects with agency, albeit in different ways and to differing extents. Although part of that process of negotiation occurs on the level of mother–daughter relation-ships, what ultimately reconnects the mothers and daughters are not their genetic ties but rather certain parallel experiences as women marked by their Chinese heritage—particularly experiences of patriarchal oppression within familial relationships, racially marked oppression within American culture, and the difficult negotiation of a Chinese American identity.[78] Moreover, the parallels between the four mother–daughter relationships and the existence of the Joy Luck Club as a community that encompasses and at times helps to negotiate these relationships highlights an interdependence that extends beyond the mother–daughter relationships. *The Joy Luck Club* thus partici-pates in what Chu describes as a tendency within Asian American writing to invent "a subject who combines independence, mobility and outspokenness with a deep sense of affinity with familial and communal others."[79]

The novel's positioning of the four mother–daughter relationships within the larger context of the Joy Luck Club community not only shifts atten-tion away from an exclusive focus on the mother–daughter dyads but also offers a larger, more dynamic familial structure that does not depend solely on genealogy and thus offers the flexibility that Chinese immigrants and their descendants require if they are to create communities to sustain their Chinese heritage while living in the United States and within the context of Ameri-can culture.[80] For example, Jing-mei's reconnection with her mother through her meeting of her twin half sisters and with her Chinese heritage through both her physical trip to China and her understanding of the function of her family as a bridge to her Chinese heritage occurs as a consequence of the existence of the Joy Luck Club. Without the caring, interdependent relation-ships that the Joy Luck Club provides for the mothers, Suyuan's search for her daughters would most likely have died with her own physical death. Not only do the Joy Luck Club aunties know of Suyuan's relentless quest—which she had not shared with either her husband or daughter—but they organize the meeting between Jing-mei and her twin half sisters by writing to the twins in Chinese (something Jing-mei cannot do) and raising the money necessary to send Jing-mei to China. The aunties' assertion as Suyuan's friends-sisters and their collective agency in making Suyuan's wish come true, as well as Jing-mei's assertion of self and of individual agency in undertaking the trip to China, thus both depend on the Joy Luck Club as a collective entity with collective agency that makes possible individual agency. As Chu notes, *The Joy Luck Club* is "a novel whose multiple narratives construct both mothers and daughters as Asian [more specifically, Chinese] American subjects";[81] but I want to add that this construction occurs crucially within the context of a dynamic, extended family-community.

Through its depiction of the Joy Luck Club, Amy Tan's novel offers a useful model for reimagining agency at the turn of the twenty-first century within the context of the United States as an immigrant nation that is growing increasingly multicultural. This multicultural aspect of the United States creates not only tensions but also the possibility of coalition building to deal with those tensions and of creating new frameworks out of the various traditions brought to this country in order to negotiate an ever-changing contemporary culture.[82] The Joy Luck Club borrows the Chinese valuing of the family and its relationships of interdependence but alters traditional Confucian notions of the family to get rid of the hierarchies of power and dependence on patrilineage that structure them. Through a more symmetrical distribution of power, the Joy Luck Club retains different roles for its various members while simultaneously rejecting a hierarchical structure. For example, although the mothers cook the meals for the club gatherings and play mah jong while their husbands play cards after the meal, the mothers share with their husbands an equal, democratic voice and vote in Joy Luck Club decisions. Moreover, the club values but does not privilege blood ties; indeed, the novel depicts a number of connecting threads between the various members of the Joy Luck Club, with the primary ones being a function of their positions as first- or second-generation Chinese immigrants to the United States. Positionality and affect rather than blood ties prove to be the real glue between Joy Luck Club members, even between mothers and daughters. Moreover, the characters' sense of hope, derived from a blend of the Chinese notion of fate and the American dream, both of which contain and celebrate a participatory element, provides the impetus for their developments as agents within the context of the collective.

Although some critics have objected to the novel's ending as overly utopian, I see this utopian ending as serving the vital function of consolidating its hopeful evocation of an alternative form of familial community as necessary both for the characters' survival and for their assertion of agency. Indeed, the novel offers an alternative model of kinship based on affinities deriving from specific cultural positioning, which creates a familial community that values caring interdependence as politically efficacious in that it makes possible the negotiation of collective identity and agency and in turn of individual identity and agency within the context of the collectivity. Tan's novel thus offers a vision of Chinese American women characters who are contributing to what Ho calls "an American culture-in-the-making"[83] through their active construction of alternative, hybrid forms of identity and agency that emphasize the interconnectedness of the individual and the collective.

NOTES

1. Elaine Kim notes in her groundbreaking *Asian American Literature* (1982) that "the theme that underscores the contemporary body of Asian American literature is the need for community" (278). Tan's novel continues this trend.

2. Shanahan, *Toward a Genealogy of Individualism*, p. 128.

3. Brannigan, *Striking a Balance*, p. 242.

4. Shen similarly notes that *The Joy Luck Club* "presents a continuous whole more meaningful than the sum of its parts" ("Born of a Stranger," p. 235).

5. McAlister, "(Mis)reading *The Joy Luck Club*," p. 103.

6. Ho, *In Her Mother's House*, pp. 149, 150.

7. Ibid., p. 151.

8. Tan, *The Joy Luck Club*, 45. Excerpts from *The Joy Luck Club* by Amy Tan, copyright © 1989 by Amy Tan. Published by G. P. Putnam's Sons, a division of Penguin Group (USA) Inc. Subsequent citations of *The Joy Luck Club* will appear parenthetically in the text by page number.

9. Tronto argues that "women remain almost entirely excluded from power in political, economic, and cultural institutions of importance in the United States" (*Moral Boundaries*, pp. 1–2).

10. Ibid., pp. 21, 162, 3, 157, 172. Tronto further notes that "care is also devalued conceptually through a connection with privacy, with emotion, and with the needy" within the context of Western cultures that value "public accomplishment, rationality, and autonomy" (117); and she argues for a "shift from the dilemma of autonomy or dependency to a more sophisticated sense of human interdependence" (101). This argument nicely complements my discussion of Tan's novel as presenting a notion of individual identity and agency *within* the collective.

11. Jaggar, "Toward a Feminist Conception," p. 132.

12. Davis argues that the novel's structure is that of "the short story cycle," in which "the constituent narratives are simultaneously independent and interdependent" ("Identity in Community," p. 4). Souris refers to Tan's use of multiple narrators and stories as "the decentered, multiple monologue mode" in the style of Woolf and Faulkner and examines "the possibilities of connection across segments" using the theories of Mikhail Bakhtin and Wolfgang Iser ("'Only Two Kinds of Daughters,'" p. 2).

13. Singer, "Moving Forward to Reach the Past," p. 334.

14. Davis argues that "the short story cycle [as a literary form] looks back to oral traditions of narrative" ("Identity in Community," p. 4).

15. Ho, *In Her Mother's House*, p. 82.

16. Grice, "Asian American Fiction," p. 135.

17. Ling, "Chinese American Women Writers," p. 219. Ling further adds that "for women brought up in the old Chinese tradition that for eighteen hundred years codified their obedience and submission to the men in their lives [. . .] any writing at all was unusual, even an act of rebellion" (219).

18. Ling, *Between Worlds*, p. 1.

19. Chu, *Assimilating Asians*, p. 3.

20. I thus disagree with critics who argue that the characters blend or dissolve into each other. For example, Heung asserts that the "interconnections between motif, character, and incident finally dissolve individualized character and plot and instead collectivize them into an aggregate meaning existing outside the individual stories themselves" ("Daughter-Text/Mother-Text," p. 612). Rather than dissolving, I am arguing that the individual characters retain their integrities at the same time they contribute to a collective representation.

21. In a much more general sense, Singer also argues that "Tan's form and content are complementary rather than counterpoised" ("Moving Forward to Reach the Past," p. 328).

22. Shear similarly notes that "the Joy Luck Club itself is the determination to hope in the face of constantly altering social situations and continually shifting rules" ("Generational Differences," p. 195).

23. Manning, *The Common Thread*, p. 33.

24. Lee, "Organizing in the Chinese American Community," pp. 120, 121.

25. Ling, *Between Worlds*, pp. 1, 2.

26. For example, Slote and De Vos make the sweeping argument that "the family constitutes the central element of those societies that have been profoundly influenced by the Confucian, and later Neo-Confucian, mandate" (Introduction, p. ix).

27. Tu, "Probing," p. 124.

28. Cua, "Confucian Philosophy, Chinese," p. 540.

29. Brannigan, *Striking a Balance*, p. 190.

30. Slote, "Psychocultural Dynamics," pp. 37, 46.

31. Ling, *Between Worlds*, pp. 6, 3.

32. Slote, "Psychocultural Dynamics," p. 38.

33. Ling, *Between Worlds*, pp. 1, 6.

34. Ibid., p. 9.

35. Tu, "Confucius and Confucianism," p. 33.

36. Chu, *Assimilating Asians*, pp. 156, 165.

37. Kuo, "Confucianism and the Chinese Family," p. 244. Although Kuo's discussion focuses on Chinese immigrants to Singapore, some of his broad statements such as this one seem potentially applicable to Chinese immigrants to other places, such as the United States.

38. The formation of the Joy Luck Club thus exemplifies Lowe's more general claim that "the making of Asian American culture includes practices that are partly inherited, partly modified, as well as partly invented" (*Immigrant Acts*, p. 65). Furthermore, using Ho's terms, I would argue that the Joy Luck Club "articulate[s] the private and domestic/familial experiences as significant sites in which identity and culture are negotiated and contested" (*In Her Mother's House*, p. 102).

39. Slote, "Psychocultural Dynamics," p. 38.

40. Ho, *In Her Mother's House*, p. 183. Although Ho's argument parallels mine as she focuses on how the women form "an extended family," "a network of women loving, nurturing, learning, and caring for each other collectively" (183), I would add

that the Joy Luck Club includes the women's husbands and children and thus is a larger extended family and collectivity.

41. Heung, "Daughter-Text/Mother-Text," p. 602.

42. For example, Bow criticizes *The Joy Luck Club* on the basis that "the maternal connection is mystified as a genetic inheritance" so that the novel "uses a racialized discourse of genetics to explain [. . .] women's connection" (*Betrayal and Other Acts of Subversion*, p. 95); and Li blasts the novel's "appeal to blood heritage and ancestral subconscious" as being "regressively feudal and antidemocratic" (*Imagining the Nation*, p. 124).

43. Hamilton, "Feng Shui," pp. 11, 7.

44. Chu, *Assimilating Asians*, pp. 157, 152.

45. Sau-Ling Wong, "'Sugar Sisterhood,'" p. 185. Although Wong is on target when she warns that these retrospective stories fall into a "quasi-ethnographic, Orientalist discourse" even if the novel at the same time offers "anti-Orientalist statements" (181), I would argue that the novel's overt framing of the stories with references to the present-day United States highlights that Orientalist potential and thus implicitly criticizes it. Bow notes that "Asian American literary texts may also replicate normative American values (and apply them to Asia)" (*Betrayal and Other Acts of Subversion*, p. 20). Yuan's argument that the mothers' stories are "informed by a complex process of translation, translocation, and transfiguration of the original experiences in China" ("The Semiotics of China Narratives," p. 292) most clearly approximates my point.

46. Yuan, "Mothers' 'China Narrative,'" p. 352. Yuan further explains that "recollection" is "a dialectical process in which the past and the present engage each other in a continuous dialogue, each revising and configuring the other endlessly" (353).

47. Heung, "Daughter-Text/Mother-Text," p. 607. Yuan also notes that, for the mothers in Tan's novel, "recollection becomes an imaginative process of self-creation," a "strategy for self-affirmation and self-construction" ("Mothers' 'China Narrative,'" pp. 358, 356).

48. Indeed, many critics read the mothers as more static characters: Bow argues that individualism is "denied the mothers' generation" (*Betrayal and Other Acts of Subversion*, p. 97); Kafka argues that "the mothers remain fixed, of the past" (*[Un]doing the Missionary Position*, p. 18); and Li argues that the mothers' "minds and memories are forever mummified in their ancestral land" (*Imagining the Nation*, p. 115). In contrast, I read Tan's novel as presenting the mothers as evolving characters who must themselves negotiate a Chinese American identity.

49. Gupta, Introduction, p. 11. Although Gupta focuses primarily on South Asian immigrants from India in her discussion, these particular comments are in concert with Tan's presentation of the mothers in her novel.

50. Ho, *In Her Mother's House*, p. 23.

51. Espiritu, "Race, Class, and Gender," p. 140.

52. Bow, *Betrayal and Other Acts of Subversion*, p. 28. Bow further argues that "the gender position of Asian women improved upon immigration as a direct result of the disruption of the social fabric of the family" (28).

53. Slote, "Psychocultural Dynamics," pp. 39, 41.

54. Lee, "Organizing in the Chinese American Community," p. 121.

55. Kafka argues that Ying-ying "has traded in the harshest forms of gender asymmetry in China for inauthenticity—for a benign gender asymmetry in the

United States [and in her marriage to a white Irish man], but gender asymmetry, nevertheless" (*[Un]doing the Missionary Position*, p. 18).

56. Lowe, *Immigrant Acts*, p. 64.

57. Maffesoli, *The Time of the Tribes*, p. 17.

58. Tu, "Confucius and Confucianism," p. 13.

59. Pahl, *On Friendship*, pp. 1, 8. Pahl also notes that "friendship is about hope" (165), which further links his argument to Tan's text.

60. Ling, *Between Worlds*, p. 20. Hagehorn makes the point that, for Chinese Americans, "our ethnic roots can indeed be traced to Asia, but the ties to America are just as binding" ("Foreword," p. ix).

61. Ho, *In Her Mother's House*, pp. 165, 166.

62. Ibid., p. 157.

63. Hum, "Articulating Authentic Chineseness," p. 67.

64. Ho, *In Her Mother's House*, p. 171. McAlister develops more fully the notion that "the embarrassed and angry responses the daughters have to their mothers are often class- as well as racially-based" ("[Mis]Reading The Joy Luck Club," p. 113).

65. Ho, *In Her Mother's House*, p. 168.

66. Hum, "Articulating Authentic Chineseness," p. 73.

67. Tu, "Confucius and Confucianism," p. 4.

68. Slote explains that, "although all Confucian societies are male dominant, within the home it was the mother who was the primary force. It was she who ran the household and brought up the children" ("Psychocultural Dynamics," pp. 40–41). Chu notes that, "for Asian American women, the culturally assigned roles of materially preserving the family and upholding traditional ways pose multiple problems in their efforts to claim authorship, Americanness, and agency" (*Assimilating Asians*, p. 5).

69. Slote, "Psychocultural Dynamics," p. 42.

70. Ling, *Between Worlds*, p. 11.

71. Bow notes the mothers' and daughters' "recognition of a commonality of experience based on their subordination as women" (*Betrayal and Other Acts of Subversion*, p. 93), but I would argue that this recognition occurs among peers—mothers and mothers, daughters and daughters—as well as among mother–daughter pairs.

72. Hum, "Articulating Authentic Chineseness," pp. 62, 67.

73. Davis notes that the Joy Luck Club "prevails in the renewed relationships between first and second generation women who gather around the mah-jong table" ("Identity in Community," p. 14).

74. Chu reads the novel's ending with Jing-mei's trip to China "as gesturing beyond intercultural understanding within America toward a horizon of international cooperation between China and the United States" (*Assimilating Asians*, p. 143).

75. Hum, "Articulating Authentic Chineseness," pp. 61, 68, 79–80.

76. Li, *Imagining the Nation*, p. 124.

77. Heung argues that Jing-mei's reunion with her sisters performs a "melding of cross-cultural linkages" ("Daughter-Text/Mother-Text," p. 610).

78. Bow argues that Tan's novel "locates the mother/daughter relationship as the site for a reenvisioning of self both based on and potentially transcending a maternal legacy" (*Betrayal and Other Acts of Subversion*, p. 71). My argument focuses

on the Joy Luck Club as encompassing the mother–daughter relationships and thus as the site for such a reenvisioning of self and of agency.

79. Chu, *Assimilating Asians*, p. 18.

80. As Heung similarly notes, "Mutual nurturance does not arise from biological or generational connections alone; rather, it is an act affirming consciously chosen allegiances" ("Daughter-Text/Mother-Text," p. 613).

81. Chu, *Assimilating Asians*, p. 22.

82. Matsuda notes that "our [Asian American] coalition does not originate in Asia. It is American" (*Where Is Your Body?* p. 173).

83. Ho, *In Her Mother's House*, p. 39.

Chronology

1952   Amy Ruth Tan born on February 19 in Oakland, California, to John Yueh-han, a Baptist minister and Beijing-educated electrical engineer, and Daisy (Tu Ching) Tan, a vocational nurse and member of a Joy Luck Club.

1960   First published work, "What the Library Means to Me," appears in the Santa Rosa *Press Democrat*.

1967   Older brother Peter dies of a brain tumor; seven months later, father dies of a brain tumor; shortly afterward, doctors discover that mother has a benign brain tumor. Mother reveals that she had been married to an abusive man in China and has three daughters whom she lost track of after the Communists came to power. After deaths of brother and father, mother takes Amy and her younger brother, John Jr., to live in Switzerland.

1970   Mother sends Amy to Baptist college in Oregon; Amy abandons pre-med studies to pursue study of English and linguistics; follows her boyfriend, Louis M. DeMattei, to San Jose City College.

1973   Receives B.A. in English and linguistics from San Jose State University. Holds various odd jobs.

1974   Receives M.A. from San Jose State University. On April 6 marries DeMattei, a tax attorney.

173

1974–1976	Enrolled in doctoral program at University of California, Santa Cruz, and later at Berkeley, through 1976. Leaves doctoral studies to pursue interest in working with the developmentally disabled as a language development consultant to the Alameda County Association for Retarded Citizens.
1976–1981	Language consultant to programs for disabled children, Alameda County Association for Retarded Citizens.
1980–1981	Project director, MORE Project, San Francisco. Freelance business writer.
1981–1983	Reporter, managing editor, and associate publisher for *Emergency Room Reports*.
1985	Short story, "Endgame," published in *Seventeen* magazine. Publishing agent asks her to write a book outline.
1983–1987	Freelance technical writer; begins writing fiction and taking jazz piano lessons as a form of therapy to engage her workaholic energies. In 1987, accompanies her mother to China for a reunion with the three other daughters. Publishing agent asks her to write a book based on the 1985 outline. Quits business writing to finish the work, complete in four months, which becomes *The Joy Luck Club*.
1989	*The Joy Luck Club* published; nominated for National Book Critics Circle award for best novel; on *New York Times* bestseller list for eight months. A short story, "Two Kinds," published in *Atlantic*.
1990	Critical essays, "The Language of Discretion" and "Mother Tongue," published.
1991	*The Kitchen God's Wife* published. Receives Best American Essays award.
1992	*The Moon Lady*, a children's book, published.
1993	Writes screenplay, with Ronald Bass, for *The Joy Luck Club*.
1994	*The Siamese Cat*, a children's book, published.
1995	*The Hundred Secret Senses* published.
2001	*The Bonesetter's Daughter* published.
2003	*The Opposite of Fate: A Book of Musings* published.
2005	*Saving Fish from Drowning* published.

Contributors

HAROLD BLOOM is Sterling Professor of the Humanities at Yale University. He is the author of 30 books, including *Shelley's Mythmaking*, *The Visionary Company*, *Blake's Apocalypse*, *Yeats*, *A Map of Misreading*, *Kabbalah and Criticism*, *Agon: Toward a Theory of Revisionism*, *The American Religion*, *The Western Canon*, and *Omens of Millennium: The Gnosis of Angels, Dreams, and Resurrection*. *The Anxiety of Influence* sets forth Professor Bloom's provocative theory of the literary relationships between the great writers and their predecessors. His most recent books include *Shakespeare: The Invention of the Human*, a 1998 National Book Award finalist, *How to Read and Why*, *Genius: A Mosaic of One Hundred Exemplary Creative Minds*, *Hamlet: Poem Unlimited*, *Where Shall Wisdom Be Found?*, and *Jesus and Yahweh: The Names Divine*. In 1999, Professor Bloom received the prestigious American Academy of Arts and Letters Gold Medal for Criticism. He has also received the International Prize of Catalonia, the Alfonso Reyes Prize of Mexico, and the Hans Christian Andersen Bicentennial Prize of Denmark.

GLORIA SHEN is part of the faculty in the Department of Asian Languages and Culture at Rutgers University. She teaches classical Chinese poetry, Chinese classics and thought, and modern Chinese fiction.

M. MARIE BOOTH FOSTER has been a professor of English and vice president for instruction at Central Florida Community College. She is the author of *A Bibliography of Southern Black Creative Writers, 1829–1953*.

STEVEN P. SONDRUP teaches in the Humanities Classics and Comparative Literature Department at Brigham Young University. He is the author of *Expanding Borders: Studies in Nonfictional Romantic Prose* and has been a coeditor of titles as well.

ZENOBIA MISTRI is an associate professor of English at Purdue University Calumet, where she has also been acting head of composition. She has written reviews and essays for journals. Among her areas of specialization is mothers and daughters in literature.

RONALD EMERICK is a professor in the English department at Indiana University of Pennsylvania. He is the coauthor of *The Influence of Music on American Literature Since 1890: A History of Aesthetic Counterpoint.*

PATRICIA L. HAMILTON is an associate professor in the English department at Union University in Tennessee. Her work has appeared in *Eighteenth-Century Fiction.*

MARC SINGER received his Ph.D. from the English department at the University of Maryland, where he completed a dissertation on alternate modes of temporality in twentieth-century American literature. He has published essays in *African American Review.*

YUAN YUAN is a professor in the Literature and Writing Department at California State University, San Marcos, where he has also been chairperson of the department. He is the author of *The Discourse of Fantasy*; translator of Saul Bellow's novel *The Adventures of Augie March*; editor of the *Journal of the Fantastic in the Arts,* Special Issue on Dream and Narrative Space; and associate editor for the *Journal of the Association for the Interdisciplinary Study of the Arts.*

BELLA ADAMS has been a lecturer in English at Liverpool Hope University College. She is the author of *Amy Tan* and *Asian American Literature.*

MAGALI CORNIER MICHAEL is a professor of English and the department chairperson at Duquesne University. She is the author of *Feminism and the Postmodern Impulse: Post-World War II Fiction.* Her writing has also appeared in various texts and journals.

Bibliography

Adams, Bella. "Becoming Chinese: Racial Ambiguity in Amy Tan's *The Joy Luck Club*." In *Literature and Racial Ambiguity*, edited by Teresa Hubel and Neil Brooks, pp. 93–115. Amsterdam, Netherlands: Rodopi, 2002.

———. *Amy Tan*. Manchester; New York: Manchester University Press, 2005.

Arfaoui, Sihem. "Feeding the Memory with Culinary Resistance: The Woman Warrior: *Memoirs of a Girlhood Among Ghosts, The Joy Luck Club* and *The Kitchen God's Wife*." *Interactions: Aegean Journal of English and American Studies* 15, no. 2 (Fall 2006): 37–48.

Boldt, Chris. "Why Is the Moon Lady in Amy Tan's *The Joy Luck Club* Revealed to Be a Man?" *Notes on Contemporary Literature* 24, no. 4 (September 1994): 9–10.

Bow, Leslie. "Cultural Conflict/Feminist Resolution in Amy Tan's *The Joy Luck Club*." In *New Visions in Asian American Studies: Diversity, Community, Power*, edited by Franklin Ng, Judy Yung, Stephen S. Fugita, Elaine H. Kim, pp. 235–47. Pullman: Washington State University Press, 1994.

———. "*The Joy Luck Club* by Amy Tan." In *A Resource Guide to Asian American Literature*, edited by Sau-ling Cynthia Wong and Stephen H. Sumida, pp. 159–71. New York, N.Y.: Modern Language Association of America, 2001.

Braendlin, Bonnie. "Mother/Daughter Dialog(ic)s in, around, and about Amy Tan's *The Joy Luck Club*." In *Private Voices, Public Lives: Women Speak on the Literary Life*, edited by Nancy Owen Nelson, pp. 111–124. Denton: University of North Texas Press, 1995.

Chen, Xiaomei. "Reading Mother's Tale—Reconstructing Women's Space in Amy Tan and Zhang Jie." *Chinese Literature: Essays, Articles, Reviews (CLEAR)* 16 (December 1994): pp. 111–132.

177

Cheng, Sinkwan. "Fantasizing the *Jouissance* of the Chinese Mother: *The Joy Luck Club* and Amy Tan's Quest for Stardom in the Market of Neo-Racism." *Savoir: Psychanalyse et Analyse Culturelle* 3, nos. 1–2 (February 1997): 95–133.

Conceison, Claire A. "Translating Collaboration: *The Joy Luck Club* and Intercultural Theatre." *TDR: The Drama Review: A Journal of Performance Studies* 39, no. 3 (Fall 1995): 151–166.

Davis, Rocio G. "Identity in Community in Ethnic Short Story Cycles: Amy Tan's *The Joy Luck Club*, Louise Erdrich's *Love Medicine*, Gloria Naylor's *The Women of Brewster Place*." In *Ethnicity and the American Short Story*, edited by Julia Brown, pp. 3–23. New York, N.Y.: Garland, 1997.

Delucchi, Michael. "Self and Identity among Aging Immigrants in *The Joy Luck Club*." *Journal of Aging and Identity* 3, no. 2 (June 1998): 59–66.

Dunick, Lisa M. S. "The Silencing Effect of Canonicity: Authorship and the Written Word in Amy Tan's Novels." *MELUS* 31, no. 2 (Summer 2006): 20.

Elbert, Monika. "Retrieving the Language of the Ghostly Mother: Displaced Daughters and the Search for Home in Amy Tan and Michelle Cliff." *Ghosts, Stories, Histories: Ghost Stories and Alternative Histories*, edited by Sladja Blazan, pp. 159–172. New Castle upon Tyne, England: Cambridge Scholars, 2007.

Green, Suzanne D. "Thematic Deviance or Poetic License? The Filming of *The Joy Luck Club*." In *Vision/Revision: Adapting Contemporary American Fiction by Women to Film*, by Barbara Tepa Lupack, pp. 211–225. Bowling Green, Ohio: Popular, 1996.

Heung, Marina. "Daughter-Text/Mother-Text: Matrilineage in Amy Tan's *Joy Luck Club*." *Feminist Studies* 19, no. 3 (Fall 1993): 597–616.

Ho, Wendy. "Swan-Feather Mothers and Coca-Cola Daughters: Teaching Amy Tan's *The Joy Luck Club*." In *Teaching American Ethnic Literatures: Nineteen Essays*, edited by John R. Maitino and David R. Peck, pp. 327–345. Albuquerque: University of New Mexico Press, 1996.

Hum, Sue. "Articulating Authentic Chineseness: The Politics of Reading Race and Ethnicity Aesthetically." In *Relations, Locations, Positions: Composition Theory for Writing Teachers*, edited by Peter Vandenberg, Sue Hum, and Jennifer Clary-Lemon, pp. 442–470. Urbana, Ill.: National Council of Teachers of English, 2006.

López Morell, Beatriz. "Chinese Women's Celebration in America in *The Joy Luck Club*." In *Evolving Origins, Transplanting Cultures: Literary Legacies of the New Americans*, edited by Laura P. Alonso Gallo and Antonia Domínguez Miguela, pp. 77–85. Huelva, Spain: Universidad de Huelva, 2002.

Macedo, Ana Gabriela. Amy Tan's *The Joy Luck Club*: Translation as a 'Trans/Cultural' Experience." *Hitting Critical Mass: A Journal of Asian American Cultural Criticism* 4, no. 1 (Fall 1996): 69–80.

Mandal, Somdatta. "Ethnic Voices of Asian-American Women with Special Reference to Amy Tan." In *Indian Views on American Literature*, edited by A. A. Mutalik-Desai, pp. 141–152. New Delhi, India: Prestige, 1998.

Mountain, Chandra Tyler. "'The Struggle of Memory against Forgetting': Cultural Survival in Amy Tan's *The Joy Luck Club*." *Paintbrush: A Journal of Poetry and Translation* 22 (Autumn 1995): 39–50.

Reid, E. Shelley. "'Our Two Faces': Balancing Mothers and Daughters in *The Joy Luck Club* and *The Kitchen God's Wife*." *Paintbrush: A Journal of Poetry and Translation* 22 (Autumn 1995): 20–38.

Romagnolo, Catherine. "Narrative Beginnings in Amy Tan's *The Joy Luck Club*: A Feminist Study." *Studies in the Novel* 35, no. 1 (March 1, 2003).

Shear, Walter. "Generation Differences and the Diaspora in *The Joy Luck Club*." *Critique: Studies in Contemporary Fiction* 34, no. 3 (Spring 1993): 193–199.

Souris, Stephen. "'Only Two Kinds of Daughters': Inter-Monologue Dialogicity in *The Joy Luck Club*." *MELUS* 19, no. 2 (Summer 1994): 99–123.

Tseo, George. "Joy Luck: The Perils of Transcultural 'Translation.'" *Literature Film Quarterly* 24, no. 4 (1996): 338–343.

Wang, Qun. "The Dialogic Richness of *The Joy Luck Club*." *Paintbrush: A Journal of Poetry and Translation* 22 (Autumn 1995): 76–84.

Wong, Sau-ling Cynthia. "'Sugar Sisterhood': Situating the Amy Tan Phenomenon." In *The Ethnic Canon: Histories, Institutions, and Interventions*, edited by David Palumbo-Liu, pp. 174–210. Minneapolis: University of Minnesota Press, 1995.

Xu, Ben. "Memory and the Ethnic Self: Reading Amy Tan's *The Joy Luck Club*." *MELUS* 19, no. 1 (Spring 1994): 3–18.

———. "Memory and the Ethnic Self: Reading Amy Tan's *The Joy Luck Club*." In *Memory, Narrative, and Identity: New Essays in Ethnic American Literatures*, edited by Amritjit Singh, Joseph T. Skerrett Jr., and Robert E. Hogan, pp. 261–277. Boston: Northeastern University Press, 1994.

Zeng, Li. "Diasporic Self, Cultural Other: Negotiating Ethnicity through Transformation in the Fiction of Tan and Kingston." *Language and Literature* 28 (2003): 1–15.

Acknowledgments

Gloria Shen, "Born of a Stranger: Mother–Daughter Relationships and Storytelling in Amy Tan's *The Joy Luck Club*." From *International Women's Writing: New Landscapes of Identity*, edited by Anne E. Brown and Marjanne E. Goozé. © 1995 by Anne E. Brown and Marjanne E. Goozé. Reproduced with permission of Greenwood Publishing Group, Inc., Westport, CT.

M. Marie Booth Foster, "Voice, Mind, Self: Mother–Daughter Relationships in Amy Tan's *The Joy Luck Club* and *The Kitchen God's Wife*." From *Women of Color: Mother–Daughter Relationships in 20th-Century Literature*, edited by Elizabeth Brown-Guillory. Copyright © 1996. By permission of the University of Texas Press.

Steven P. Sondrup, "Hanyu at the Joy Luck Club." From *Cultural Dialogue and Misreading*, edited by Mabel Lee and Meng Hua. © 1997 by Wild Peony Pty. Ltd. and contributors. Reprinted by permission.

Zenobia Mistri, "Discovering the Ethnic Name and the Genealogical Tie in Amy Tan's *The Joy Luck Club*." From *Studies in Short Fiction* 35, no. 3 (Summer 1998): 251–257. © 1998 by Newberry College.

Ronald Emerick, "The Role of Mah Jong in Amy Tan's *The Joy Luck Club*." From *The CEA Critic* 61, nos. 2–3 (Winter and Spring/Summer 1999): 37–45. © 1999 by the College English Association. Reprinted by permission.

Patricia L. Hamilton, "Feng Shui, Astrology, and the Five Elements: Traditional Chinese Belief in Amy Tan's *The Joy Luck Club*" was first published in *MELUS*: The Journal of the Society for the Study of the Multi-Ethnic Literature of the United States and is reprinted here with permission of *MELUS*.

Marc Singer, "Moving Forward to Reach the Past: The Dialogics of Time in Amy Tan's *The Joy Luck Club*." From *JNT: Journal of Narrative Theory* 31, no. 3 (Fall 2001): 324–352. © 2001 by *JNT: Journal of Narrative Theory*. Reprinted by permission.

Yuan Yuan, "Mothers' 'China Narrative': Recollection and Translation in Amy Tan's *The Joy Luck Club* and *The Kitchen God's Wife*." From *The Chinese in America: A History from Gold Mountain to the New Millennium*, edited by Susie Lan Cassel. © 2002 by AltaMira Press. Reprinted by permission.

Bella Adams, "Identity-in-Difference: Re-Generating Debate about Intergenerational Relationships in Amy Tan's *The Joy Luck Club*." From *Studies in the Literary Imagination* 39, no. 2 (Fall 2006): 79–94. © 2006 by Georgia State University. Reprinted by permission.

Magali Cornier Michael, "Choosing Hope and Remaking Kinship: Amy Tan's *The Joy Luck Club*." From *New Visions of Community in Contemporary American Fiction: Tan, Kingsolver, Castillo, Morrison*. © 2006 by the University of Iowa Press. Reprinted by permission.

Index

Adams, Bella, 123–137
agency
    assertion of, 161, 162, 167
    Chinese forms of, 159
    collective and individual, 144, 167,
        168
    communal form of, 154
    familial structure and, 142
    identity and, 140
    women's collective, 164
alienation, 9, 15
Althusser, Louis, 131
ambivalence, 19, 88, 158
America, 32, 36, 111
    as adopted country, 64, 145–146
    American dream, 140, 146, 149,
        167
    "Americanness," 129
    fabled American successes, 45–46
    hyphenation and, 26
    multicultural aspect of, 167
American English, 37. *See also*
    perfect American English
"American Translation," 19, 28, 49,
    80, 99–100
ancestors, 50. *See also* genealogical
    ties
animals, astrological. *See* dragons;
    tiger theme; zodiac
An-mei Hsu, 9, 12, 25, 116, 126,
    149

childhood burn injury of, 26
Christian faith of, 40
lessons from mother of, 26–27
not knowing mother and, 48–49
rape story, 12, 141, 161
son Bing's death, 27, 41, 72
swallowing desires, bitterness,
    misery, 6, 26
See also "Magpies," "Scar"
Arcana, Judith, 23–24, 32
    Our Mothers' Daughters, 21
arranged marriage, 30, 141
As I Lay Dying (Faulkner), 88
Asian-American literature, 36
Asian-American writers, 29, 98
assertiveness, 29
assimilation, 32, 98, 154
    Chinese language and, 42
    immigration and, 35–36
    one-way information flow and, 97
    perfect American English and, 37
astrology, 66, 74, 80, 82
    Chinese zodiac, 65–66
    feng shui, five elements and,
        63–82
asymmetry, 63–64, 134
aunts. *See* mothers, the
auspiciousness
    colors and, 81
    dates and, 66–67
    See also *feng shui*

authenticity, 109
autonomy, struggle for, 11

Bagua map, 76
Bakhhtin, Mikhail
    "Concluding Remarks," 87
    "Forms of Time and the
        Chronotope in the Novel," 87
Bakhtinian theory, 84–85, 87, 168
balance, 18, 19, 27, 58
    Chinese sense of, 28
    of East and West, 29
    Five Elements and, 69–70
    imbalance and, 30, 70, 72
    at mah jong table, 94
    See also feng shui; yin and yang
Baptist Church, First Chinese, 27
Belensky, Mary Field, 17
belief system, 78, 80
"Best Quality," 21, 81, 99, 100
Betty St. Clair. See Ying-ying St.
    Clair
Between Mothers and Daughters
    (Koppelman), 21
Between Worlds (Ling), 15, 135
biblical references, 40–42, 43, 72
biculturalism. See under culture
bing, Chinese word/name, 40–42, 43
biography, 15, 18, 29
birthright, 68
blame, 19, 117
"blood ties," 49, 127, 130, 148, 167
    "Mongol blood," 164
    See also genealogical ties
Boelhower, William, 47–48, 50–51
    Through a Glass Darkly: An
        Ethnic Semiosis in American
        Literature, 45
bonds, familial, 15, 37
Braendlin, Bonnie, 85
broken English, 9, 49, 64
Buddha/Buddhism, 65, 82

calendar. See astrology
"Can the Subaltern Speak?" (Spivak),
    125

cannibalism, 127
Canning Woo, 97, 103
Canton, 51
Cantonese language, 36, 37
capitalist economy, 64, 104, 151–152
Carlson, Kathie, 18
causality, 79
central axis, 46, 51. See also Jing-mei
    Woo
central themes, 56, 60, 61
character, 59, 66, 68, 73
characterization, testimonial mode
    of, 6–7
Cheng, Sinkwan, 124
chess prodigy. See Waverly Jong
Chevigny, Bell Gale, 29
chi/ch'i (spirit/positive life force),
    55–56
    feng shui and, 74, 75, 76
    fluctuations in, 13, 66, 78, 79
Chih, Wang, 74
Chin, Frank, 98
China, 92–93, 129, 164
    China narratives, 117–119
    communism, shift to, 165
    Fujian province, 39
    misogynist culture in, 142
    national game of, 54–55
    pre-revolutionary, 99, 147
    Republic of, shift to, 147–148, 149
    Tienanmen Square, 104
    truths and hopes from, 8
    See also Japanese invasion;
        "motherland"
Chinese American. See under identity
Chinese cosmology, 65, 80–81
Chinese culture, 12, 6, 32, 67
    bicultural heritage and, 47
    centrality of family in, 147
    Chinese thinking, 6, 23, 50, 56
    Chineseness, 157, 164
    group vs. individual in, 152
    mythology in, 59, 84, 87
    "raised the Chinese way", 26
    superstitions and, 64, 65, 66
    women's status in, 67, 147

worldview and, 65, 71, 74, 78
  See also Confucianism; languages,
    Chinese; culture; patriarchal
    system
Chinese diaspora, 37
"Chinese Exclusion Acts," 144
Chinese subjectivity, 87, 88
chronology. See dialogics of time
chronotypes, 87
Chu, Patricia
  on Asian-American subjects, 167
  on family system, 147, 166
  on individual identity, 149–150
  on international cooperation, 171
Chungking, 20, 51
Clifford St. Clair, 68, 77, 78, 100
colonial imagination, 128
colors, significance of, 81
communication
  broadening lines of, 17
  miscommunication and, 9, 39, 48
Communist revolution, 15, 83, 104,
    147, 165
community, 47, 157, 158, 160
  Chinese heritage and, 166
  interdependence and, 142, 143, 144
  rituals in, 153
concubinage, 18, 26, 147, 161
Conduct of Life, The (Emerson), 1
Confucianism, 140, 147, 148, 153,
    158, 167
contradictions, 19
cosmology. See Chinese cosmology
cultural gap, 12, 8, 38
  asymmetry and, 63–64
  Chinese/American ways, 9
  geographical cleft and, 10, 15
  incomplete cultural knowledge, 64
  between mothers/daughters, 46, 73
culture
  acculturation, 97–98
  American culture, 71
  Asian-American culture, 106
  biculturalism, 32, 110
  cultural inheritance, 50
  cultural nationalism, 98

cultural positioning, 168
hybridized traditions, 140
materialistic culture, 65, 146
natal culture, 35
See also Chinese culture

daughters, the, 79, 156–157
  American-born, 116, 130, 131
  Americanization of, 150, 155
  mah jong game and, 60–61
  names of, 18, 124, 140
  not understanding mothers, 50
  See also mother-daughter
    relationships
"Daughter-Text/Mother-Text:
    Matrilineage in Amy Tan's The
    Joy Luck Club" (Heung), 115
de Crèvecoeur, Jean, 47
defiance, 127, 144
deracination, 35. See also racial ties
destiny, 70. See also fate
dialogics of time, 83–107
  double chronology, 99–103
  literal dialogue and, 99
  temporal dialogicity, 84–89
  "Typological Time," 92
dialogism, 143
Doten, Patti, 19
"Double Face," 97, 100, 102
dragons, 18, 56, 59

East, the
  Eastern inheritance, 51
  Eastern worldview, 77
  East-West binarisms, 128
  and West, balancing, 29
Emerick, Ronald, 53–61
Emerson, Ralph Wald, 1
emigration, 35
empowerment. See power
Espiritu, Yen Le, 151
essentialism, 128, 132–133, 134
ethnic identity, 6, 10–11, 12, 47, 85,
    87, 154
  "consent and descent," 50
  ethnic minority, 64

ethnic self, finding, 46
ethnic semiosis, 43, 47
    See also identity
ethnicity school, 36

familial structure
    agency and, 142
    extended family, 154, 167
    genealogy and, 166
    See also community
fate, 65, 71, 63, 77
    manipulation of, 64, 78
    traditional Chinese belief in, 149,
        151, 167
Faulkner, William, 88, 168
"Feathers from a Thousand *Li*
    Away," 19, 89, 93, 99, 100
femininity, 159
feminism, 24, 28, 134, 142
feng shui, 73–78, 80
    astrology, five elements and, 63–82
    See also mirrors
Five Elements, the, 82
    feng shui and, 63–82, 75
    imbalances, clashes in, 25, 70, 76
    list of, 65, 69
foot binding, 18, 27, 147
"Forms of Time and the Chronotope
    in the Novel" (Bakhtin), 87
Foster, M. Marie Booth, 17–33, 117
"Four Directions," 102–103
fragmentary structure. *See*
    postmodernism
"From Anderson's *Winesburg* to
    Carver's *Cathedral*" (Kennedy), 96

Gately, Patricia, 126
gender/gender roles, 67, 85, 148, 158
    gendered positioning, 157
    gendered shift, 158–159
genealogical ties, 48, 83, 149, 164,
    165, 166
    blood-based "togetherness," 130
    obliteration, fear of, 49, 50
    trip to China and, 48
generation gap, 53, 65, 94–95

archetypal, 36
intergenerational isolation, 99
geographical gap. *See under* cultural
    gap
geomancy, 73. *See also feng shui*
Gerrard, Nicci, 123
ghost, 26, 92
    becoming a, 29, 68, 113
    being devoured by fears and, 28
    at bottom of lake, 27
    of man sentenced to death, 56–57
goddess, 22, 29. *See also* Lady
    Sorrowfree
good fortune, 59. *See also* 'joy-luck'
Govert, Johndennis, 72
grand récit ("grand narrative"),
    88–89
Guangzhou, China, 51, 104, 165

Hamilton, Patricia L., 63–82, 149
Han dynasty, 74
"happily-ever-after" ending, 124,
    131, 134
happiness, balance and, 28, 37, 60
Heung, Marina
    on alternate affiliations, 148
    on audience participation, 89
    on character, 169
    "Daughter-Text/Mother-Text:
        Matrilineage in Amy Tan's *The
        Joy Luck Club*," 115, 170, 171,
        172
    on empowerment, 150
    on foregrounding of voices, 79
    on temporal theme, 86, 103
Hirsch, Marianne, 19
Ho, Wendy Ann
    on English language, 155
    In Her Mother's House, 169–170,
        171
    on social network, 148
    on stereotypes and racism, 154
    on storytelling, 116, 141
Hong Kong, 50, 51, 74
hope
    dreams and, 60, 140, 149, 154, 167

generation to generation, 49, 60, 65
as only joy, 80, 145
of reunion, 60, 164
stock market and, 151–152
Hornik, Susan, 74
Huang Tai, 24
Hum, Sue, 157, 163, 164
Huntley, E.D., 97, 119
Hwang, Henry
    M. Butterfly, 36
"hyphenated" American females, 18

I Ching, 76
identity, 29, 67–68, 86, 90, 127, 168
assertion of, 71, 73
chi and, 78
Chinese-American, 150, 152, 156, 164, 166
Chinese identity, 14, 105, 159
hybrid identities, 140, 163, 164
"identitarian" terms, 124
"identity-in-difference," 125–126, 131, 132, 133
"imbalance" and, 70
re-creation, recollection and, 110
tiger zodiacal symbol and, 68
See also ethnic identity; selfhood
ideological claims, 87, 88
imagery. *See* symbols and imagery
imbalance. *See under* balance
immigration, 35–36, 41, 50
"Chinese Exclusion Acts," 144
first-generation immigrants, 80
immigration nation, 140, 167
second-generation immigrants, 142, 154
In Her Mother's House (Ho), 169–170, 171
independence, struggle for, 11
individualism, 64, 139, 140, 157–158
inheritances, 13
intergenerational relationships, 124–125
difference and indifference, 129
ideologization and, 132–133

See also mother-daughter relationships
"inter-monologue dialogicity," 54
invisible strength, art of, 24

Jaggar, Alison, 143
Jameson, Frederic, 4
    The Political Unconscious, 15
Japanese invasion, 12, 40, 144–145
Jehlen, Myra, 1–2
Jing-mei Woo ("June"), 25, 90–91, 146
"becoming Chinese," 164
China trip, 3, 13–14, 48, 50–51, 166–167
ethnic identity and, 47–48
father's stories and, 50
leitmotif, story as, 45, 46
miscommunication and, 64
mother's death and, 14, 153, 163
as mother's voice, 19, 46, 112, 143
names, significance and meaning, 14, 20, 51
in narrative, 59, 91, 94, 95
at New Year crab dinner, 8
not knowing mother and, 8, 48
piano prodigy attempt and, 9, 11, 14, 21, 23
sisters, reunion with, 9, 60, 91, 164, 165–166
sisters' abandonment, story of, 20
taking mother's mah jong place, 3, 8, 20, 47, 51, 53, 90, 129, 153, 163
worst insult to mother, 11–12
See also "Best Quality," "Joy Luck Club, The," "Pair of Tickets, A," "Two Kinds"
"joy luck," 49, 59–60, 131, 134
daughters not understanding, 155
mothers/daughters and, 65
philosophy of, 61
stock market and, 151–152
Joy Luck Club, The, 140, 166, 169
in America, formation of, 146
"aunties," 63

in China and America, 20, 90,
    140, 144, 145, 151, 166
  as family entity, 146, 149, 153–154,
    162
  initiation and membership, 18, 94
  initiation of first, 20, 48, 90, 145
  functions of, 148, 151
  philosophy of, 60
  rituals in, 153
  stock market and, 151–152
"Joy Luck Club, The," 51, 99, 129
  formal and thematic preludes in,
    89–95
  as opening tale, 84
June Woo. See Jing-mei Woo
juxtaposition, 41, 94

Kennedy, J. Gerald, 106
  "From Anderson's *Winesburg* to
    Carver's *Cathedral*," 96
Kim, Elaine H., 36, 128, 168
  on interchangeability, 126
  on structural unity, 86
Kingston, Maxine Hong, 5, 98
  The Woman Warrior, 36, 139, 144
kinship. See patriarchal system;
  familial structure
Kitchen God's Wife, The (Tan), 17–33,
  29–32, 36, 109–121, 113
  hearing, understanding and, 21
  Jade Emperor in, 32
  Jimmie Louie in, 31
  Lady Sorrowfree in, 22–23
  narrative, 22
  Pearl Louie Brandt in, 19, 22,
    29–32, 112
  secrets/revelation in, 30, 31
  Wen Fu in, 30–31
  Winnie Louie in, 19, 22, 29–32,
    112
  Zhang story in, 31–32
Koppelman, Susan
  Between Mothers and Daughters,
    21
Kuo, Eddie, 148, 169
Kuomintang, the, 20

Kweilin, 20, 48, 51, 80, 90, 95, 114,
  118, 144–145
  description of, 92–93

Lady Sorrowfree, 22–23, 31, 32
  characteristics of, 27
  role of, 25–26
  voice and, 29
Langdon, Philip, 78
language barrier, 9–10
  class status and, 145
  between mothers/daughters, 64
languages, Chinese, 36–37, 56
  Chinese tone, 40–41
  dialects, 35, 39, 153
  homophones, 37, 41
  linguistics/syntax, 37, 38, 117–118
  oral tradition, 37–38
  phonological struggles, 38–39
  Pinyin and Yale systems, 39–40
  romanized Chinese words, 39–40
  translation to English, 118
Lee, Peter Ching-Yung, 146
leitmotifs, 3, 45, 46, 61
Lena St. Clair, 12, 27–29, 113
  marital conflict and, 13, 55–56,
    160
  overhearing through wall, 11, 57,
    78–79
  See also "Rice Husband," "Voice
    from the Wall, The"
Li, David Leiwei, 123–124, 165
"life's importance," 133
Lindo Jong, 9, 24, 25, 55, 118,
  148–149
  arranged marriage of, 12, 141
  Chinese culture and, 10–11, 23,
    117
  explaining feelings, 13, 163
  in narrative, 49, 56
  Taiyuan/Taiwan mistake and, 38
  See also "Double Face," "Red
    Candle, The"
Ling, Amy, 171
  on authenticity, 109
  Between Worlds, 15, 135

on interchangeability, 126
on mother-daughter theme, 53
on old ways, 147
on themes, structure, 61, 86
on women writing, 169
Literature of Marilineage, The, 19–20
losing face, and regaining, 27
"Lost Lives of Women" (Tan), 18
Lowe, Lisa, 98, 106, 152–153, 169
luck, 66, 80
    peach-blossom luck, 81, 131
    See also auspiciousness; "joy luck"
lunar calendar, 66
Luscher, Robert, 46
Lyotard, Jean-François, 4, 15, 88–89

M. Butterfly (Hwang), 36
Maffesoli, Michel, 153
Maglin, Nan Bauer
    The Literature of Marilineage,
        19–20
"Magpies," 26, 60, 100
mah jong game, 37, 53–61, 145
    as central metaphor, 54–55
    as cultural bridge, 60
    elements in, strategies for, 56
    Jewish vs. Chinese, 55, 94, 95
    June taking mother's place at, 20
    reformulated game, 59
    stories told around, 90
male domination, 17
male Eurocentrism, 37
Mandarin language, 36–38
marginalization, 35, 37, 143, 151
Maspero, Henri, 69
matrilieal heritage, 98
matrilineal fears, 50
Matthew, Mark, Luke and *Bing*,
    40–42
maturity, 14, 15, 37
McAlister, Melanie, 98, 106, 128,
    141, 171
memory
    cultural inheritance and, 50
    ethnic project and, 47
    memnotechnical strategy, 51

recollection and, 48, 110–111
shrouding China in, 93
voices and, 26
Memory, Narrative, and Identity:
    New Essays in Ethnic American
    Literature, 115
Metahistory (White), 112
metaphor
    central metaphor, 46
    loss as, 112–113
    mah jong game as, 54–55
    of power, 58
    Schumann's music as, 14
    voice as, 17, 30
    of the wall, 56–57
    See also tiger theme
Michael, Magali Cornier, 139–172
mirrors, 28, 75, 80–81. See also *feng
    shui*
misogyny, 142, 147
Mistri, Zenobia, 45–51
"Moon Lady, The," 28, 67–68
mother-daughter relationships, 36,
    53, 56, 60, 61
    alienation in, 9
    battles in, 162, 163
    biculturalism and, 32, 46
    blame and shame in, 19, 47
    blood bond in, 49
    indirect love, criticism and, 127
    maternal authority, 8, 94
    pairs, mothers/daughters, 18
    prologue setting tone for, 7
    rebellion of daughters in, 23–24
    storytelling and, 29
"motherland," 8, 14, 115–116, 130.
    See also China
mothers, the, 79, 150
    America/Americanization, 64,
        147
    at mah jong table, 54
    names of, 18, 49, 124, 140
    storytelling by, 12
Mr. Old Chong (piano teacher), 9
"mutuality, principle of," 147
myth, American Dream as, 146

mythologized Chinese past, 88, 92, 94, 101, 105, 111–112

narrative technique
China narratives, 117–119
Chinese language and, 40–41, 42
flashbacks and, 92, 95, 100, 103
foreshadowing, 95
four main sections, 3, 19, 46, 126
historical narratives, 112
as implicit conversation, 46, 92
"master narrative" term, 88–89
monologues, 7, 88, 96
mutual narrative drives, 88
narrative isolation, framing of, 96–99
"narrative paradigm," 3, 4
narrative tension, 85
"progressive" sections, 101
prologues to sections, 7, 19
self-identity and, 90, 110–111
short story sequence, 46, 93
sixteen "her stories," 3, 18, 54, 55, 84, 126
supranarrative structure, 84, 89, 98
See also juxtaposition; storytelling
national identity. See ethnic identity
"nativeness," 109
nativism, 98
necklaces, 13, 22, 49, 71, 133
neoconservatism, 124, 130, 131
novelistic element, 88, 127

obedience/disobedience, 11
Occidentalist, 130
Of Woman Born (Rich), 24
Old World/New World, 10
"oneness," 127
Opposite of Fate, The (Tan), 124, 130
oppression, 141, 150
in marriage, 160
patriarchal oppression, 159, 161, 166
Orientalist, 87
binary logic, 128
neo-Orientalism, 124, 130, 131

"otherness," 154
Our Mothers' Daughters (Arcana), 21

Pahl, Ray, 154
"Pair of Tickets, A," 21, 97, 100
narrative and temporal closure in, 103–105
Pak, Gary, 123, 126
passivity, 29, 68, 73, 160. See also victimization
patriarchal system, 141, 142, 152, 159, 160
peach-blossom luck, 81
pendants, 13, 22, 49, 133
perfect American English, 38, 81
mothers' inability to speak, 10, 22
in narrative, 37
swan emblem and, 7
personal responsibility, 65, 79
personality, 68, 73
philosophy. See 'joy luck'
piano recital, 14
plot, overarching, 88–89, 98
point of view, 19
Polaroid photograph, 127, 165
Political Unconscious, The (Jameson), 15
Poppo, 26–27
portents, 78
Post-colonial Critic, The (Spivak), 132
Postmodern Condition, The (Lyotard), 15
postmodernism, 4, 15, 61, 88–89, 124, 135
power, 141–142, 161, 167
economic power, 159
ethical relationships and, 131, 133
metaphor of, 58–59
"patriarchal power," 141, 146, 149
of reflection, 81
self-empowerment, 115
vertical power hierarchy, 152–153
prologues. See under narrative technique

psychiatry, 25–26
psychological development, 61
psychological gap, 8, 11, 15

"Queen Mother of the Western
    Skies," 19, 51, 94, 100–102, 104
    recursions in, 105
    tale prefacing, 27
quest
    for reunion, 47, 166–167
    for understanding, 21
    See also voice

racial biases, 10–11, 144, 157
    neoracism, 124, 130, 131
    See also marginalization;
        stereotypes
rebellion, 23, 30, 37
    against Chinese heritage, 158
    escaping development as, 21–22
reconciliation, 13
"Red Candle, The," 24, 63, 81
    matchmaker in, 66
    narrative, 49
Reed, Evelyn
    Woman's Evolution, 27
reflection, power of, 81
rejection and resistance, 12
religious beliefs, 64, 79. *See also*
    Confucianism
"Rice Husband," 79, 82, 102
Rich, Adrienne
    Of Woman Born, 24
rituals, 153
Rose Hsu Jordan, 117, 155
    as born without wood, 25
    brother *Bing*'s drowning, 27,
        40–42, 72
    doll selection and, 11
    marital conflict and, 9, 25, 71, 73,
        160
    in narrative, 128–129
    See also "Without Wood"
Rossbach, Sarah, 81

"sameness," 128, 129, 153

San Francisco, California, 51, 59, 66,
    92, 100
    Joy Luck Club in, 90, 140, 144,
        145, 151, 166
"Scar," 26, 100
    blood bond in, 49, 127
Schell, Orville, 126, 128, 129, 136
Schueller, Malini Johar, 86
Schumann's music, 14
See, Carolyn, 28
self-affirmation, 114, 115, 144, 150
self-hatred, 27, 157
selfhood
    determination and, 24
    instilling sense of self, 6
    mothers and, 19, 20, 131–132
    See also identity
self-punishment, 77
sentimentalism, 124, 125
sexism, 140, 144, 157
Shanahan, Daniel, 140
Shanghai, 7, 51
Shear, Walter, 86
Shen, Gloria
    on dialogicity, 85
    on intragenerational similarity,
        126
    on mother-daughter theme, 3–15
    on novel's ending, 134
    on repeated themes, 61
    on storytelling, 3–15, 53, 96, 97
Shenshen, China, 51
Shostak, Debra, 115
signifying system, 40, 117–118
silence, 18, 24, 98
Singer, Marc, 83–107, 143, 169
Skinner, Stephen, 74
Sloate, Walter, 148
social reality, 118, 119
Sollors, Werner, 45, 50
Sondrup, Steven P., 35–44
Song of Myself (Whitman), 1–2
sorrow, swallowing one's own, 6, 26,
    27, 37, 111
Souris, Stephen, 54, 85, 86, 168
Spivak, Gayatri Chakravorty, 43

"Can the Subaltern Speak?," 125
The Post-colonial Critic, 132
Squaw Valley writer's workshop, 15
stereotypes, 128, 129, 130, 134, 144,
    154
    China Doll, 130, 160
    "model minority" Asian
        Americans, 128, 136
    submissive Chinese woman, 159
Stone, Oliver, 38
storytelling, 12, 19, 29, 32, 42, 54
    frame-story, 90
    purposes for, 91, 115
    voice and, 150
    See also narrative technique
subalterns, 38, 43
suicide, 161
Suyuan Woo, 9, 25, 91, 92–93, 146
    abandoned twins of, 12, 20
    child prodigy molding attempt of,
        21, 23
    daughter as storyteller for, 112
    death of, 3, 66, 99, 130, 131, 133
    Five Elements and, 69
    "Joy Luck" creation by, 80, 144–
        145
    in Kweilin war refuge, 20, 48, 95,
        114
    long-cherished wish of, 131, 165,
        166
    mah jong game and, 54, 55
    meaning of name, 14, 60
    miscommunication and, 64
    in narrative, 39, 93
    two types of daughters, 11
swan emblem/swan feather, 7, 8, 13,
    22, 111
Swillinger, Heidi, 76
Syi Wang, 27
symbols and imagery, 7, 46, 117–118
    jewelry and, 13, 22
    Lady Sorrowfree, 31
    names and, 13–14
    in sisters' reunion, 51
    See also dragons; swan emblem/
        swan feather

Taiyuan, 10
Taoism, 82
Three Powers theory, 69
*Through a Glass Darkly: An Ethnic
    Semiosis in American Literature*
    (Boelhower), 45
tiger theme, 28, 50, 130
    astrology and, 67, 68
    "tiger spirit," 13, 55–56, 68
time/temporal theme, 60. *See also*
    dialogics of time; mythologized
    Chinese past
tragedy, 72, 112–113, 150
    family secrets and, 29
    passivity and, 80
    "unspeakable tragedies," 145
Tronto, Joan, 142, 168
truths and knowledge, 12
Tu, Wei-Ming, 147
TuSmith, Bonnie, 127
    on interchangeability, 126
    on mother-daughter theme, 53
    on structural unity, 86
Twenty-Six Malignant Gates, The,
    66, 72
"Twenty-six Malignant Gates,
    The," 19, 56, 99
    tale prefacing, 22–23
"Two Kinds," 21
typographical devices, 94

United States. *See* America
unity
    bing, Gospel of John and, 42, 43
    fragmentation and, 4, 15, 61
    Polaroid photograph and, 127

Vertretung over *Darstellung*, 132, 133,
    134
victimization, 27, 53, 73, 150
    servitude position and, 160
    storytelling and, 115
voice, 18, 24, 26, 79, 150
    for Chinese-American women,
        144
    journey to, 19–20

listening and, importance of, 32
    as metaphor, 17, 30
    of mothers and daughters, 5, 32
    multivocality, 85
    for subalterns, 38
"Voice from the Wall, The," 56–57,
    73, 75
vulgarity, *Fukien* misunderstanding,
    39

"Waiting Between the Trees," 63,
    77–78, 96, 100, 102
walls, 56, 57
Walters, Derek, 69, 74, 80
Walters, Suzanna Danuta, 19
war and political strife, 37, 144–145
    effects of war, 64
    Sino-Japanese War, 135
    Tienanmen Square, 104
    Vietnam War, 129
    World War II, 31
    See also Communist revolution;
        Kweilin, China
Waverly Jong, 8, 9, 10–11, 12, 118,
    162–163
    art of invisible strength, 55
    as child prodigy chess player, 11,
        23, 24, 59
    China trip of, 14, 162–163
    defiance of, 127, 158
    fiancé, situations, 24–25, 155–156,
        162
    origin of name of, 13
    Taiyuan/Taiwan mistake and, 10,
        41
    wedding preparations for, 163
    See also "Four Directions"
Welch, Holmes, 68, 82
West, the, 14, 51, 100, 140
    capitalistic economy in, 151
    East-West binarisms, 128, 142
    See also America; assimilation
White, Hayden
    Metahistory, 112
Whitman, Walt, 1–2
winds, 56, 57–58, 59, 75

"Without Wood," 5, 25, 63, 70–71,
    79, 102
Witke, Roxanne, 17
Wolf, Margery, 17
Woman Warrior, The (Kingston), 5,
    36, 139, 144
Woman's Evolution (Reed), 27
Women in Chinese Society (Martin,
    Wolf & Witke), 17
women's rights. *See* feminism
Women's Ways of Knowing (Belensky),
    17
Wong, Sau-ling Cynthia, 43, 135
    on authenticity, 109
    on ethnic identity, 87, 89
    on historical specificity, 104
    on ideologies and truth, 130
    on narrative framing, 92, 100, 150,
        170
    on novel's ending, 124
wounds, hyphenation and, 26
wu-hsing, 68, 69–70, 80. *See also* Five
    Elements, the

xenophobia, 155
Xu, Ben
    on ethnic identity, 89
    on Five Elements, 69
    on mah jong game, 59
    on mother-daughter theme, 53
    on recollection, 114

Yen, Tsou, 68
yin and *yang*, 69, 72
Ying-ying St. Clair, 25, 39, 50, 55,
    113, 152
    abortion and, 77, 100
    balance, *feng shui* and, 74, 75, 78
    becoming "Betty," 29, 68, 113
    childhood outing, rescue and, 28
    depression bouts of, 57
    as a ghost, 27–28
    identity-altering incident, 67–68
    infant's death, guilt and, 76–77
    mother's story, balance and, 27
    name, meaning of, 27

in narrative, 49–50, 58
storytelling and, 12–13
as a tiger, 67, 68, 77, 113
See also "Moon Lady, The,"
    "Waiting Between the Trees"
Youngblood, Ruth, 67

Yuan, Yuan, 109–121, 150, 170
Yue language, 36
Yün-Sung, Yang, 74

Zhou dynasty, 41
zodiac, 65–66, 68, 113